EDITED BY ESTHER CHARLESWORTH

CITYEDGE: CASE STUDIES IN CONTEMPORARY URBANISM

ELSEVIER

AMSTERDAM • BOSTON • HEIDELBERG • LONDON • NEW YORK • OXFORD
PARIS • SAN DIEGO • SAN FRANCISCO • SINGAPORE • SYDNEY • TOKYO

Architectural Press is an imprint of Elsevier

Architectural
Press

Achitectural Press
An imprint of Elsevier
Linacre House, Jordan Hill, Oxford OX2 8DP
30 Corporate Drive, Burlington, MA 01803

First published 2005

British Library Cataloguing in Publication Data
A catalogue record for this book is available from the British Library

ISBN 0 7506 63537

For information on all Architectural Press
publications visit our website at architecturalpress.com

Typeset by Newgen Imaging Systems Pvt Ltd, Chennai, India
Printed and bound in Great Britain

CONTENTS

CREDITS

Cover phto provided by Leigh Shutter
Figure 3.2 and 3.4 Photographs by John Gollings
Figure 4.1 Based on maps from 1. Hoshen (2001) 2. Younan (2003)
Figure 8.1 Institute for Urbanism, Belgrade
Figure 8.2 Slavija Project, architects Djordje Bobic and Vladimir Macura
Figure 8.4 and 8.5 Darko Radovic
Figures 9.1 to 9.5 All photographs courtesy of Graeme Reid
Figure 11.2 and 11.3 Photographs by David Brazier, Harare

FOREWORD

PHILLIP ADAMS

Edges are interesting. They are places of tension, of transformation, of discovery, creativity and disaster. And edges are – yes – edgy. Dangerous places where people teeter or topple. All too easily and often the exhilarating edge becomes the fatal precipice.

The cutting edge, that place of experiment, is deemed admirable: the bravest place to be. And again and again it's truly productive. A few years back, a major breakthrough was found at a cutting edge, involving the legendary Mandelbrot sets, wherein scientists discovered edges, beautifully filigreed, in infinite recession, leading down into endless fascination… giving birth to Chaos Theory. And it's recently been argued that we humans are creatures of the edge – that our original niche was on that narrow strip of sand between land and sea, with the terrors of the deep on one side and the mysteries of the jungle on the other. This is held to explain the aquatic abilities of the newborn baby – and perhaps the lifelong obsession of the Australian, that denizen of the Dicky's towel and slip slap slopping.

The edge is where waves pound the shore, retreating to leave tidal pools full of evolutionary experiment. The edge is where old ideas run out of currency and philosophers search for new ones, like kids seeking shells on the shore. But an edge is also a border, a fence, a wall that contains you and blocks the view.

It's on the edge of science, literature, painting, politics and philosophy that you find the most innovative and, as well, the most eccentric ideas. The place of invention is also the realm of madness. Thus, hardly a week passes when another improbable manuscript arrives from someone combining both ratbaggery and genius. For example, take the immense volume, the work of a lifetime's research, from an English scholar, proving beyond reasonable doubt that ancient Troy can be found in close proximity to Cambridge University! Dig here. And the phrase, 'going over the edge', reminds us that for centuries the edge terrified oceanic explorers. For it was there, at the end of the world, that their ships would topple into the bottomless abyss.

The notion of the edge conjures notions of the extremity, the fringe, the margin, the brim, the brink, the verge, the perimeter, the circumference, the periphery. It invokes, in the same breath, notions of limits and boundlessness. Thus the edge is the line in ink or charcoal that defines the form, that creates the drawing. The skin, as traced by the fingertips, is an edge. The orbiting satellite is at the edge of space. The dawn is an edge, as is the sunset. And the opposite of the edge is, of course, the middle. It's boring, the middle. The realm of the middlebrow, the middle-of-the-road, the middling, the accepted and the ordinary. And sometimes the edge is a no-man's land, a place of abandonment. Then, of course, it's an invitation to renewal. There's nothing like a wasteland to create opportunities for new communities. And new buildings.

I'm no architect, planner, academic or theorist. Nonetheless I've spent a lifetime as a writer and broadcaster trying to intrigue and educate on any and every imaginable topic. In the course of a week my wireless programme might tackle the edgier aspects of theology, economics, ethics, science – anything edgy. In the hope of producing the sort of abrasive ideas that irritate, unsettle and provoke.

And in Melbourne's CityEdge conferences, more than any others I've attended, and I visit far too many of them, I've found an edginess of ideas that stirs the synapses. At a CityEdge conference, the edge becomes the place where intersections between politics, design, history and economics produce new urban environments from Barcelona to Beirut. And it was at a CityEdge conference that the case studies in this book had their first airing. The case study approach is particularly valuable, as it is here that the complexities of problems can be explored and answered – not theoretically but in reality. And the answers have tended to exhilarate because, by and large, they've not come from habit or the filing cabinet but from the fresh thinking that you only get at – yes – the edge.

CityEdge has attracted architects, politicians and planners who've been responsible for reshaping cities, or parts of them, in France, Spain, China, the Lebanon, Thailand, Holland and Germany. But for me, one of the most fascinating experiences was to be taken to East Timor, to learn of attempts to rebuild the burnt-out communities using cheap, low-tech approaches that were in harmony with communal traditions. The answer isn't always big, bold and innovative. As much as anything, City Edge has been about cultural specificity – about answers for this time, that place, a unique sets of circumstances. The homogeneous has been rejected in favour of heterogeneity and originality.

Several thousand professionals have attended the four conferences between 1998 and 2005. And what they had to say was, at its best, edgy in the sense of urgent, edgy in the sense of energizing. When edges rub together, you produce friction and heat – and sometimes City Edge has been somewhat uncomfortable for those attending. But the heat has produced light and you'll find much of that in this book. More and more, issues of urban design, issues of rebuilding following natural or political catastrophes, of reconfiguring the no man's lands that surround central business districts, of containing and encouraging the current dramatic changes in demography, are becoming of wider interest. Where architectural and urban planning matters were once the province of experts, they are now a major part of the cultural and political conversations of the entire community – and areas of endless controversy and conflict. In the City Edge conferences we've seen some of the bravest, boldest thinking applied to the problems of bricks and mortar, flesh and blood, and soul and spirit that struggle for equilibrium and harmony in our societies. Get it wrong and you've got ghettoes for both rich and poor, an economic counterpart to ethnic cleansing. Get it right and you've magical places where life can begin again.

What Esther Charlesworth and her colleagues have achieved with this book of City Edge case studies will, I hope, have you on the edge of your seat. It will certainly have the professionals and the wider community edging towards better understandings.

CONTRIBUTORS

PHILLIP ADAMS, the presenter of the acclaimed radio programme, Late Night Live, is a prolific and sometimes controversial broadcaster, writer and filmmaker. He is the recipient of numerous awards. In 1998 he was elected by the National Trust as one of Australia's '100 Living National Treasures'. His latest book is *Adam's Ark* (2004).

ESTHER CHARLESWORTH is Director of the CityEdge International Urban Design series and Founding Executive Director of Architects Without Frontiers (Australia). She has taught and practiced architecture and urban design in Melbourne, Sydney, New York, Beirut and Brisbane.

ANGUS GAVIN is currently Planning Adviser to the Chairman of Solidere, the Lebanese company for the development and reconstruction of the regions central district. He has practiced as an urban planner and designer in the UK, the USA, the Middle East, Turkey, Greece and West Africa and has also taught at the University of Virginia in the USA and at the Bartlett School, University College, London.

JOAN BUSQUETS is the Principal of BAU-B Arquitetura/ Urbanisme in Barcelona and Martin Bucksbaum Professor in Practice of Urban Planning and Design at Harvard, Boston. He has previously been head of the Barcelona Planning Department (1983–1989) and was in charge of planning for the Barcelona Olympics of 1992.

ROB ADAMS is Director of Design and Culture at the City of Melbourne and a Professorial Fellow in the Faculty of Architecture, Building and Planning at the University of Melbourne. He has over thirty years' experience working in urban design and architecture, with both local government and the private sector in Australia and Africa.

ARIE RAHAMIMOFF is a Jerusalem-based architect and urbanist. He has consulted widely for the City of Jerusalem and is an active and passionate advocate for this most loved and contested of cities. He has lectured and taught around the world, including recently at Harvard's Graduate School of Design in Boston.

JOHN MONTGOMERY is Managing Director of Urban Cultures Ltd., specializing in urban development and cultural planning consultancy. His work deals with the connections between city and city–region economies, place, urban design and culture. He is currently based in Australia.

FRANCINE HOUBEN is co-founder and director of Mecanoo Architects in the Netherlands. In 1999 she introduced the concept of 'mobility aesthetics' the better to connect highways with the urban development and landscape through which they pass. She is a professor at the University of Technology in Delft and at the Universita della Swizzera Italiana, Accademia di archittura, in Mendrisio, Switzerland.

AJMAL MAIWANDI is an Afghan-American architect and planner. He is currently a consultant architect working for a major international organization in Kabul. His previous work includes consulting the Center on International Co-operation in New York on their reconstruction of Afghanistan project, in co-ordination with the UN Foundation and the office of the UN Special Representative of the Secretary-General and the Interim Administration of Afghanistan.

ANTHONY FONTENOT is a visiting assistant professor in the School of Architecture at Tulane University. His writings have appeared in several books, including: 'Waiting for Kabul' in *At War With The City* (2004), and 'Instant Kabul' in *Space Troubles* (forthcoming, 2004), both co-authored with Ajmal Maiwandi. He has worked with many international architecture firms, including, Frank O. Gehry and Associates, and in 1998 he established an independent office, f-architecture, for architecture and urban research and practice, based in New Orleans.

DARKO RADOVIC is currently Senior Lecturer and Head of Urban Design in the Faculty of Architecture, Building and Planning at the University of Melbourne. He has taught, researched and practised architecture and urban design in Europe, Australia and Asia.

GRAEME REID, a lawyer by profession, was the City of Johannesburg's Inner City Manager before joining the Johannesburg Development Agency as founding Chief Executive Officer. As a lawyer he practiced and taught law before joining Planact – an urban non-governmental organization offering advice and assistance to civic associations and trade unions.

JANICE PERLMAN is part of the Graduate School of Architecture, Planning and Preservation at Columbia University, New York, having previously been the University Professor of Comparative Urban Studies at Trinity College, Harford. She is also President of the Megacities Project, which she founded in 1986 as a non-profit network of collaboration among the world's largest cities.

MICK PEARCE is the Principal Design Architect at the City of Melbourne. In over thirty years of practice in Africa, England and Australia, he has specialized in the development of buildings which have low maintenance, low capital and running costs and renewable energy systems of environmental control.

CASSIO TANIGUCHI is the Mayor of the Brazilian city of Curitiba, currently serving in his second term (2001–2004), having been first elected in 1997. He actively participated in Curitiba's urban planning process for over thirty years, as a member of the highly regarded Jaime Lerner's team.

STUART NIVEN is Director of Urban Design at the Victorian Government's Department of Sustainability and Environment. As the state's principal public design advisor, he leads a specialist team on a programme that supports and strengthens the state's urban design function across the whole of Victoria. This responsibility includes providing urban design advice, strategic direction and implementation strategies into Melbourne 2030.

CATHY WILKINSON is the Executive Director of Metropolitan Development at the Department of Sustainability and Environment which implements the Victorian Government's Melbourne 2030 plan. She brings to this position broad experience in policy development and project management within both state and local government, as well as the private sector.

MICHAEL SORKIN is the principal of the Michael Sorkin Studio in New York City and is the Director of the Graduate Urban Design Program at the City College of New York. His books include *Variations on a Theme Park, Exquisite Corpse, Local Code, Giving Ground* (edited with Joan Copjec), *Wiggle, Some Assembly Required, The Next Jerusalem*, and *After the Trade Centre* (edited with Sharon Zukin).

JOHN FIEN is Professor of Sustainability at RMIT University, Melbourne, Australia. A regular consultant to UNESCO and UNEP, he is co-editor of the IUCN book, *Education and Sustainability: Responding to the Global Challenge*.

ACKNOWLEDGEMENTS

This CityEdge book has been a long time coming and owes its existence to the persistence of many individuals involved in its conception and final editing. I would like to thank all the writers involved in this project for their wonderful blend of design experience and scholarship and all the efforts involved in writing their chapters. The support of Rob Adams (Director, City Projects, City of Melbourne) is especially significant for without Rob, there would be no 'CityEdge'. Kamini Pillay, Andrew Martel and our editor, Carole Pearce, deserve endless praise in making this book a reality and I would also particularly like to thank Alison Yates and Catharine Steers from Architectural Press (UK) for taking this book to print. Finally I would like to thank John Stilgoe (Harvard University) and Sultan Barakat (York University) for encouraging me to investigate urbanism, in all its contentious shapes and forms and John Fien for providing boundless wisdom in helping keep together all life's multiple edges.

Esther Charlesworth

CITY EDGES

Esther Charlesworth

To investigate the city is therefore a way of examining the enigmas of the world and our existence.
Lea Virgine, *La Citta e l'immaginario, Mazzoleni*

A city is composed of different kinds of men; similar people cannot bring a city into existence.
Aristotle

one

THE CITY AS PARADOX

Why are cities, paradoxically, such significant repositories for human knowledge and global capital yet, simultaneously, such fertile targets for division, partition, evisceration and destruction? As sites of both triumph and resistance, cities have always provided intellectual platforms for thinking about social justice, civil society and democracy. Yet they have also been the focus of much disputed political territory. Many twentieth century writers expand on these critical contradictions of urban life. For example, the celebrated urban historian, Lewis Mumford, suggests, 'The city is one of the central discursive sites of society' (Mumford, 1938, p. 23). Similarly, Robert Beauregard comments, 'to speak of the city is to articulate who we are, how we want to live, and what our society does or should look like' (Beauregard, 1986, p. 195). Yet, in much contemporary of urban literature, cities are also referred to as 'fragmented', in 'quarters', in 'bits and pieces', 'divided', 'chaotic' and, 'anarchic' (Davis, 1993; Mitchell, 1998).

While cities are both places of hope and sites of despair, many have increasingly come to see – and experience them – as 'environments of marginalization, disempowerment, alienation, pollution and degradation' (Harvey, 1992). When cities are pushed right to the edge, as we see in post-war cities such as Belgrade, Kabul and Beirut, existing social and economic fractures can become chasms or fault-lines that further fragment disempowered, ethnic and financially marginalized groups.

Indeed, the literature on cities reflects a curious double-sidedness, a binary construction of night–day, dark–lightness and peace–conflict, within the same urban centres. The Old Testament speaks of 'cities of light' and 'cities of darkness', with parallel graphic depictions of paradise and hell, heaven and purgatory. The nineteenth century cities of Europe were represented in many sociological accounts as repositories of disorder, pollution, chaos, ill health and immorality. For example, a 1903 essay by sociologist Georg Simmel, entitled 'The metropolis and mental life', used Berlin as a case study to depict the inner life crisis produced in individuals by the modern city. Such images foreshadow the sinister portraits of cities in later science-fiction novels such as Aldous Huxley's *Brave*

New World (1983), where urban order is maintained by sexual promiscuity and the easy availability of drugs, and *1984*, where George Orwell describes his fantasy city as 'puritanical, harsh and bitter'.

The study of cities is on the cutting edge of many professions and academic groups, including sociologists, geographers, journalists, architects and economists, with many writers debating the construction and, often simultaneous deconstruction, of urban centres and cultures. For many urban theorists, such as Castells (1992); Harvey (1990); Hayden (1997); Sassen (1991) and, Zukin (1991), theorizing about the city and its inherent contradictions is a critical part of comprehending the rapidly changing post-industrial, capitalist and, essentially, chaotic world in which we all now live.

Cities also present an enormous challenge purely in quantitative terms. For example, in 1900 no more than 7 per cent of the world's population could be classified as urban. Yet, within one century, and for the first time in human history, by 2001, more than half the world's population lived in cities and there were over 500 cities with a population size of more than a million. Thus, Girardet comments, '[T]he footprint of the city on the earth is now more massive than ever' (in Watson and Bridge, 2000).

In summary, the essential role that cities have of mixing diverse social, ethnic and economic groups that, in the end, collapse together all different kinds of peoples, has the potential to produce antagonism and chaos and, in many cases, does so. However, this mixing also has the potential for creativity, new cultures, new languages and new built environments. Thus, the political philosopher Iris Marion Young proposes an ideal of the city as a 'metaphor for a politics of difference, at its best, city life embodies an ideal form of social relations between strangers' (Young, 1990, p. 227). Indeed, just as Plato proposed a concept of the ideal city or utopia for Greek citizens in *Critias*, *The Republic* and *The Laws*, David Harvey (1992) argues that cities provide the framework within which the debate about the future of civilization can take place. In this regard French urban sociologist, Henri Lefebvre, claims:

> *To think about the city is to hold and maintain its conflictual aspects, constraints and possibilities, peacefulness and violence, meetings and solitude, gatherings and separation, the rival and the poetic, brutal functionalism and surprising improvisation. One can hope that it will turn out well but the urban can become the centre of barbarity, domination, dependence and exploitation.*
> (Léfebvre, 1985, p. 110)

two
CITYEDGE

Amidst such contradictory discourses on the urban condition, design colleagues from Beirut to Bangkok and Berlin to Bogotá have been debating the most appropriate comparative urban design models for today's cities. Such debates gave rise to the CityEdge series of international urban design conferences in the late 1990s. Hosted by the City of

Melbourne, the aim of the CityEdge series has been to provoke discussion on the critical urban design, architecture and planning issues facing cities in the new millennium. Through specific local and international case studies, the CityEdge series has provided a forum for architects, landscape architects, urban designers and planners to review the rapid and radical development of contemporary metropolises.

Four CityEdge conferences have been held between 1999 and 2005. Organized around four different themes that have become the framework for collating this book, these conferences were:

- Private development versus public realm (1999)
- Centre versus periphery (2000)
- Cities on the edge: reconstruction, deconstruction and architectural responsibility (2002)
- The eco edge: urban environments or urban disasters? (2005)

The chapters in this book do not duplicate the original conference presentations. Rather, leading speakers from the conferences have been asked to write concrete and practical, but reflective, case studies on how their work in their cities might provide ideas and lessons for other cities and city planners and managers seeking to make their cities more sustainable and liveable. Thus, each of the case studies was written by a practitioner, among whom are many well-known 'design politicians' and 'design actors' across a range of European, North and South American, Australian, British and Asian cities. The case studies investigate the political, design, historical and economic reasons that have produced the specific urban environments of their cities, which range from Barcelona, Beirut, Dublin and Rotterdam in the 'Old World' to Melbourne, Johannesburg, New York and Curitiba in the New. There is a plethora of urban design theories in recent urban planning literature but these are few accounts by the individuals who are actually responsible for shaping contemporary urban metropolises. Providing some of these accounts is the purpose of this book and it is hoped that out of their practice, praxis for the present and future city will result.

THEME 1: PRIVATE DEVELOPMENT VERSUS PUBLIC REALM

The central paradox framing the theme of the first CityEdge conference, and the theme of the first set of case studies in this book – 'Private development versus public realm' – is clearly not a new one. Hannah Arendt, the social theorist whose work investigates the typological structures of society, explored the same territory in her landmark text, *The Human Condition* (1958). Tracing the origins of the 'polis', the Greek city-state, Arendt exposed the contradictions in the public–private debate through her analysis of the ethical imperatives faced by Greek city leaders, concluding that

> *To be political, to live in a polis, meant that everything was decided through words and persuasion and not through force and violence. Historically, it is very likely that the rise of the city-state and the public realm occurred at the expense of the private realm.*

Arendt's observations about the demise of the private realm through the enlargement of the public state or polis, can now four decades later, almost be reversed. The private realm no longer implies the domain of the family but, instead, the corporate forces that increasingly control our urban planning processes and the resultant spatial outcomes. What balance of public interest and private aspiration best serves the city today? And what does the way each city decides this balance say about the nature of democracy and social well-being in a city?

In his case study of Barcelona, Spanish architect, Joan Busquets, argues that the transparency of the urban design process, that is, its openness to public scrutiny, is intertwined with the quality of the urban design outcome. Yet, democratic processes alone cannot bring about good cities overnight. Thus, Busquets suggests a layered approach in which 'artificial cities' can start being 'real cities' over time, through reflective public planning and intelligent public-minded design. During the 2000 conference, he commented that the city: 'needs a lot of designers producing good layers, layers that are respectful of others that will introduce a new richness'.

This layered approach of public-controlled planning was not the chosen approach in Beirut. With a European background tinged by the *laissez-faire* planning agenda of the Middle East, Scottish architect and planner, Angus Gavin, is a strong advocate of the capacity of the private sector to deliver good urban design. As the manager of planning and urban design of Solidere (the private company formed to manage the reconstruction of the *centre ville* district of Beirut after nearly 20 years of civil war), Gavin argues in his chapter that only independent, privately funded development can overcome the inertia, clash of vested interests and lack of funding that often plague urban renewal. Only a well-funded private company can have the resources to implement a master plan without deviation. But, then he would say that, as the representative of a real estate company that owns the entire city centre of Beirut, the only city in the world to be listed on the stock market.

Joan Busquet's Barcelona had to respond to a different social and economic agenda; one more embedded in centralized public-good city planning. It thus offers an alternative catalytic model of urban reconstruction. In his chapter, Busquet discusses how to consolidate 'the methodological gaps between the practiners in the disciplines of architecture, engineering, management', through urban projects targeted towards needy precincts in a city rather than the achievement of a grand master plan. Melbourne represents a variation on this approach. Rob Adams's chapter on Melbourne's urban renaissance redescribes Busquet's layered design approach as planning according to a philosophy of 'incrementalism'. Adam's essay shows how a 1985 master plan from Melbourne has been implemented flexibly over a 20-year period through a combination of central planning, design standards, government example and public–private partnerships. Like Busquet's, the result of Melbourne's approach has been a number of key urban projects (from Federation Square to the pedestrianization of the city's grand axis, Swanston Street, reconfiguring the city's inner urban landscape).

four

THEME 2: CENTRE VS. PERIPHERY

The debate over private–public design models for city centres touches but the tip of the urban design 'iceberg' and often neglects the greater and more significant processes shaping the wider urban region. While not losing sight of the central city debate, it is the battle between the 'centre' and the 'periphery' that is the ultimate challenge that urban designers will face in coming years. Yet, one may ask, why is there so little design innovation at the periphery of most large urban centres, from Melbourne to Johannesburg? Architects and planners have always been fascinated with historic cores and how to protect them, and yet the vast majority of urban dwellers inhabit the city's edge rather than its centre. In the vacuum of interest in the periphery, the so-called 'new urbanism' of gated communities for the wealthy and middle classes all but dominates discussion of design ideas for this outer city. The case studies in this section seek to redress this neglect.

Working with the idea of cultural precincts that so often have been confined to the city centre, John Montgomery's chapter provides four case studies – Dublin, Sheffield, Manchester and Adelaide – of the development of cultural quarters in previously abandoned industrial precincts. These case studies show how much needed social and economic (and related employment) renewal can be encouraged both in the centre and outskirts of declining urban centres. In making the case for integrating artists and 'cultural producers' within the urban design strategy at large, Montgomery argues:

> Urban peripheries are not a single type of place and we have choices in what sort of places we wish to make. This should be governed by the relationship of any given site to the wider urban structure, the balance of uses that have already been established across the urban area and the need to improve networks of movement.

Francine Houben's concept of the 'aesthetics of mobility', elaborated through case studies of Rotterdam and Delft, extends the centre–periphery paradox to yet another dimension, the dynamics of motion. Her interest as an architect and urban designer is the moving perspective of the everyday mobile person. She claims that a critical part of the urban designer's toolbox is to recognize both the aesthetic and logistic of mobility as urban dwellers commute between the *urb* and the *suburb*. Houben claims that

> Mobility is not just about traffic jams, asphalt, delays and tollgates, but also about people deriving a sensory experience from their everyday mobility … . One might wonder whether the traditional methods of urban planners, in the form of future scenarios depicted statically in maps coloured red, blue, yellow and green are truly appropriate. These maps are not merely static – they are two-dimensional. The third dimension is missing, as are the dynamics of motion.

Arie Rahamimoff's study of Jerusalem posits an interesting angle on the centre–periphery debate. In his essay, Rahamimoff suggests that the city 'edge' can be interpreted not only as the 'periphery', but also as the 'forefront' – as a starting point. He reminds us that

> *When the ancient Greeks felt that they had reached the edge of a city – its limits – they did not expand the periphery of the existing city, but rather went on to build a new one.*

The centre versus periphery battle in Jerusalem thus extends well beyond a mere discussion of urban projects in the holy city, to a provocative platform about the 'holiness' of Jerusalem's historic centre, upon which thousands of lives have been lost in only the last few years. Rahamimoff's paper leads us into the increasingly urgent dilemma of 'cities on the edge'.

five
THEME 3: CITIES ON THE EDGE

The chapters in this section address the challenge of how to tackle the issue of urban centres riven by urban violence – a category of cities that have grown rapidly in geopolitical relevance as a result of tragic global increases in intra-ethnic and religious warfare and the related catastrophic outbursts of targeted urban conflict and violence. These crises include (but clearly are not limited to) the destruction of much of Beirut from 1975–1991, the persistent bombing of Sarajevo and Mostar in the early 1990s and Belgrade in 1999, the attack of the Pentagon and New York's World Trade Center on 11 September 2001 and in 2004 the demolition and social debris of a 'conquered' Baghdad.

Darko Radovic's chapter on Belgrade's 'deconstruction of urbanity' illustrates the common thread among many of these cities on the edge – 'urbicide' (Charlesworth, 2002). Urbicide connotes the targeted decimation of urbanity, in the literal (rather than postmodern) deconstruction of cities by armed conflict Radovic comments that

> *The assault on the urbanity of Yugoslav cities came not only from chauvinist, retrogressive, atavistic internal reflexes. The cities embodied a pluralist, cosmopolitan and inclusive culture that ridiculed narrow particularism and the xenophobia of nationalistic exclusiveness.*

What approaches to urban design and planning are best suited to post-conflict reconstruction: centralized master planning or layered, incremental renewal? Should it be publicly or privately funded and who should have the say about this in a city traumatized by war?

Architects Ajmal Maiwandi and Anthony Fontenot address these questions in a case study of the reconstruction of Kabul, a city they claim still remains 'largely invisible to the world'. They comment:

> *Unlike many of the other large-scale post-war urban reconstruction projects, Kabul is being stitched together bit by bit. As yet, Kabul has defied the grand gestures of big business reconstruction, allowing multiple-scale projects to unfold simultaneously and slowly transform the city.*

Like Joan Busquet's layered approach to Barcelona's urban reconstruction, Maiwandi and Fontenot argue against the more traditional planning tools of master plans and generic urban planning polices that are destined to fail in political environments of such profound unrest. They suggest that

> *Planning, in its traditional form and logic, cannot save Kabul; it can only stifle a city on the edge of defining new urban forms, shapes and programmes. . . . Rather than attempting to control or stop the process, government agencies might lead initiatives that provide minimal surgical insertions to guide the flow of activities along more desirable paths.*

On the other side of the globe, urban planner, Graham Reid, argues for a more holistic, participatory planning strategy for yet another city on the edge – Johannesburg. Reid comments that by the inclusion of 'professionals, city council officials and political and business leaders who have participated in this process of reinterpreting and understanding the city centre' has helped move Johannesburg quite rapidly from being

> *a city governed by apartheid laws of exclusion to one of democratic governance premised on ideals of economic and social inclusion; from an isolated city to one increasingly integrated into the region and proud of its position as a leading African city.*

Like Montgomery's argument for seeing urban design strategies as a catalyst for both social and economic renewal, Reid's case study of Johannesburg argues for two main principles. The first is the need to see urban design as one of the critical tools for realizing development objectives at the same time as enhancing social integration and new economic opportunities. The second principle is to understand the inner city as a series of interrelated but differentiated precincts in which urban design interventions seek to 'uncover, articulate and strengthen the organic character of each area'.

In her discussion of 'mega cities', urban planner Janice Perlman extends the consideration of cities on the edge to urban centres with populations generally above 10 million people such as Rio de Janeiro and Mexico City. These sprawling cities have gone beyond the edge of conventional warfare into centres that are bursting at their physical and social seams. Perlman comments that 'the sheer size of the megacities presents a situation for which we have no collective experience.' She argues that we have no precedent 'for feeding, sheltering or transporting so many people in so dense an area, nor for removing their waste products or providing clean drinking water'. What happens, she asks, when urban services and utilities originally designed for human settlements of 50 000 or 250 000 need to accommodate many more people? They may even stretch to accommodating one million, she argues 'but will begin to break down at four million, and are blatantly unworkable at 10 million'. How can life in such cities be sustainable?

six

THEME 4: THE ECO EDGE

Perlman's examination of the social, economic and environmental crisis faced by the ever-increasing group of megacities leads us into the final 'edge' discussed in this book – the eco edge. What experiences and principles might architects, planners and policymakers utilize to mitigate impending social and environmental collapse – and the subsequent economic decline of cities? How can cities be part of the slow transition to sustainability, from the design of individual buildings to the development of strategic frameworks for sustainable urban metropolises?

In a chapter grounded in core ecological principles, architect Mick Pearce describes how two buildings he has designed, Eastgate in Harare, Zimbabwe, and CH2 in Melbourne, Australia, respond to the imperatives of sustainability. Pearce uses these examples to position a wider charter for all built environment professionals through the recognition that the 'lifeblood or energy that is necessary to power cities, is not only disastrously harming the environment and social order, but it is also running out'.

Pearce's wakeup call for the pressing need for urban designers to pay much more than lip service to the environmental cause is well illustrated in Cassio Taniguchi's examination of Curitiba, Brazil. Taniguchi's response, as mayor of Curitiba, to the increasing environmental awareness in his city was a comprehensive master plan that integrated projects in transport, environmental preservation, jobs and income generation. Through a streamlined urban management process at Curitiba's City Hall all the municipal offices across the 'social', 'urban', 'environmental' and 'economic' areas were synthesized into a highly sophisticated and transferable model of urban sustainability. Stuart Niven and Cathy Wilkinson's chapter on 'Merging sustainability and metropolitan planning' continues Taniguchi's call for a comprehensive sustainability strategy, encompassing both local and state actors and related projects. In Niven's case study, the 'Melbourne 2030' plan is the blueprint for regulating environmental improvements in the State of Victoria's sprawling capital city and its hinterland of small regional cities and towns. Illustrating the interconnectedness of environmental and economic sustainability, Niven and Wilkinson argue that the philosophy underpinning 'Melbourne 2030' 'is as much about securing the city's economic future (its competitive edge) as it is about addressing the city's impact on the carrying capacity of its ecological setting'.

Michael Sorkin uses his experiences in New York and other major cities to conclude the consideration of the eco edge with a five-element 'formulary for a sustainable urbanism'. Arguing for compact, green, self-sufficient, localized 'garden cities', Sorkin suggests that our lives actually depend on 'green cities', bringing us right back to the *moral* edge of urbanity.

Like Sorkin, we could then comment that, because cities challenge the most fundamental 'natural' principles of ecological and biological survival, sprawling urban centres cannot always be considered the most resilient entities in the world, as Mumford perhaps too readily claimed at the start of this essay. The multiple urban edges described in the following chapters, however, suggest that the city can be transformed, so that, as Cassio Taniguchi states: 'people can feel at home and naturally develop their civic and artistic spirits and livelihoods within its boundaries'.

REFERENCES

Arendt, Hannah (1958). *The Human Condition*. University of Chicago Press.

Beauregard, Robert (1986). Civic culture and urban discourse, a rejoinder. *Journal of Architectural and Planning Research*, **3,** 183–98.

Castells, Manuel (1992). The world has changed: can planning change? *Landscape and Urban Planning*, **22,** 73–8.

Charlesworth, Esther (2002). Beirut: city as heart. *Open House International*, **27,** 4.

Davis, Mike (1993). *City of Quartz: Excavating the Future in Los Angeles*. Vintage Books.

Harvey, David (1992). *The Urban Experience*. Blackwell.

Hayden, Dolores (1997). *The Power of Place: Urban Landscapes as Public History*, 2nd edn. MIT Press.

Léfebvre, Henri (1985). *The Production of Space*. Blackwell.

Mitchell, William (1998). *City of Bits*. MIT Press.

Mumford, Lewis (1938). *The Culture of Cities*. Harcourt, Brace & World, Inc.

Sassen, Saskia (1991). *The Global City*. Princeton University Press.

Simmel, Georg (1968). *The Conflict in Modern Culture, and Other Essays*. (Translated with an introd. by K. Peter Etzkorn). Teachers College Press.

Watson, Sophie and Bridge, Garry (2000). *A Companion to the City*. Blackwells.

Young, Iris Marion (1990). *Justice and the Politics of Difference*. Princeton University Press.

Zukin, Sharon (1991). *Landscapes of Power: From Detroit to Disney World*. University of California Press.

Part One

PRIVATE DEVELOPMENT VERSUS THE PUBLIC REALM

#01
REMAKING BEIRUT

Angus Gavin

one

INTRODUCTION

Behind the discussion of 'private development versus the public realm' lies the growing concerns of many urban designers, sociologists and city authorities over the continuing decline of the public realm, the loss of civic value and the lack of maintenance and increasing privatization of public space. Private corporate interests that have ghettoized the city into gated communities and incorporated the green space and former public arena of the city into private ownership and development are seen as the principal scapegoat.

As part of their route of recovering from a sixteen-year civil war, the Lebanese government privatized in 1994 the entire city centre of Beirut, transferring the ownership of virtually all land, including the former public realm, to a private development corporation, Solidere. On the face of it, Beirut seemed to confirm the worst fears observers might have about the private annexation of public space, presaging the ultimate demise of the public realm. As an example of inner city renewal, Beirut might be seen to represent this extreme. This chapter seeks, however, to demonstrate that the reverse is in fact the case.

Solidere is required, under its formation decree, to build up the entire infrastructure and public domain of the city centre, defined in the master plan as constituting almost half the land area of the city, and to deliver it to the public authority on completion. The company finalized most of the infrastructure in 1996 and continues to work through a rolling programme of design, construction and handover of some 60 public parks, gardens, squares and promenade areas.

Since these green spaces are perceived by the company to exert a significant impact on land sales, as well as creating a strong focus of attraction in the city as a whole, Solidere has been motivated to build a public realm of the highest quality, which is much admired by Beirutis and visitors alike. Key factors are the Mediterranean climate and lifestyle that permit and encourage the social use of public space for promenading in ways that are inconceivable elsewhere in the Middle East. What is gradually emerging in the downtown area is very distant from the impoverished or privatized public realm decried by critical observers of the modern city. Fine public spaces that are owned by the city and create the main meeting points, social arenas and attraction to visitors are rapidly emerging as one of central Beirut's unique assets, differentiating it from all other cities.

two
ENERGY OF THE MULTI-LAYERED CITY

For 5000 years Beirut has provided a link between Europe and the trade routes of the east. Lying at a watershed of cultures and religions, the city has absorbed the legacy of twelve civilizations. Destroyed several times in its long history by war, invasion, earthquake and tidal wave, it has nevertheless each time succeeded in regaining its role as a regional focus and gateway between Europe and the Arab world. Now recovering from the 1975–1990 Lebanese war, Beirut lies again at just such a crossroads.

In spite of the destruction it experienced during the war and its resulting loss of regional influence, Beirut remains a fascinating place of contrasts, complexity and cultural depth,

figure 1.1
CITY CENTRE CONTEXT – SATELLITE IMAGE OF BEIRUT PENINSULA

figure 1.2
CITY CENTRE MASTER PLAN

compared with many of its neighbours. The booming cities of the Gulf, which thrived on Beirut's wartime decline, seem by comparison like global city implants on the Dallas model, or superficial place-marketing constructs. In Beirut, the energy for renewal seems to radiate from the ground – the very soil that, through postwar clearances and excavations in the downtown area, has revealed the archaeological riches of past city layers from the Canaanite Phoenicians through the Classical, Arab, Crusader and Ottoman periods to the recent past. All these layers exist within the area dedicated for postwar renewal as the 'Beirut Central District', a zone which contains the entire extent of the city from ancient times until the 1830s but now defines the city centre of the Lebanese capital. These past city layers which represent simultaneously both constraint and opportunity, carry the risks of conflict between archaeology and development. At the same time, however, the preservation and display of the key features of the city's past is also helping create a unique destination for visitors in the downtown area.

three

AFTERMATH OF WAR

Much of the outside world's perception of modern Beirut derives from televised reportage of the sixteen-year civil war that was incomprehensible in its complexity, destroying the central area and costing the city its hitherto undisputed role as the Middle East's first city and regional centre for banking and trade, culture and tourism, higher education and health care.

The war left Beirut polarized into many different enclaves – a pattern more complex than the east–west divide between Christian and Moslem communities that the Green Line implied. The city centre bore the brunt of destruction, and in postwar surveys the entire infrastructure and two-thirds of the fabric was assessed as being beyond salvage. At the same time the population was almost totally dispersed from the core to the relative safety of outlying areas, accompanying other major population shifts in Lebanon caused by the war and by Israeli occupation of the south. In the latter years of the conflict and immediate postwar period this flow was reversed, with some 20 000 refugee families squatting in derelict properties in the abandoned city centre. Meanwhile, throughout the war years, the downtown foreshore had become the city's fly-tip and dumping ground for domestic waste from West Beirut, which had been deprived of the city's waste services, since they were located on the east side. By the close of the war this uncontrolled landfill extended some 25 ha into the sea, causing an environmental hazard in the eastern Mediterranean.

In reviewing the options for the recovery of the city centre these were perhaps the starkest of the dilemmas facing Lebanon's immediate postwar government, but there were others. Fifteen years of war had left an institutional vacuum so that no public sector agency was capable of taking on such complex, large-scale urban restructuring. The government's resources were already stretched to the limit on an ambitious nationwide postwar programme of recovering the nation's physical and social infrastructure and institutional investment, dubbed 'Horizon 2000'. Furthermore, such was the destruction that it seemed impossible that anything other than very small-scale incremental redevelopment could take place using the existing private stakeholders in city-centre land and buildings. Lebanese property law has generated multiple ownership over the generations that has frequently resulted in paralysis. The ownership of one parcel of land in the souks, for example, was claimed by more than 4700 people. It was hard to imagine establishing a consensus for action among so many vested interests.

The metropolitan plan for Greater Beirut, completed in 1986 during the war years, recognized the vital importance of restoring and redeveloping the city centre, both to symbolize postwar national renewal and to help recover Beirut's lost regional pre-eminence. It was clear that this could not be achieved through small-scale, piecemeal redevelopment. What was needed was a grand vision.

Mindful of these factors and rising to the challenge, the country's first postwar government under Prime Minister Hariri, was determined to turn Beirut's downtown disaster into a rising phoenix through a unique form of public–private partnership. Lebanon's modern economy has always been heavily service-oriented and private-sector driven. Beirut's postwar urban recovery was therefore best directed, neither through conventional public sector investment and management, nor through reliance on aid-agency funding, as in the Balkan cities, but through concerted and rapid private sector investment into a carefully constructed institutional framework and regulated by government decree.

PUBLIC–PRIVATE PARTNERSHIP

While incremental development remains the city's normal process of renewal, large-scale urban restructuring and regeneration call for more drastic measures. With some exceptions, traditional public sector urban renewal has generally not fared well. Today there is widespread acceptance that the most successful model is some form of public–private partnership that combines the regulating powers of the state with the investment capability and market awareness of the private sector. Beirut offers one such model and, to that extent, lies in the mainstream of contemporary urban regeneration.

One of the largest inner city and waterfront regeneration projects in the world, the renewal of Beirut's war-torn city centre was initiated in 1994. In the first decade of a reconstruction that is likely to take some thirty years in all, central Beirut has attracted considerable international interest, for the quality of its urban development, its unique form of public–private partnership and the remarkable speed of its regeneration. This has enabled Lebanon's flagship postwar reconstruction project to attract significant inward investment and bring life back to a destroyed city centre in less than a decade, without recourse to scarce public funds. No government resources whatsoever have been expended on Beirut's downtown renewal.

Beirut's unique private sector institutional framework must be seen in the context of world trends. The increasing dominance of free-market capitalism has been matched, in urban development, by the gradual decline of traditional, centralized, public agency control. This has been replaced by more flexible, market-driven models of urban development that have shown they can respond to shifts in demand, attract investment and implement projects rapidly. Unlike traditional models, commonly based on a single fixed vision, they are by definition more adaptable and have the capacity to create mixed, viable synergies of land use that reflect the complexity of the organic urban patterns of the past.

The past quarter century has, therefore, seen the gradual weakening of public sector control over large-scale urban development and an increase in direct private sector engagement. There are examples of successful public–private partnerships, where private investment is leveraged through tax or other concessions or by means of public agency pump-priming in infrastructure development. In Beirut, under very special circumstances, the government elected to privatize its city centre renewal through the government's power of eminent domain and under the regulating control of a publicly approved master plan.

The reconstruction is being carried out by a unique private development corporation, Solidere, which combines a majority shareholding of some 60 000 former owners and tenants in city centre property, with new shareholders investing some $650 million of the initial operating capital. All former stakeholders were, therefore, required by government decree to relinquish their property rights in exchange for acquiring controlling shares in the company. Established by Council of Ministers' decree, the company, thereby owned at the outset virtually all land in the central district and by 2003 had achieved its first objective of re-activating the city centre and bringing life back to Beirut's historic core. To date some $2 billion worth of direct investment has been committed to the project, divided about equally between Solidere (in infrastructure, land development and real estate development) and other investors in land and building acquisitions and development.

The broad principles of the Solidere model are as follows:

- Government delimited the city centre area, and commissioned and approved a master plan prior to the formation of Solidere.
- Government established judicial committees to identify existing owners and tenants and assess the value of their property assets as the basis for the distribution of Type A shares in the company.
- After a successful initial public offering of Type B shares to new investors, Solidere was formed by government decree in May 1994. The company was initially granted a twenty-five-year life, subsequently extended by shareholders' vote to seventy-five years.
- With the exception of government and religious buildings and more than half the other preserved buildings whose owners elected to retain and restore them, Solidere became the owner of the remaining land in the city centre.
- The company was required to implement the master plan, to finance and carry out the necessary reclamation of the landfill and to design, finance and construct the entire infrastructure and public domain for the city centre, constituting 49 per cent of the total land area, and to hand it over to government on completion.
- In return for this significant initial and ongoing investment in the infrastructure and public realm the government granted Solidere ownership of some 21 ha of future development land on the reclaimed area, or the New Waterfront District.
- All development in the city centre takes place in accordance with the master plan and its regulations and under the normal permit and planning procedures of the state.
- Under its formation decree, Solidere's profits may derive from real estate development, the sale of land and buildings, property rental and management, and from certain concessions, including marinas and the operation of cable TV and broadband network services restricted to the city centre area.

five

URBAN MODELS THAT HAVE INFLUENCED BEIRUT

Inner city urban redevelopment has been through a steep learning curve since the questionable successes and frequent failures of large-scale public sector urban renewal of the 1950s in the US and Europe. Those involved in large urban projects today constantly learn from the successes and failures of their peers, transforming experience from one project to another. Three broad categories of such projects have had an influence on

Beirut: postwar reconstruction, inner city regeneration and waterfront development. Examples from around the world of these different forms of city restructuring have offered useful parallels and important lessons, both in the urban planning and the implementation of Beirut's central area renewal.

Postwar parallels have been drawn from the reconstruction of European cities following World War II and from the contemporary reconstruction of the Balkan cities. Important parallels also exist between modern central Berlin and central Beirut, both with regard to the city-making process and regimes of urban design control, and on issues of reunification and national identity that have emerged during the process of reconstructing divided cities.

Post-war reconstruction offers a very case-specific and highly-charged range of paradigms. For a major project of downtown renewal on the scale of Beirut, contemporary models of urban regeneration and revival of the inner city have provided an equally valid and often more relevant source of inspiration. These have included examples of successful inner city renewal and cultural regeneration in the US and European cities, such as Boston, Bilbao, Glasgow and Dublin, as well as examples of the successful pedestrianization of the central area in many historic European cities; urban regeneration through the stimulus of world events such as the Olympics, Expos and other international forums in Barcelona, Lisbon and Vancouver, and lessons drawn from different approaches to the creation of new inner-city business and financial districts taken from Paris's La Défense, London's Canary Wharf and Shanghai's Lujiazui.

As a Mediterranean city with new waterfront opportunities, even though the latter are the result of a wartime environmental disaster, Beirut has also been influenced by contemporary projects of waterfront development from around the world. Rediscovering the value of the urban littoral is a recurring theme of contemporary urban interventions, from the reactivation of abandoned dockside areas in London, Rotterdam and Cape Town, to the mending of severed connections between city and the waterside in Genoa, Boston, San Francisco and New York and the creation of major new urban poles of attraction on the waterfront in Baltimore, Yokohama, Sydney and Melbourne.

six
CHANGING URBAN IDEOLOGIES

While grand ideas and policies are less evident in the piecemeal urban interventions that characterize any city's everyday pattern of renewal, projects of large-scale urban restructuring often become polemic statements of contemporary urban ideology. When change is in the air they can become battlegrounds of conflicting ideals.

In Beirut's last major restructuring of its central area, during the early French Mandate period of the 1920s and 1930s, the last remnants of the medieval city were swept away, to be replaced by the radiating beaux-arts streets of the Etoile and orthogonal street blocks of the Foch-Allenby district. These districts now form the Conservation Area of the twenty-first century city. The making of these fine Haussmannian streets and the recent painstaking restoration of this area have been extensively recorded in a recent book. The buildings are not from local, vernacular tradition but are in the French classical style, many with a veneer of neo-orientalist detailing in their ornate stonework. Both urban design and architecture convey a well-meaning, if paternalistic, sense of 1930s nation-building. Inescapably, in terms of urban plan and ideology, the composition remains a colonialist implant in the grand planning tradition.

As if during a strange time-warp, in the same period that Beirut was being rebuilt in this way, Corbusian modernism was rapidly becoming the avant-garde ideology in Europe. Modernism, as urban ideology, came into its heyday immediately after World War II and the postwar reconstruction of the European cities took place under its dominant influence. This called for a *tabula rasa* restructuring, sweeping away much of the surviving city fabric capable of being restored and imposing a new 'rational' city diagram on the old. Along with their rejection of history and urban context, the main features of these diagrams were the zoned separation of land use, a preference for the elimination of residential use in the city core, a reduction in its population density and a concentration there of administrative and business functions – the central business district. The modernists' emphasis on functionalism gave high priority to the nascent science of transport planning that favoured the car and promoted the widening of traffic arteries and the construction of new inner-city ring roads and through routes, causing further destruction to the urban fabric. With hindsight, the modernist dogma that guided much of Europe's postwar reconstruction is now often perceived as having inflicted more damage to the city than the war itself.

Downtown Beirut's immediate postwar planning efforts of the early 1990s harked back to both preceding influences: Lebanon's colonial traditions of French grand planning and the by now outmoded ideology of modernism. The original plan was structured around three *grands axes* which, placing little value on the preservation of the urban fabric, proposed infilling the First Basin of the port and a new financial centre on the reclaimed land, together with a general reduction in densities elsewhere, and emphasized a heavy infrastructure of urban highways separated by grades. A battle of ideologies ensued. The master plan that emerged and is now directing the urban development of Beirut's new downtown is based on a more contemporary urban ideology that is diametrically opposed to this modernist model. The plan encourages mixed-use instead of the separation of functions, breaks the central business district mould by infusing the downtown area with residential dwellings as the predominant use of this land, almost triples the number of buildings preserved and places higher value on conservation, historical and urban context, public space and pedestrianization than on traffic arteries, curbing the impact of the car on the urban environment.

seven

MASTER PLAN FOR A NEW KIND OF CITY CENTRE

Planning law in Lebanon assumes the preparation of fixed master plans of a traditional kind. Beirut's central district plan was, however, conceived within a more flexible development framework to facilitate adaptations to it over time. It contains, for example, no fixed land-use or zoning plan, which is normally the core regulating document of a traditional master plan, and has already been through a series of amendments. Behind the master plan there are several core concepts and a regulatory framework designed to encourage their realization. The first concerns the changing role of city centres. Beirut's postwar reconstruction is taking place at a time when the role of the downtown in general is being called into question. Almost everywhere, and for more than half a century, the central areas of cities have been declining relative to outlying centres and 'edge cities' in the suburban fringe. The former model of the city centre as a predominantly single-use, employment-based central business district is breaking down and is widely perceived as having failed. What is envisaged in Beirut is a new kind of city centre that is mixed-use, emphasizing downtown living, heritage and civic value. It is to be a magnet for shopping, entertainment, culture and leisure, with a continually changing programme of festival events, while at the same time maintaining the city centre's traditional focus of government, business and banking. Such a mixed-use pattern of development is unlikely to arise from traditional land-use zoning. Instead, the master plan adopts an essentially market-driven approach guided by planning regulations that encourage mixed use, with an emphasis on housing in traditional residential districts. In practice, choices are made by individual developers depending on the market, the location and the physical assets of each particular site. Solidere exercises an influence at the strategic level, in order to avoid overbuilding in a specific land use beyond the market's rate of absorption.

The second core idea is that the master plan should stimulate the growth of the unique identity of the place, rather than imposing on Beirut the collective identity of a global city. Beirut should stand by its differences and not adopt the ubiquitous sameness of the globalizing world. This means the plan should be less of an imposed diagram on a clean slate, and more of an approach that grows out of the context – its landform, views of the sea and mountains, historical layers, the value of its heritage buildings, the surviving street patterns and public spaces, local architectural traditions and the individual character of the separate city quarters.

A third principle is that the master plan mandates an extensive public realm as a form of armature to development. This framework defines a hierarchy of green spaces from those of a metropolitan scale, like the waterfront city park and Corniche promenades, to local squares and gardens. These public spaces are linked on a network of pedestrian routes, including many mid-block easements across private land that are designed to guarantee desire-line continuity and permeability. In its extent and total area, the public realm was planned to the highest international standards and constitutes almost half the land area. An important intention of the master plan was to create an almost irresistible attraction in the centre of a very dense city, in order to establish there the city's meeting point. The public realm was to assume a role in the postwar reconciliation process by reconstituting in the city centre the common ground for all Lebanese communities.

A fourth core idea was to create a street-based master plan, moving away from the modernist-inspired city of object buildings and internal private malls, to a city of active public streets and public spaces befitting the Mediterranean climate. Rebuilding the street was seen as an appropriate mechanism for the reconstruction of a war-damaged city. It could bring back to life key elements of the historic street pattern and with it the identity of neighbourhoods that had been destroyed. Furthermore, these streets would emanate from and connect to the fine surviving streets of the historic core. Elsewhere, in the new waterfront area or in areas where few buildings survived, the street network could be rationalized to allow orthogonal parcellation within an overall scheme that defined corridors providing views to the sea and the mountains.

Behind the master plan's emphasis on the street as the building-block for city-making lay other convictions. The forming of streets requires that individual buildings be constructed on a continuous frontage to a defined building line, creating not individual object buildings but a connected, urban architecture that is subordinate to the higher order of the street. Coincidentally, however, streets are formed by placing development around the edges of city blocks instead of central to them, as in the podium-and-tower form favoured by the modernists. Perimeter development provides an extremely efficient distribution of floor space, enabling the quantity of high-rise tower development to be significantly reduced. The techniques used in the master plan to achieve built forms that combine to create streets with their sense of enclosure, pedestrian scale and continuity, are those of the streetwall control and various forms of build-to-line and mandated setback. These derive from an analysis of the dimensional rules behind the design of buildings on the colonnaded Maarad Street and Foch Street, with its distinctive 'jetty' form. Streetwall controls are applied along all main streets connecting to the historic core, stepping up in scale through new development areas. The scale and form of the street is maintained, with any permitted high-rise elements set back from the street façade.

A final principle behind the master plan is reflected in the form in which it all comes together; a three-dimensional massing plan that determines, not the zoning of land use, but the maximum heights, building envelopes and control surfaces of the new architecture of the downtown. It is these envelopes that regulate the floor space of any given parcel.

In areas where these are retained, heritage buildings, heights and envelopes prescribe a scale of new development that matches the existing low- and medium-rise buildings. The exploitation factors that apply elsewhere in Beirut, and are a principal cause of the continuing destruction of the city's heritage, allowing an owner to replace a two-storey Levantine villa with a twelve-storey apartment tower, have been abolished in the city centre. They apply only in the calculation, at an exploitation factor of 5:1, of the overall legal capacity of the entire downtown: 4.69 million m^2. This floor space is distributed by the master plan to permit, for example, two-storey development in the souks, up to six storeys in heritage areas and over forty storeys on selected landmark sites.

Considerable variety in the massing of built form is, therefore, a visible feature of the master plan. This massing is used to form streets, enclose public space and shape view cones and corridors. Within clusters of preserved buildings the envelope controls will prescribe new infill development that is in scale with its urban context. Elsewhere, high density development is located on carefully selected landmark sites. High-rise marker buildings are located at key entry points into the city centre. Towers are otherwise restricted to existing high density zones and as symbols of contemporary development at key sites on the new waterfront, commanding spectacular views seaward and towards the mountains.

eight
ASPECTS OF URBAN DEVELOPMENT

Three main aspects of urban development are now shaping Beirut's renewed downtown: infrastructure and the public realm; archaeology and restoration; and new development and future opportunities for new strategic areas.

INFRASTRUCTURE AND THE PUBLIC REALM

Solidere's formation decree required the company to design, finance and build all the city centre's infrastructure and public space. Since no substantive development could take place before the infrastructure was completed and authorized cadastral plans defining parcellation were issued, these aspects of renewal were pushed forward as quickly as possible during the early years of the project. The main infrastructure contracts were completed a year ahead of schedule in 1996. A very high standard of infrastructure and public space design and execution was established from the outset, since the company perceived that there was a direct relationship between this and the protection and enhancement of the value of its main asset – development land.

The master plan had defined an extensive public realm and landscape framework constituting almost half the land area. When implemented, this will create a public realm of some sixty green spaces, squares, gardens, parks and pedestrian promenades totalling 39 ha in area. This is close to the area allocated to such spaces in the rest of municipal Beirut. On completion, Beirut's new downtown, constituting about 10 per cent of the city's total area, will therefore contain about half its green space. The generous provision of public space had been an important principle of the master plan, designed to relieve the oppressive density of much of the city.

In retrospect, Solidere's policy of building high standard streetscape and public space has been amply rewarded. The quality of the pedestrianized public realm and the integrated street furniture design of Beirut's historic core is a tangible and recognized asset of substantial value. Along with the high quality of stonemasonry in the restoration of historic buildings, this has been the main contributing factor behind the extraordinary success of the historic core as Beirut's primary visitor destination, now attracting some 3 million visitors a year. The area is already the city's main focus of promenading, café life and specialty shopping, even before completion of the souks, Beirut's main retail and entertainment attraction.

Figure 1.3
CONSERVATION AREA: A COMBINATION OF HIGH QUALITY RESTORATION AND PEDESTRIANIZED
STREETSCAPE

Outside the historic core a mechanism that relates adjacent green space to successful land sales and rising land values is clearly evident to Solidere. Investors prefer, and often compete for, sites overlooking public space and green corridors. For this reason the company is now bringing forward as quickly as possible the design and execution of some 20 public spaces ranging from major public gardens, such as Hadiqat As-Samah (the Garden of Forgiveness) to small local squares and pocket parks. For the future, a substantial impact on development is anticipated from the implementation of the Martyrs' Square Grand Axis as well as the waterfront City Park and contiguous Corniche promenades, waterside squares and public quaysides in the New Waterfront District.

ARCHAEOLOGY AND RESTORATION

During the height of its archaeological excavations, from 1993 to 1998, central Beirut became the largest urban archaeological site in the world. Solidere has been the principal source of funding for many foreign and local teams, with site archaeologists appointed by the Direction Générale des Antiquités. As a result of these and other excavations many gaps have been filled in Beirut's urban history. Decisions whether to preserve the exposed artifacts in situ, or relocate or remove them, have been made on the basis of a UNESCO protocol. It would be unrealistic not to admit that under the pressure for development some losses have occurred. Nevertheless, the overall record is positive and probably at least as good as that experienced in other similar urban projects overlying historic sites.

Solidere enjoys a good working relationship with the Direction Générale des Antiquités and has developed a strategic approach to the integration of archaeological finds within the urban fabric and landscaped spaces. These past city layers are seen as a significant cultural asset, and their display and celebration as an important attraction to visitors as well as an opportunity to project the uniqueness of Beirut in comparison with competing cities in the region. Key features of the strategy are the heritage trail and the site museum. The first stage of the heritage trail is due to be inaugurated in the near future. Encircling the conservation area, it will link together the main historic and archaeological sites and heritage buildings on a four-kilometre walking tour that will start and finish at the proposed Tell Site Museum, to be built at the location of Beirut's most important recent finds, the remains of ancient fortifications to the Canaanite–Phoenician city. Other smaller site museums are planned at key historic sites along the trail. Their unique feature is that they will be built over, and celebrate, the place where discoveries have been made, in contrast with the traditional museum, where artifacts are displayed out of the context in which they were found.

As the heritage trail is launched, an extensive restoration programme of close to 300 buildings is nearing completion. Most of this is concentrated in the historic core conservation area, with other significant clusters in the city centre's traditional residential districts. About one-third of the undestroyed urban fabric has been salvaged, creating a significant impact on the overall project. As a total environment of restored urban fabric in a reconstructed and pedestrianized public realm of the highest quality, the restoration of Beirut's historic core represents a major urban regeneration achievement on a global scale. Constructed in a variety of Lebanese limestones varying in colour from rich gold to pale ochre, with intricately carved details, most of these buildings had been badly damaged in the war. Their external fabric required an average of 40 per cent renewal, with some buildings being entirely reconstructed. Fortunately, traditional artisan skills still exist in Lebanon and Syria and the majority of this work, including the carving of intricate detail, was carried out by hand using traditional stonemasonry techniques.

NEW DEVELOPMENT AND FUTURE OPPORTUNITIES

The variety of new developments now completed, under construction or in design, illustrates the success of the mixed-use policy. New projects include commercial and government offices, embassies and hotels, retail, entertainment and leisure facilities, health care and cultural uses and a significant content of high-value waterfront and mid-range hinterland housing. The success of Solidere's urban village housing and the restored historic core's pedestrian milieu for shopping and street cafés has resulted in a strong current demand for occupation in both residential and retail sectors. While this seems set to continue, the range should broaden in the near future to include hotel and office development, as a result of continuing growth in the tourism sector and the advent in the downtown area of advanced broadband telecom services.

There is no doubt that Lebanon's war left the country with a crisis of identity and a strong sense of nostalgia for a lost past. These themes are reflected in current architectural expression, and the city centre is clearly a major contributor to contemporary architectural debates. However, the master plan envelope controls stay clear of prescribing an architectural style. They operate in the sphere of urban design, not architecture, and originate from the scale of the challenge – that of reconstituting an urban typology from the often isolated elements of context and remembered places that were virtually obliterated by war. While architects and their clients may see individual buildings as opportunities for personal and corporate expression, the key concerns of the master plan remain at the urban scale. Individual buildings should contribute to the street, and the street to the remaking of the city. While encouraging for the most part a modest, urban architecture of the street, the master plan also identifies key or landmark sites at city gateways, focal viewpoints, strategic and waterfront locations. On these sites, a much freer regime of planning controls is applied; creating major architectural and development opportunities intended to attract world-class designers.

This is now happening with many international architects attracted to Beirut. The move to bring world-class designers to the city was initiated by Solidere as part of the process of repositioning the city. Such architects are working both on the company's own projects and for key sites acquired by other developers. These plots are sold with a list of international architects incorporated in the contract of sale, specially selected for the particular site and agreed with the purchaser.

So far the response has been very favourable and many celebrated architects are now working in Beirut. They include Rafael Moneo, Jean Nouvel, Steven Holl, Michael Graves, Kohn Pederson Fox, Philippe Starck, Ricardo Bofill, Architecture Studio, Axel Schultes, Robert Adam, Vallode et Pistre, Kevin Dash and Jean-Michel Wilmotte. Solidere has also retained a number of leading architects to undertake urban village residential schemes: Abdel Wahed el Wakil, Demetri Porphyrios, Giancarlo de Carlo and Rassem Badran. Other architects who have expressed an interest in working here, some of whom having completed design studies, include Norman Foster, Nicolas Grimshaw, Zaha Hadid, Renzo Piano and Frank Ghery. While star architects, working with local partners, are generally selected for landmark sites, the complementary urban architecture of the street, constituting most of the city fabric, is seen as the domain of Lebanese designers.

In this way three distinctly different design approaches have emerged to the architectural identity that is now being played out in the city centre: vernacular, modernist and contextual. The vernacular architecture of Saifi Village, offering the nostalgic comfort of a familiar past, is popular with the general public and a tempting and easy route to follow. Uncompromising modernism breaks with this legacy but has a relatively recent pedigree in Lebanon's last golden age of the 1950s and 1960s. Successful examples of this include Pierre Khoury's UN House, waterfront towers by Ricardo Bofill and KPF, now under construction, and Jean Nouvel's Landmark project, in design. The last category, a sometimes eclectic contextualism, seems to offer a unique and relevant way forward: an architecture that responds to its urban, cultural and climatic context. Cosmopolitan Beirut has a strong, eclectic architectural tradition that has always combined new influences from abroad with its own distinctive cultural inheritance. Examples of this approach include Mounir Saroufim's Embassy Complex, Rafael Moneo's souks and Kevin Dash's Banque Audi Plaza, a beautiful exercise in contextual urbanism now recognized as an exemplary model. Meanwhile Solidere is exploring these themes in a series of residential projects now in design, each bringing new ideas from outside to combine with traditions of the place. For the future, new development opportunities designed to internationalize and reposition Beirut will soon be opening up on the Martyrs' Square Grand Axis and Beirut's New Waterfront District.

Martyrs' Square, almost entirely destroyed in the war and its aftermath, is currently the subject of an international urban design competition. This focuses on the new identity

figure 1.4
SAIFI: PUBLIC WALKWAYS AND GREEN SPACES PERMUTE THE URBAN VILLAGE; A
COMBINATION OF RESTORED BUILDINGS AND VERNACULAR DEVELOPMENT

figure 1.5
KEVIN DASH'S BANQUE
AUDI PLAZA

figure 1.6
EAST MARINA: QUAYSIDE,
SHOPPING, MUSEUM, CON-
VENTION HOTEL AND
WATERFRONT HOUSING
AROUND THE MARINA.

and surrounding development of this historic public space, now open to the sea on Beirut's new grand axis extending from the Damascus Road gateway to the public quay-sides of the port. Martyrs' Square, the Bourj (a tower) and the Place des Canons has existed at this location since medieval times, changing its identity through the centuries with the passage of civilizations, the trauma of war and the impact of city growth and social change. The goal of the competition is to conceptualize an urban design for Martyrs' Square and the Grand Axis that can give this historic place a new identity, drive the repositioning of the city within the region and help reconcile the divisions that polar-ized Beirut during the war. With the implementation of broadband multimedia telecom-munications infrastructure, it is envisaged that there will be opportunities to develop the corridor as a city centre media and communications hub, stimulating Beirut's rapid adaptation to the new economy and globalizing world of the information age.

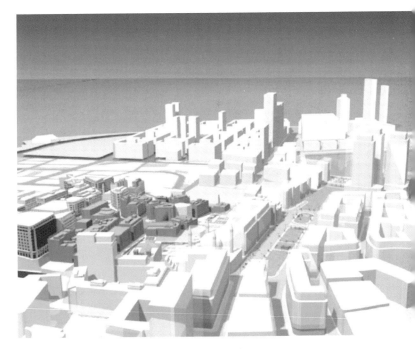

figure 1.7

MARTYRS' SQUARE AND THE GRAND AXIS OF BEIRUT: SUBJECT OF AN INTERNATIONAL URBAN DESIGN COMPETITION

On Beirut's New Waterfront District the landfill decontamination works are nearing completion. Once the master plan amendment for the sector is confirmed by ministerial decree, work will proceed on the infrastructure and landscaping of the waterside city park and Corniche promenades. Short-term uses are already active, including the city's main exhibition and leisure centre. Meanwhile the city centre's first new marina is open and in use, with completion due in 2006 of the yacht club and residential buildings, quayside restaurants and shops.

Solidere's vision for the city's new waterfront has evolved differently from the original concept of a new financial district proposed in early postwar plans. Although demand for corporate office space is expected to grow with Beirut's re-emergence as a regional capital centre for markets and private banking, this is unlikely to dominate the character of the waterfront. This is expected to remain broadly mixed use in character with an emphasis on recreation, leisure and quayside festival retail, cultural or tourism activities. Waterside and parkside sites are most likely to attract high-value residential use. High-rise buildings, sited to command spectacular views of the Mediterranean and the mountains, are expected to be used either as hotels or offices or for housing.

Beirut will consolidate its rediscovered role as the region's leisure, cultural and entertainment centre. This is perhaps best exemplified by the Monaco-style Formula One Grand Prix circuit, to be built by Solidere on city streets, predominantly in downtown's New Waterfront District. Within the next decade, Beirut's New Waterfront District will come alive. At the moment it is too early to tell, but for the future this will produce development opportunities, juxtapositions of activities and a fine and unique architecture.

nine
CONCLUSIONS: CRITIQUE AND PARADIGM

Large urban projects attract considerable public debate and that of Beirut has been no exception. Here, the debate has been about both the urban plan and the project's institutional framework, involving as it does large-scale private intervention in the city. Criticism of the urban planning, much of it well-founded, has been directed mainly at the early postwar plans. The critique in the media replaced what might elsewhere have been a very lengthy public inquiry process with a nine-month public debate that probably had greater impact than any alternative. The new planning team, established in late 1992, was able to set about preparing a revised master plan in an atmosphere of constructive criticism and with a client that was receptive to new ideas.

Criticism of the institutional framework has been more deep-seated and politically charged. Fears that privatization would lead to a sell-out of the city centre to foreigners proved unfounded: over 90 per cent of the shares issued in the initial public offering were taken up by Lebanese. It is true that much of the direct investment into development projects has so far come from the Gulf and Saudi Arabia. However, there is nothing new in this: Lebanon has always appealed to these markets and there is a long tradition behind these regional connections. After 9/11, this pattern of investment has increased to the benefit of Beirut, as many Arab nationals return to the region and repatriate funds.

Private property rights are considered inalienable in Lebanon and their seizure by government decree in exchange for shares in Solidere was contested and highly controversial.

Individual right-holders' assets were claimed to have been undervalued by the judicial committees responsible for the process. However, these valuations were based on the post-war damaged state of property and infrastructure, as had been the case in Europe after World War II. The splitting of ownership of such property over the generations, as applied under Lebanese property law, also had the effect of reducing individual valuations below expectations. It took the judicial committees three years to undertake this immensely complex process and, after Solidere was formed, a further seven years for the company to locate all the shareholders, many of whom were dispersed throughout the world and to issue them their shares.

Although almost all stakeholders had abandoned the city centre during the war, so that the cancellation of their ownership rights, except for those who owned preserved buildings, prevented them from taking part directly in the renewal process. Stakeholder involvement, an important objective in large urban projects, was achieved in a novel way in Beirut, by making them majority shareholders in the company. Although many small shareholders had no interest in grasping the necessary long-term view, one advantage to them was that these shares made their assets liquid, enabling them to sell and realize their capital. This would not have been possible had these assets remained tied to derelict, war-damaged buildings surrounded by totally destroyed infrastructure.

Criticism has also been levelled on matters of broad principle: those of assigning the reconstruction process to a private agency, claims of exercising inadequate public control and of involving the state directly in real estate risks. These arguments, however, do not take account of the global shift towards co-ordinated public and private sector action in urban development in the form of public–private partnerships. Instead they hark back to socialist ideals of centralized public sector control and strong public institutions – in the Lebanese context, to the Chehabist era of the late 1950s and early 1960s – institutional models that have a poor record in the complex field of city-making and regeneration.

Other criticisms have had a more direct political stamp. Prime Minister Rafic Hariri is recognized as the creative inspiration behind the project and its institutional framework. In Lebanon's confessional political climate this has meant that his opponents have attacked the project as part of his political agenda, rather than accepting it as a flagship of postwar recovery and in the national interest. However, after some difficult early years, the project reached critical mass, gained a momentum of its own and it is now widely regarded as a driving force in the national economy, attracting inward investment and beginning to change the external perceptions of the country.

These changing perceptions of a new, emerging Lebanon were demonstrated in a recent *Newsweek* cover story featuring Beirut as one of 12 'capitals of style', illustrated with a night-time view of café life in the city's restored historic core. Beirut's central area renewal is also arousing interest as a model that may offer solutions elsewhere, exemplified by requests for consulting advice in such varied locations as Armenia, Malta, South Africa, Cuba, the Caribbean, Brazil and Iraq. Some relate to post-disaster situations – war and earthquake devastation – others to mainstream urban renewal and restoration. In the broader debate on inner city regeneration the institutional framework of Solidere has attracted much interest, for example, for possible application in cases of severe central area decline in US cities. It is, however, questionable whether such a model could be directly replicable elsewhere, since it developed out of the particularities of an extreme disaster with its own political and economic circumstances.

After a decade of implementation several aspects of Solidere's central area renewal are a visible success and may hold lessons for others. The first is the successful restoration of the historic core. Key factors are the combination of high grade restoration and stonemasonry with attention to detail and quality in the pedestrianized public realm. Secondly, Beirut holds relevant experience for others in the development of a new kind of livable, mixed-use city centre, visitor destination and meeting point. Many cities are searching for new roles for their own downtown area and there may be useful parallels here. Thirdly, Beirut's unique approach to the design, financing and execution of the public domain as a whole may offer inspiration for others. The transfer of responsibility for this to Solidere has created inherent incentives to build to a high specification and quality with low long-term maintenance costs. International talent is being commissioned to design the landscaped spaces, street furniture and public-area lighting, with the overall objective of creating a superb public social arena for the city that is appropriate to its Mediterranean lifestyle and climate.

On one final issue the jury is still out: can the private sector deliver on the public, cultural and social aspirations of the city? With the increasing privatization of urban development, is the city-making process in safe hands? The new breed of market-oriented public–private partnerships – like Solidere – needs to demonstrate their ability to deliver on this essential public agenda. Beirut shows some promise. A critical issue is that the large size of the project allows public, cultural and social benefits to be internalized, as they are perceived to be important to the success of the whole. Solidere is gradually and pragmatically evolving a holistic city-making vision with its own social and cultural infrastructure and funding mechanisms. This includes many children's and youth facilities, archaeology site museums, art galleries and an arts district, a cultural and entertainment centre, many outdoor performance venues and the 'Garden of Forgiveness' with its own museum space.

#02

BARCELONA REVISITED: TRANSFORMING THE CITY WITHIN THE CITY

Joan Busquets

FRAMEWORK

In the course of the last thirty years Barcelona has undergone a major process of enhancement affecting both the restructuring of its urban spaces and principal infrastructures and a transformation of its former industry-based economic system. The city was originally founded beside the Mediterranean in a natural geographical position between the coastal mountain system and the sea, framed by two rivers. This is the natural space of the central city of 1.6 million inhabitants, in a metropolitan territory of approximately 4.5 million covering in the region of 1000 km².

Barcelona's modern history therefore presents a rather small city in the early nineteenth century, when the walled city of 130 ha and barely 150 000 inhabitants was the centre of everything, including Catalonia's growing textile industry. It is important to bear in mind the initial work of Cerdà's project for the Eixample (city expansion). This laid the basis for an open grid structure that enabled dense yet harmonious extension over the Barcelona Plain. Alongside this central development, the outer ring saw a series of hundreds of small-scale projects in the former villages in the plain that constituted suburban Barcelona. Gràcia, Poblenou and Sant Andreu are examples of some of these villages, which gradually grew and were modified by interesting small projects of various kinds. This dual model continued to operate until the post-war years, when intense speculative residential development interspersed with scattered industrial growth shaped a great metropolitan periphery. This considerable quantitative growth was set in the context of an authoritarian political system that allowed excessive development without the services and infrastructure that mark the image and urban planning conditions of the contemporary city. As a result, the advent of democracy in the late 1970s led to the possibility of a radical change in urban planning strategy, whose effects on the city can be clearly seen (Busquets, 2004).

URBAN PLANNING STRATEGIES IN BARCELONA

Having observed the difficulties of a form of modern planning that attached great importance to the quantitative side of the reconstruction of so many cities after the war, it became necessary to improve on it by means of systems of intervention that recognized the great complexity of the urban phenomenon and the agents operating in it, and that were able to channel projects of urban form to ensure that the transformation of the

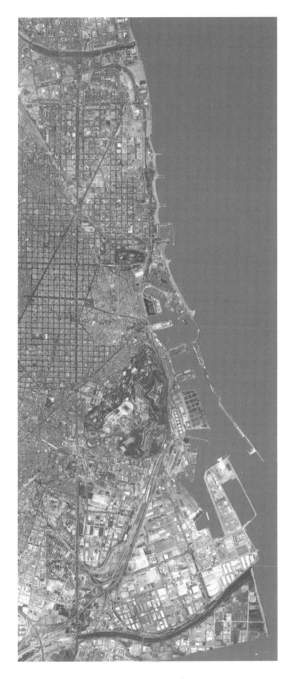

figure 2.1
AERIAL PHOTOGRAPH OF BARCELONA IN 2001, SHOWING ITS NATURAL POSITION BETWEEN THE COASTAL MOUNTAIN RANGE AND THE SEA, FRAMED BY TWO RIVERS

existing city involved rehabilitation and implement restructuring projects based on spatial quality.

This could be seen as a new type of urban planning, a kind of new master plan, that brought together the contents of the innovative planning of the first decades of the century. It was, however, based on a different concept: it recovered the urban form project with all its potential highlighting its operative capacity to resolve social or functional problems that had been clearly spelt out. This seemed to be the only solution to the deadlock and the fragmentation imposed by functional planning, which separated the plan (as a mid-term view) from the actual operational projects, segregating each specific function (such as housing, work or traffic) and thereby consolidating the methodological gaps between the practioners in the disciplines of architecture, engineering, management and so forth.

Instead of organizing urban planning operations according to existing planning documents or a master plan that would be applied sector by sector, the European experience showed that a good mid-term structure or vision was more effective in renovating the city. This involved approaching the problem at different scales and implementing works that were generated by redesigning small existing interstitial spaces with landscaped squares and specific rehabilitation. All this led to the reorganization of the city with a particular emphasis on infrastructure and new urban spaces. It is not easy to summarize the ideas and the strategy underlying such varied interventions, but I would like to highlight the role of the urban project as a common denominator in the majority of these operations, including the plans, programmes and strategies of intervention.

In the early 1980s Barcelona launched a strategy of constructing squares and gardens inside the city as a way of reinstating the quality of urban spaces and improving the residential condition of existing neighbourhoods. Successful minor improvements made in suburban districts also demonstrated the general scope of this initially dispersed and rather disjointed strategy. These initial interventions served to create the image that the city could be improved and also to generate the confidence necessary to make improvements to the road and public transport system, thereby reactivating derelict areas or unoccupied interstitial spaces. A programme of promoting 'new downtowns in town' made these interventions possible, together with the backing of joint public–private co-operation. As part of this strategy, the 1992 Olympic programme served to consolidate the transformation of four of these areas: Montjuïc, Diagonal, Vall d'Hebron and Vila Olímpica. The relative success of these interventions at different scales consolidated this process and led to the formulation of more ambitious strategies. We will now go on to look at two of these, located in the city's most singular spaces: the old walled town and the waterfront.

three

CITY DESIGN IN THE EUROPEAN CONTEXT

City design calls for a specific, in-depth study of the existing city and an understanding of the situation as it exists and the phenomena that influence and mark its dynamic.

An analysis of the existing situation calls for an understanding of both its urban and social forms and the tradition underlying its projects and strategies in the mid-term. Only a thorough interpretation of the existing conditions can channel or formalize a view, or a system of interventions, of the future, set in the conditions or style of the present.

The city has shown itself to be an enduring social artefact in the course of time. However, the urban territory we commonly refer to as the city has come together over the last 200 years, during which period it has come to the fore as the dominant 'lifestyle' and economic basis of nations. Its major growth in population and surface area occurred in the twentieth century, following in the wake of the evolving industrial system. The nineteenth century city is still familiar to us as the 'city of yesterday', and we easily identify with the advances to have taken place since then, which we continue to regard as phenomena of our times. Here, for example, I refer to the implantation of industry, the railways, the Great Exhibitions, working-class neighbourhoods and so on. Today we speak of the growth of the post-industrial system, but almost without realizing it we continue to obey the models and referents of this same system. Nonetheless, our cities are indirectly experiencing changes that are sometimes strongly marked by the presence of the models of the past. This transition has been in force for the last twenty years and involves:

- Taking a new look at the city of the past and directing it towards new uses. This recycling of what already exists involves the recovery of public space, a search for new contents and symbols and the improvement of residential conditions.
- The decreasing value of the traditional model of growth based on spatial continuity between the parts of the city and its long-term evolution over time. Cities and their hinterlands now behave like open territories, due to the power of mobility and communication infrastructures in current times.
- An increase in the mobility of persons and products and, as a result, an increasing importance of the nodes of interchange between different forms of mobility.

In short, we see the need for an in-depth investigation into the new urban forms that the city of the future will ultimately organize, understanding that the 'city of yesterday' will play a major part in this new urban framework.

four
REVISITING TWO CRUCIAL AREAS

In this context it is interesting to evaluate the development of the various projects and strategies listed above in the two critical sectors of particular relevance in Barcelona: the waterfront and the Ciutat Vella (the Old Town). Both areas have gone from a state of abandonment to become very active elements in the city's new dynamic.

THE WATERFRONT

Historically, like many capitals, Barcelona expanded inland, never taking advantage of its waterfront potential. The port began to expand westwards and the construction of the

figure 2.2
THE POBLENOU WATERFRONT IN 1985 (TOP), INDUSTRIAL ACTIVITIES AND SEWERS BY THE SEA
AND IN 1992 (BOTTOM), RESIDENTIAL AREA — VILA OLIMPICA

railway along the coast in the nineteenth century attracted industry, cutting the city off
from the water. Its spatial and functional transformation, made possible by various strategies, has been spectacular. An observer comparing the site today with photographs of it
from the 1970s might think that there was an excellent master plan or development

agency behind an integrated change. Yet it was a sequence of interventions that made this possible.

These interventions have all become linked together as part of the ambitious overall vision of recovering the city's access to the sea. It is through a series of projects and interventions on different scales and within different contents that this is becoming a reality. The sequence began with the recovery of the first port space of the Moll de la Fusta when, in 1983, Manuel de Solà-Morales created pedestrian access to the old timber wharf and gave the space a two-level section, confining through traffic and underground car-parking to the lower level, and allowing pedestrian access from the historic city to the port. This was a pilot project that addressed a fundamental issue in the rehabilitation of the built city: the combination of traffic control and the enhancement of prime public spaces.

The clarity and success of the project led to the introduction of a new approach to long-distance traffic in the form of Barcelona's Ronda ring roads that run the length and breadth of suburban Barcelona and enabled the large-scale reorganization of the port. The change introduced by this project served to focus on the ambitious restructuring of the water-front from La Barceloneta to the river Besòs, on the basis of four systems of infrastructural intervention:

- Changing the layout of the railway line inland from the coast by means of a false tunnel.
- Reorganizing the city's drainage system, which until then had emptied its sewage into the Mediterranean via the Bogatell, and creating an interceptor and a treatment plant beside the river Besòs.
- Drawing up a coastal strategy to create five kilometres of urban beaches, protected by perpendicular breakwaters that adopt the modular system of Cerdà's grid.
- Providing new access for private mobility and public transport. The former comprised the integrated mixed model used in the Moll de la Fusta. The latter promoted the completion of streets and avenues in this sector, such as the Diagonal and Avinguda Icària.

Today, this vast infrastructural programme may appear to have more coherence than the individual projects actually had in themselves. A careful observer will probably find many inconsistencies, but the programme obeyed a general common logic that prioritized access to the sea and sought a clear dividing line between space that could be privatized and spaces that should be public or communal. This overall vision, in which the Olympic theme of the area next to the Ciutadella Park represented a major contribution, was carried out at different times and rates, and comprised a whole series of urban projects of varying scopes and initiatives.

The Vila Olímpica (the Olympic Village) developed on either side of the extended Avinguda Carles I, was the keystone of this new construction. With a surface area of over 20 ha and a programme for 1200 dwellings with services, it became the spearhead of the waterfront. A marina and two flagship buildings completed the intervention. With regard to urbanism, Martorell, Bohigas and Mackay's project played with the general

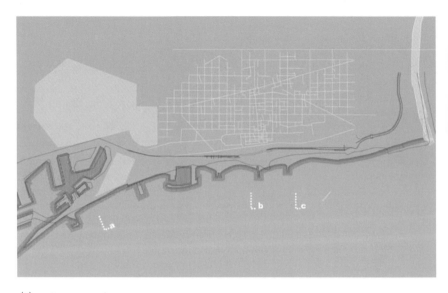

(a)

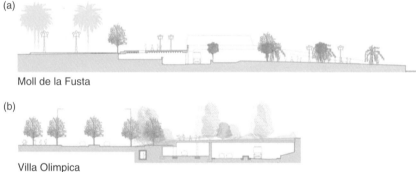

Moll de la Fusta

(b)

Villa Olimpica

(c)

Poblenou

figure 2.3
THE RONDA LITORAL RING ROAD. THE NEW SYSTEM OF ACCESS WAS BASED ON THE CONSTRUCTION
OF THE COASTAL RING ROAD, DRAWN WITH AN INTEGRATED SECTION OF URBAN TRAFFIC AND
PUBLIC SPACE. THREE MODEL SECTIONS: (a) MOLL DE LA FUSTA; (b) VILA OLIMPICA;
(c) POBLENOU

urban morphology of the Eixample, introducing a maxi-block system that combines buildings of various scopes (Martorell, Bohigas and Mackay, 1992). The Vila Olímpica was developed by VOSA, a publicly-owned, privately-run company, and the dwellings went on the market before the Olympics took place, although they were not occupied until the Games were over. The dwellings were of standard size and were purchased mainly by middle-class and professional buyers who received tax benefits because the apartments had been built for the Olympics. Two smaller Olympic villages were constructed in Poblenou and Vall d'Hebron which, though privately developed, accepted the

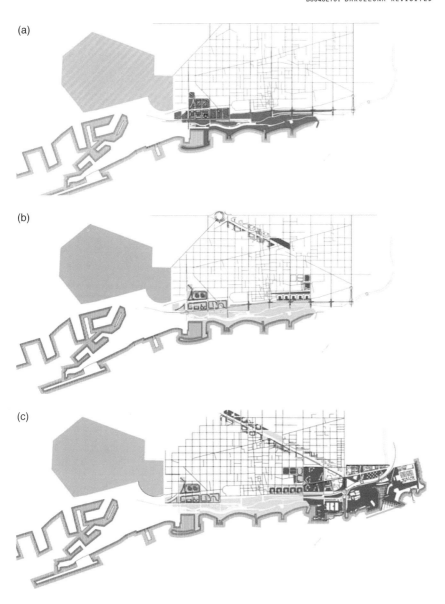

figure 2.4
MORPHOLOGICAL RECONFIGURATION OF THE WATERFRONT FABRIC. THERE ARE THREE SECTORS,
EACH CORRESPONDING TO A PHASE: (a) VILA OLIMPICA; (b) FIVE STREET BLOCKS;
(c) DIAGONAL MAR

municipal strategy according to which new developments should comprise at least
one-third affordable housing. The Vila Olímpica introduced high quality urban spaces
and its beaches became an attraction for the whole metropolitan region.

The second urban development was created near Poblenou with the construction of five
street blocks on the waterfront. Further inland, street blocks replaced abandoned factory

buildings and contributed new residential units that also included one-third affordable housing. Here, the urban morphology returned to the initial form of the Eixample, though now introducing different types of open street blocks with communal landscaped spaces in the interior of the block. The most important urban spaces were the waterfront and the inland axis of Passeig del Taulat, forming a transition between the existing city and the new street blocks.

The third leap was Diagonal-Mar, coinciding with the extension of the city's largest avenue as far as the sea. Here, the urban morphology is organized according to open city patterns, with apartment blocks around a large park. The transformation of this 30 ha industrial site was carried out independently of the city's formal patterns and the dwellings constructed responded to direct market demand. The complex includes a large, inward-looking shopping centre that has little to do with the tradition of open urban commercial spaces so characteristic of the Mediterranean climate. This transformation was accompanied by another major public operation, the Forum of Cultures 2004, completing the waterfront with a system of large buildings in a programme that centres on meeting places, recreation and leisure. The event itself will last six months and is intended to provide the city with a series of service spaces that also aim to recycle the energy and water-treatment plants and change the negative ecological image of this part of the city.

The city's waterfront therefore presents an integrated vision of a city open to the sea, as a result of the various infrastructural projects and a sequence of morphological interventions intended to define the city's coastal façade and plant new uses there. It is logical to think that the waterfront complex will one day be considered as a single project or unitary idea and as a way of enhancing and recycling the minor inconsistencies marking a process that has lasted two decades. At the same time, the port is expanding westwards and rationalizing its functions in an unprecedented transformation. This reinterpretation of its separate parts is clear while new activities are incorporated into the whole. The old port in the heart of the city is being opened up to urban uses.

After the Moll de la Fusta, the next step was the Moll d'Espanya with commercial operations, shopping and leisure as the foremost elements. The central wharf has come into its own as a passenger terminal that is well positioned with regard to the city. Unfortunately, a new office building at the end of the wharf exceeds the scale of the whole. To the west, warehouses storing goods and inflammables (the commercial port) have been clearly laid out. After this is new logistics plant with an efficient motorway and, in the near future, high-speed train connections will be put in place to meet the needs of the new functions of a central port development. The location of the port beside the airport even suggests rerouting the traditional course of the river Llobregat, though this could lead to high environmental costs in the long term.

This rationalization of the port will allow its reintegration into the old 'Free Zone', the largest industrial estate in Catalonia, originally designed as a service area for the port and used for decades as an industrial area where major industries such as SEAT are located.

Relocating some of these industries could create space for the future expansion of activities induced by the port. The re-vision of the construction of the waterfront in Barcelona shows the frenetic dynamic of this city in the reconquest and rationalization of its contacts with the water.

THE REVITALIZATION OF CIUTAT VELLA

Another interesting development is the in-depth rehabilitation of Ciutat Vella that has taken place over the last 20 years. This is the walled centre of the city that was Barcelona for nineteen centuries, until the town wall was demolished in the latter half of the nine-teenth century, when the city began its expansion inland across the plain. As in other European cities, the success of this expansion led to the decline and degradation of the old town, since the only people to live there were those who could not afford to live elsewhere. While it is true that its urban fabric is interesting and its monuments remarkable, it is also very built up, with narrow streets. Its lack of prospects to expand horizontally led, in the course of the twentieth century, to the upward extensions of many properties, adding illegally constructed dwellings with a view to speculation. In 1980 Barcelona had a large and highly problematic old town, with some small, well-rehabilitated sectors, such as the central area known as the Barri Gòtic or Gothic quarter, while the rest of the district was, to a large extent, at an advanced stage of degradation with some areas that were practically ghettoes.

A problem of this kind evidently called for more than an urban development project, and a series of shock measures was applied as part of a relatively coherent urban strategy. The only way to establish a system of interventions that could lead to its integrated rehabilita-tion was to produce a precise overall evaluation of its values and difficulties. At this point it is important to remember the theoretical puzzle present in historic cities: should they be preserved or are they merely the forerunners of the contemporary city, which will always be 'better'? The sharp contrast between the old and the new – that is, the relevance of Ruskin and Viollet-le-Duc's nineteenth century discussion – is just as visible today. In fact Barcelona, like many other European cities (such as the paradigm case of Paris), has undergone major transformation in the last 150 years. The desire to improve its condi-tions of hygiene and connect it to the growing Eixample was one reason for a great deal of demolition, in the belief that the construction of broad new streets would guarantee renovation.

A recent study (Busquets, 2003) of the past and the present city illustrates the strength of this dynamic, and the different types of urban development projects underlying these transformations show that interventions such as these have been repeated over the last two centuries, offering us a critical understanding of their present-day interest and validity. The transformations respond to different ideas that are normally known as urban devel-opment plans. The interventions undertaken in the last twenty years have to be seen in the space between ideas and their realization. For many decades, the ideas of *sventra-mento,* or the opening up of a street network, prevailed in Barcelona; today, we see that in

figure 2.5
FREE SPACES. INTERVENTIONS IN PUBLIC SPACES INVOLVING TRANSFORMATION AND IMPROVEMENTS THAT ARE MORE IN KEEPING WITH
THEIR HISTORY. LEGEND: 1. COMPLEX TRANSFORMATION - AVINGUDA DE LA CATEDRAL, 2. DEMOLITION OF THE INTERIOR OF A
STREET BLOCK - PLAÇA ALLADA-VERMELL, 3. SPACES AROUND THE TOWN WALL, 4. NEW STREET - CARRER FERRAN

the historic city there are other ways of addressing transformation and improvement that are more coherent with the maintenance of its history.

Below I summarize the approaches to rehabilitating the Ciutat Vella in Barcelona.

Firstly, an improvement strategy was re-established to take into account the elements constructed in the course of the city's history and the implanted activities that still make sense in the old town. This approach called for a critical review of activities that cause congestion in or damage the centre. By abandoning the centre, it had been left open to uses associated with drugs, prostitution and so forth that required a series of drastic measures for their eradication. There were also many activities that could remain and that, in the new context, flourished. At the same time, new activities were introduced into the centre or were extended in their scope and content, provided they were compatible with the built structures. This led to the return of some university departments, museums and arts centres and their associated activities, which in turn increased the functional and symbolic role of the centre that the old town had fortunately always retained. The new functional structure for Ciutat Vella was based on its strong centrality, underpinned by the public transport systems surrounding it. The node of Plaça de Catalunya is still Catalonia's most important hub, around which all the Metro lines and most metropolitan buses circulate. The car parks around its edges also provide good support for existing and newly introduced activities, keeping most of the cars out of the centre.

Secondly, the recycling of buildings was re-examined and it was seen that the original structures could to a large extent be combined with contemporary residential use. On the basis of some prototypical experiences, housing rehabilitation programmes now address both public interventions aimed at more critical sectors and less concentrated private interventions, as they respond to agents operating with public backing. At the same time, some 2000 new dwellings were built to replace houses that it was impossible or inappropriate to rehabilitate. In strategic places, in combination with other public space projects, it was appropriate to construct small new buildings or residential blocks that addressed the difficult question of how to bring a contemporary approach to building in the historic centre. After this had been considered, questions of the scale of openings, the treatment of materials, and so on, were perhaps more important than resorting to a given style that was inappropriate and difficult to reproduce, given the circumstances and concerns surrounding present-day architecture.

Interventions in public spaces were of great importance in the recovery of the Ciutat Vella, whether by working with existing spaces or creating new ones to ease the density caused by overbuilding. The first group included many small spaces distributed throughout historic districts, whereas the second involved the necessary demolition of some small blocks, such as Allada-Vermell and La Mercè, which, once the inhabitants had been rehoused, provides key public spaces for the residential recovery of the district. This series of strategies and interventions was accompanied by the introduction of new uses and the promotion of new roles for the Ciutat Vella as a whole. This could be one positive effect of the plan in the mid-term, since in the historic city it is logical to seek the superposition of functions, attempting

figure 2.6
SUPERPOSITION OF TRANSFORMATIONS, 2000–1842. THE MAJOR TRANSFORMATION OF CIUTAT
VELLA IN 150 YEARS, CONSTRUCTING NEW STREETS TO PROVIDE CONNECTIONS WITH THE
GROWING EIXAMPLE AND SEEKING IMPROVED HYGIENIC CONDITIONS

to prevent its monopolization by its function as a museum and tourist attraction, which is
its foremost activity in the mid-term future. In this way, perhaps housing, small shops, new
artisan activities and informal cultural spaces will hold their own and evolve with time.

This is a long-term strategy. The city has experienced twenty years of shock tactics by
planners with the aim of enhancement, and this experience perhaps shows that we have
not yet reached our goal, and that the recovery of a historic city is a long process that calls
for continual attention as the only way of guaranteeing its future.

five

SOME HYPOTHESES AS TO NEW URBAN PLANNING PROJECTS IN BARCELONA

The most complete urban development experiences in recent years, such as those of
Berlin and Barcelona, among others, involve the simultaneous application of many

projects with very differing scopes and interlocutors including urban projects, general strategies, open spaces, plans for the traditional centre, major projects for intermodal stations, and so on. At the same time, combining heavy intermodal infrastructures with independently developed existing buildings and ways of approaching a run-down urban space with enormous potential in the mid-term suggest strong conditioning factors for urban development programmes. We can also see the 'real' capacity of the project on the scale of a large fragment of the metropolis.

We might add five specific dimensions of these strategies and projects:

Firstly, the scope of intervention is very varied, emphasizing approaches based on the scale of the territorial or urban fragment, or on a specific sector of urban development (such as green spaces or waterfronts). The idea of the 'cascade' of plans or projects – that is, the universal planning principles that have advocated decision-making from the general to the particular – seems to have vanished in the interests of greater efficiency. In its place we see the forceful emergence of the idea of 'trans-scale'; in which each project or strategy moves through different scales: starting with its own, but also having an impact on other, larger or smaller scales, as though to prove its urban condition (its insertion in the city), but also to demonstrate its coherence, for example, with larger infrastructures. This approach may show to what extent an abstract urban development project has the capacity to produce an 'urban part' that is coherent with the rest, while possessing spatial qualities of its own.

Secondly, this could signify greater breadth of the planning field, involving new professional disciplines to produce more effective responses to urban regeneration. Perhaps more advisable, however, is a stronger, more comprehensive disciplinary field that generates different forms of professional practice. Such a disciplinary corpus should be seen as integrating rather than exclusive, and therefore capable of overcoming the regressive aspects of the old specializations that have broken down in-depth disciplinary studies into a system of conflicting competences, leading to an excessive fragmentation of the city, its infrastructures, its functional sectors, and so on.

Thirdly, we also detect the major opening up of working methods and an end to the idea that urbanism and projects for the city mean working on two-dimensional plans, with the help of finished models explaining the final result as a preview of the image to be produced by the projects for each part of it. Today there is an unprecedented wealth of methodologies for city analysis, the formulation of alternative types of intervention and means of linking general proposals and partial developments. Some methods seem to be more suitable than others, according to the spatial dimension of the project, the specific nature of the phenomenon in hand and the necessary period of implementation. This variety needs to be exploited.

Furthermore, these proposals entail a series of programmatic determinations that are difficult to develop without taking into account other realities subject to the same tensions.

This situation leads to the use of comparative systems of case studies as instruments for discovering reasonable 'truths' to be applied to other examples. Instead of standard general models such as those put forward by the Modern Movement, analogical systems are frequently applied in order to develop specific actions. It is in this way that urban development projects incorporate the library of applied research in order to add their own contribution to the catalogue of experiences. This is where the urban development project intervenes and helps to model the urban form, its public space and its civic values. It is therefore worth insisting on the project as research in itself, capable of simulating and giving rise to alternatives to programmes that are considered unfeasible on the basis of established models.

Fourthly, the spaces of the urban development project are changing and being extended so that we may easily accept the fragmentary condition of today's city in comparison with the overall, comprehensive visions of other periods. The public space is once again being formulated as a strategy that can provide the cohesion for a city comprised of parts, each with its own independent management and projects. Other areas are being incorporated into the typical fields of urban development (such as the extension and remodelling of the city, and territorial organization) as a result of the application of the intermediate scale, concerned with discovering how improving the 'urban form' of a development project can best address new phenomena that seem to be leading to a more open territory. Furthermore, the dismantling of large monographic spaces such as ports and industrial areas has opened the door to a qualitative improvement of the city and the possibility of introducing new economic activity into what is now a wasteland. At the same time, the complex experience of urban rehabilitation has, since the 1970s, led to new ways of understanding the city and projecting it towards the future: the recycling of existing fabrics and their adaptability to new uses have produced brilliant models of the way forward in most cities.

The organization of major events (such as Expos, the Olympic Games, cultural capital, and so on), now a frequent relaunching strategy in cities, calls for urban planning projects that are capable of addressing the impact of these events. They require thorough restructuring in the short term and therefore need a two-phase design process, to consider firstly what the city will be like afterwards and secondly what it will be like during the special event. This seems to be the best guarantee to avoid large unproductive investment in the short term. It is also important to realize that the project is often a step in the process, and we are used to seeing projects that induce or guide other proposals and projects that are moving in the same direction. Here, the project, as a trigger or catalyst, must be adaptable enough to continue moving forward.

Similarly, the processual component of the project cannot be overlooked. This also includes understanding the necessary political ambition – public or private – contained in each project and the time required to deploy it. This is where the partnership between the public and private sectors comes into its own. We have to overcome the apparent contradiction between these sectors that must always be in a dialectic relation. The city has almost always been mostly privately built, but its long-term vision of a good city is a collective initiative, and the project is situated in this apparently contradictory situation as an idea that is capable of guiding and giving an image to this public-private venture, although the investment is, ultimately, fundamentally from private sources.

Fifthly, the theme of innovation in the urban planning project should draw our attention to research that contribute fresh viewpoints helping us to understand new urban phenomena, and to create proactive strategies. It is easy to pinpoint the implicit difficulties of operationalizing research in these fields, since the action is 'real', and testing and simulation are therefore complex. In the past, utopian ideas of alternative cities could find a space, and be applied, therefore, tested by measuring their difference to the traditional city. Present-day paradigm examples play with both what does exist and the new, and modern experiments therefore have first to be evaluated. However, the forward-looking nature of urban design calls for its verification in action. We might say that its theoretical dimension leads to its capacity, albeit virtual, for implementation. In the present-day situation there is an abundance of projects and experimental strategies that seek their conceptual references in scientific theories that are borrowed to introduce new logics into interventions. This indicates an endeavour to incorporate the dynamics of change into the city and extract certain conditions for the form and composition of the city that are sensitive to these variables. This is the point at which considering strong practical examples should be combined with creating models or referents to redefinite theory. This is the way to promote a substantial improvement in our cities.

REFERENCES

Busquets, J. (2004). *Barcelona, la construcción urbanística de una ciudad compacta*. Ediciones del Serbal. Soon to be published in English.
Busquets, J. et al. (2003). *The Old City of Barcelona. A Past with a Future*. Barcelona.

MELBOURNE: BACK FROM THE EDGE

Rob Adams

Like many first world cities, by the 1980s central Melbourne had taken itself to the very edge of anonymity as a functioning centralized metropolis. Private interests, poor planning strategies, the pull of suburbia, the dominance of the motor vehicle and the migration out of the central area of key central city activities, such as retailing, had resulted in a city close to achieving the 'doughnut syndrome' – a city without a strong central core.

Thirty years later, the drab, semi-deserted central city of the 1980s has all but disappeared. Voted three times in the last decade as the world's 'most liveable city', most recent by *The Economist* in 2003, even the city's most staunch critics – its own inhabitants – recognize the change. The central city has become more vibrant. Residential accommodation, almost nonexistent in the 1980s ('Australians don't live downtown' was the common belief) rose from 738 units to 9895 by 2002. Bars, cafes and restaurants increased from 580 in 1998 to over 1200 in 2003. Not a week passes without a major festival, sporting event or cultural programme. The Rugby World Cup and Grand Prix jostle with the Comedy Festival and the Melbourne International Arts Festival for a space in Melbourne's crowded calendar. Melbourne has turned a central business district, previously dominated by private interests, into a vibrant central activities district.

How has this come about? While one can point to the expected list of *grande projets* such as Federation Square, the new Museum of Victoria, the Crown Casino and the Melbourne Exhibition Centre, these alone could not account for the dramatic change since the 1980s. The change has been more subtle: the city is greener, more people live downtown, the footpaths are wider, paved with stone and featuring side walk cafes, flower stands and fruit stalls. There is more pedestrian space, as well as more bicycle routes and a better balance between the car and other forms of movement. As the result of more parkland and a cleaner Yarra River, activities are springing up on either side as the river cuts through the city. There is a feeling of greater continuity between the physical patterns that underpin the city's character; its parks, rivers, generous streets, public transport and strong central core.

It would be easy to imagine that these subtle improvements are a part of the natural development of a city, and in fact one commentator noted of Swanston Street, the city's main street, 'For years nobody knew what to do with drab old Swanston Street. Then, when no one was looking, it fixed itself.' However, this result and the public perception that things fix themselves lie at the very heart of the urban design strategy pursued by the City of

Melbourne over the last 20 years. It is this story of a local government as choreographer, delivering on a community's expectations, that is told in this chapter.

The impetus for change came in the early 1980s. The once 'Marvellous Melbourne' of the 1890s that stood proud as the rich gold mining capital of Victoria and the twenty-second largest urban conglomeration in the world (Lampard, 1973), was fast losing its purpose and its heart. Figures from the city's 1974 strategy plan tell the story. In the period 1961 to 1972 the city had experienced a drop in the number of people employed in retail by 4382 or 15.9 per cent, a drop in manufacturing employment of 6615 or 34.7 per cent and a decrease in the residential population from 5534 to 4082. This was to drop further to about 2000 by the late 1980s. Thus, by the 1980s, Melbourne was well on the way to becoming a soulless business core surrounded by leafy suburbs, its inner city relegated to the poor and disenfranchised. As freeways snaked into the centre, terraced houses were demolished to make way for slim slab blocks standing in open space (the international solution to low-cost housing). The 40 m height limit in the central city was breached for the first time in 1958 (for the ICI Building), thus opening the door for high-rise offices to erode Melbourne's strong streetscape character. Fear of the loss of the 'Paris End' of Collins Street and the looming predictable future ahead was the spark that changed the dynamics of the city.

This fear brought about a political change that was to rekindle the Melbourne of the twenty-first century. Activists with a design background and a love of Melbourne stood and won office at both state and local government levels. They put in place an administration that was as committed as they were to seeing the city regain its previous position of greatness on the world stage. While the state government was to draw up plans for the central area and kickstart the revival of the Yarra River by opening up the Southbank, the city was to put in place its 1985 Strategy Plan which was to guide the incremental improvement of the city for the next two decades.

THE 1985 STRATEGY PLAN

The strength of the City of Melbourne's strategy plan of 1985 was its strong belief in the intrinsically positive characteristics of Melbourne and the realization that the road back to 'Melbourne' was by reinforcing those aspects of the city that were positive, while working to remove those that were negative. 'Building on our strengths' became the catch-phrase. The strategy plan was heavily based in community plans that had been developed in the late 1970s and early 1980s, a process that empowered local groups who then elected their representatives to office. While these plans produced a basis for the preferred future for each neighbourhood, they also identified important heritage buildings and streetscapes and started a process towards comprehensive conservation controls designed to protect areas and buildings of special significance. These far-reaching controls saw every building in the central city surveyed and graded on a scale of significance. They also introduced graded streetscape ratings and declared all parks and gardens heritage areas. This significant action by the city's communities started the turn-around on the very slow road back to a liveable city.

The 1985 strategy plan integrated the earlier work done on community planning into a single strategic document. It clearly articulated the desired outcomes:

- The central city was to move away from its role as a five-day twelve-hour central business district and towards a seven-day twenty-four-hour central activities district. One of the main ways of achieving this was to increase the central city population by 8000 over fifteen years.
- Designated conservation areas were to be regarded as areas of stability where the existing building stock was to set the context, while the remaining areas were to become key development areas where local government would work with developers to aid redevelopment.
- The major patterns of Melbourne's cityscape which give the city its distinctive identity were to be preserved. These include its gentle, rolling topography, rising from the Yarra and Maribyrnong flood plains and the Port Phillip Bay hinterland, creating permanent sites and views which determined the location of most of the early prestigious buildings. Another feature are the major waterways, which are functional streams that at times have formed barriers to circulation and hence represent both physical and administrative boundaries. The city's formal grid system of major roads and streets marking the central activities district and aligned along the Yarra and the later north–south grid of residential streets were to be respected as well as the network of rail lines which help shape the city, cutting irregularly across it in a radial pattern, in distinction to both the street grid and major landscape features; and the city's extensive tramway system which has provided a safe, sustainable public transport system right into the twenty-first century. Other important features are the city's formal parks and gardens which are of two types – the major metropolitan parks ringing the city and the smaller, formal urban gardens and squares that extend the garden environment into the heart of the city. The central activities district's skewed street grid, aligned with the Yarra, has remained distinctive and identifiable within Melbourne and the intensive development of this area, initially within a 40 m height limit, has resulted in an impressive built form of a three-dimensional expression of the Hoddle grid with its 30 m and 10 m streets, lanes and arcades.

Having spent eighteen months preparing and adopting the plan, the city moved very quickly into the implementation phase through a balanced capital works and maintenance programme to ensure the incremental improvement of the public realm. It is the success of this phase that has seen the city transformed over the last two decades. Very broadly, three factors lay behind the successful implementation of this urban design agenda: political support, design-led delivery and private-public partnerships. These three factors have worked in concert to deliver on the aspirations of the 1985 strategy plan.

one

POLITICAL SUPPORT

This took a number of forms. Initially having put in place the process for the 1985 plan, driven its philosophy and voted it into policy, the councillors were instrumental in setting up the city's first urban design unit. This unit came into being in late 1985. Its mandate was to ensure the implementation of the urban design components of the 1985 plan, but more importantly to provide a unified design approach that balanced the demands of private interests against those of the public realm and to carry this message across the whole council. The mechanisms for achieving this, which ultimately led to a cultural change in the organization, was the setting up of an urban design subcommittee. This subcommittee, an offshoot of the planning committee, was charged with ensuring that all designs that came forward to the committee had been tested against the objectives and principles of the 1985 plan.

Chaired by a councillor who was a strong advocate of the urban design agenda, this subcommittee was instrumental in changing the internal culture of the council, in particular, that in which the council was strongly dominated by engineering solutions. In a cross-corporate role, the subcommittee oversaw the introduction of design solutions that were based on requirements for a people-friendly city over any single-purpose requirement, such as traffic movement. This included simple requirements to reduce the radii at street corners, remove slip lanes and introduce central, treed medians in roads. Combined with paving policies, pram ramps and quality street furniture, this produced strong visual clues that favoured pedestrians.

The subcommittee also oversaw major planning submissions and started to put in place requirements that new buildings were built up to their site boundaries and provided active street frontages along all major streets. New developments were also required to sit comfortably within the context of the dominant streetscape. This approach quickly recruited the combined energies of the statutory planners and the traffic engineers to the cause of designing quality streets, leading to a better understanding and delivery on Jane Jacob's philosophy that if you build good streets you build a good city.

The other major influence that the political arm had on the city was to recognize that, while trying to preserve and enhance the traditional qualities of Melbourne, this needed to be an approach to quality, built-to-last solutions rather than short-term, quick-fix remedies. This new culture saw a rise in creative people to the top of the organization and the willingness of the council to pursue ambitious goals. Many of these, such as 'Postcode 3000', a programme designed to repopulate central Melbourne; the closing of Swanston Street (the main traffic artery through the city); the promotion of arts and culture and the introduction of a $200 million investment fund designed to allow the pursuit of strategic projects that provided an economic return to the city, all represented ambitious and innovative approaches to city change.

These programmes and many others became the backbone of an innovative and risk-taking political culture that has driven the progress of the city over two decades and towards the next major step of the transformation of Melbourne so that it is not only the most liveable, but also the most sustainable city in Australia. The goal in this regard has been set high – zero emissions by the year 2020. Already in its early stages, reductions in

53

emissions of up to 14 per cent have been achieved. The city has now embarked on a significant change exercise that includes designing and building what is likely to be one of the world's most advanced environmental commercial office buildings, which is due for completion in late 2005. This building, designed to save up to 80 per cent of the energy of a conventional office building and delivering 100 per cent fresh conditioned air to its occupants will, like 'Postcode 3000', lead to a cultural shift in the way the future functioning of downtown is conceived.

two
DESIGN-LED DELIVERY

Hand in hand with the strong political culture came a strong design culture. Many of the politicians who had come into power in 1983 were from a design or cultural background. They had in 1983 called for a strategy plan and, following its adoption in 1985, put in place a high-level urban design team within the administration. As already discussed, this team had the ability and mandate to override the more traditional engineering solutions and work with the planners to deliver on a new statutory planning approach. At a time when most governments were trying to phase out inhouse design and delivery teams, the city ran against the tide and has seen the original team of five grow to a division of nearly 60 under the title of 'Design and Culture'. The design component of this division has, over the last 20 years, been responsible for the design and delivery of most of the city's key projects. These projects, both large and small, have been delivered in accordance with the vision set out in 1985. The change in approach led to the following implementation strategy.

DESIGN PHILOSOPHY

Following the 1985 plan, the urban design unit produced a publication, *Grids and Greenery*, which clearly articulated its design philosophy. This document looked at how the city had been developed and identified the key physical patterns within the city. *Grids and Greenery* also identified numerous projects such as the 'Turning Basin', the consolidation of the eastern parklands and the importance of the built form within the central area, and placed these in a readable format that enabled it to be understood by all stakeholders. With a strong design philosophy in place, the urban design unit set out to implement the plans using a combination of master plans, action plans, development control plans, streetscape plans and technical notes.

MASTER PLANS

Many of the actions outlined within the strategy plan needed to be implemented using master plans for various special areas in the city. In the main, these consisted of areas requiring long-term planning, such as the parks and gardens, the river and city edges. Below are case studies of the processes and outcomes of two such master plans, the Northbank master plan to link the Yarra River to the city, and the eastern parklands master plan, to consolidate the open space on the edge of the city. Master plans tended to concentrate on the physical aspects of these areas that allowed for the forward design, budgeting and allocation of resources that might otherwise have be formulated on an *ad hoc* basis. They also enabled the city to seek external funding from other agencies to assist in implementating them and in this endeavour it has been highly successful with public–private partnerships. The existence of the clear philosophy outlined in *Grids and Greenery* and supported by achievable master plans has enabled the efficient expenditure of money by other private and public sector agencies in a consistent, long-term strategy throughout the city.

case study
NORTHBANK

Purpose. To reconnect the central city with the Yarra River.

Issues. Road and rail infrastructure had since the late nineteenth century, increasingly isolated the central business district from the river. Ground conditions were such that placing this infrastructure below ground was not an option. The land and infrastructure was in multiple ownership and the city was not a major owner. The river is one of Melbourne's main topographic features.

Delivery strategy. In 1987 the city produced a plan based on the historical layout of the site. This plan accepted that the rail viaducts would need to stay but, as with the original fish and rabbit market site, they could be embedded within the built form of the site. This would limit their impact as physical barriers and allow for active street frontages alongside the major roads and park frontages. The road overpass could be removed and all traffic taken back down to grade. In the section where the rail viaducts could not be contained within the new buildings, the amenity of these structures would be upgraded through the following changes:

- The use of lights to transform these viaducts from dark and forbidding structures into large, sculptural landscapes.
- The old Turning Basin, the original city harbour, was to be excavated so that the river was widened and built into a more positive relationship with the new viaduct and central business district. These structures would become colonnades along the water's edge.
- The ground level was lowered around the new viaduct and the ground plane was sloped to provide better views of the water. The slope was to be grassed for seating. The lowering of the ground plane also gave the viaduct greater height and elegance.
- Artwork and simple nautical detailing were used to enhance the character of the area. Roads and parking were to be turned into parkland.

Outcome. Twenty years on, the incrementally-staged process has seen the Turning Basin excavated, and the roads and parking on the eastern site removed and returned to parkland. The Aquarium, built to enclose part of the new viaduct, the artwork and the lighting are in place. Proposals and contracts now exist to remove the road bridge and build a new mixed-use development to enclose the rail viaduct on the western site.

figure 3.1

NORTHBANK, MELBOURNE. ELEVATED VIEW LOOKING EAST ALONG THE NORTH BANK OF THE YARRA
RIVER FROM THE CENTRAL HOTEL ON CLARENDON STREET (1986)

EASTERN PARKLANDS

Purpose. To consolidate the parklands to the east of the central business district into one large park: Melbourne's 'Central Park'.

Issues. These parks are not perceived as part of a single system, but rather as separate parks such as the Botanical Gardens and Olympic Park Trust that are often under separate committees of management. The park system is divided by major rail infrastructures and the Yarra River which cuts through its middle. These separate it from the central business district. The parks house a number of significant state government facilities which have a tendency to press for their own expansion, such as museum and exhibition buildings, parliament, sports and entertainment precincts, Melbourne Cricket Ground and Government House. The design of the parks, in the main, date back to the late nineteenth century and comprise 'soft landscapes' ill-equipped for the major city festivals such as Moomba Festival, that tend to wish to be located in these areas, as they are close to the central city.

Delivery strategy. The city and state had for a number of years produced options for the greening of the Jolimont area. In 1987, as part of the publication of *Grids and Greenery* the city produced a concept plan that looked at connecting and greening the whole eastern park system. A major component of this was the removal of rail lines to decrease the impact of the rail corridor. Between 1987 and 1997 through a process of incremental change, the council removed approximately 1 ha of asphalt from the precinct through the greening of carparks, the removal of central road parking and its replacement with treed and grass medians and the removal of slip lanes. This programme was accompanied by the improvement of the parklands through tree planting, path upgrading and improvements to facilities such as fountains and conservatory buildings. A major step was needed to get the government to rationalize the rail maintenance workshops so as to free up large tracts close to the central business district. This opportunity arose in 1996 when the city floated

figure 3.2
NORTHBANK, MELBOURNE. AERIAL VIEW SHOWING BATMAN PARK BETWEEN KINGSWAY (TOP) AND
QUEENS BRIDGE (BELOW). THE TURNING BASIN IS ON THE NORTHERN BANK (RIGHT) JUST
ABOVE QUEENS BRIDGE (1996, PHOTO BY JOHN GOLLINGS)

the idea of building a new public square and buildings on the Swanston Street edge of the
rail corridor opposite the cathedral known as the centenary centre. The adoption of the
proposal, now known as Federation Square, led to the rationalization of rail lines from
fifty-six to twelve. This released 8 ha of land adjacent to the Yarra River which were converted into Melbourne's first new major park since the nineteenth century, Birrarung
Marr. This park, designed and built by the city, was a hard-wearing park capable of
accommodating festivals and events.

Outcome. Nine hectares of asphalt and rail lines were converted to greenery and parkland.
A reduction in the barrier effect of the rail corridor was achieved and the central business
district was better linked to the river and the eastern park system.

figure 3.3
AERIAL VIEW OF CENTRAL MELBOURNE FROM THE EAST, SHOWING CONTINUOUS PARKLANDS
DIVIDED BY RAIL INFRASTRUCTURE (LATE 1980S)

ACTION PLANS

Unlike master plans, action plans tend to cover precincts and deal with both physical actions as well as activities. The most successful of Melbourne's action plans has been the 'Postcode 3000' project. This plan required the city to increase the number of residential units in the central city by 8000 over fifteen years. With the crash of the property market in the 1990s the city was given the opportunity to provide incentives and guidance as to how this could be achieved. Through pilot projects, the changing of regulations and providing marketing and financial incentives, the city has achieved an outstanding success and has seen residential units within the central city climb from 736 in 1992 to 9895 in 2002. Other action plans have examined particular areas of cultural identity such as the Greek precinct and Chinatown and these have all been supported through these plans. The importance of the action plans is that they are not always physically based and look to partnerships with communities and the private sector.

case study
POSTCODE 3000

Purpose. To change the central city to a central business district to the central activities district over fifteen years, thus creating a 24/7 city.

Issues. By the early 1980s the predominant use in the central city was commercial office space. Residential units in the central city area numbered less than 750 and the city had become a five-day, 8 a.m.–5 p.m. city that was dead at night and at the weekend. The 'doughnut' syndrome of an empty central core was well advanced. As a result the central city was beginning to suffer economically, with retail and entertainment moving out of the city to be closer to suburban locations. A large number of historic buildings were unused or underutilized and were in danger of demolition by neglect. Nightclubs, bars and restaurants were on the decline.

Delivery strategy. Through positive discrimination in favour of residential schemes, the aim was to increase the central city's population by 8000 units over fifteen years. The Postcode

figure 3.4
AERIAL VIEW OF THE MOST RECENT ADDITION TO THE PARKLANDS OF THE CITY OF MELBOURNE,
BIRRARUNG MARR, FOLLOWING REMOVAL OF SECTIONS OF THE RAIL INFRASTRUCTURE
(PHOTO BY JOHN GOLLINGS, 2003)

3000 programme developed in the early 1990s had four key platforms: financial incentives, technical support, street level support and promotion. The incentives included fee relief. No open space fees were payable on any type of residential development, saving owners 3 per cent of the value of the land. Performance-based refunds were provided on permit fees for planning, subdivision, building approvals and site services. Residential and council rates during the construction period were given special treatment. A free housing development advisory service giving special advice was introduced. Building recycling guidelines for residential and mixed use were produced and released. The City of Melbourne gave a commitment to streamline approvals and developed a City of Melbourne housing preference register to help identify demand and assist in the marketing of projects. The city also

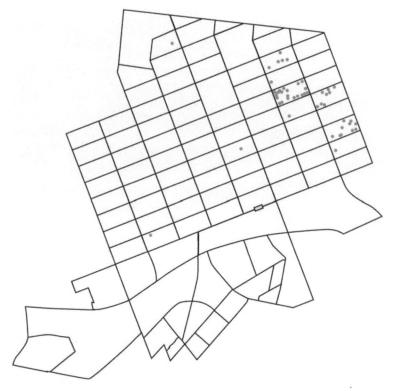

figure 3.5
POSTCODE 3000: 1983. EACH GREY DOT REPRESENTS FIVE DWELLINGS

produced market reports, using data obtained from the housing preference register. Capital works at street level supported private development projects. On-street parking in a resident priority parking scheme was offered for a twelve-month trial and off-street parking in a residential rate parking scheme was offered to selected buildings and operators. Finally, public relations and media programmes were initiated together with the production of regular project newsletters and the distribution of information packs for key groups, including leading institutions, investment groups, property owners, developers and prospective residents. Demonstration projects were also set up by Melbourne City Council.

Outcomes. Over the period 1992–2002, over 9000 new residential units were added to the central city area. The impact of these new residences was to deliver, for the first time, a truly mixed-use area in the central city with a dramatic increase in convenience stores, supermarkets, bars, cafes and restaurants. In the late 1990s the number of bars, cafes and restaurants rose from 587 to 1200 within the central area.

DEVELOPMENT CONTROL

Without a doubt the most important mechanism for the implementation of an urban design strategy in achieving a balance between the private and public realm is development

figure 3.6
POSTCODE 3000: 2002, SHOWING A TOTAL OF 9895 DWELLINGS. THE BLACK DOTS REPRESENT
CONVENIENCE STORES

control. If used correctly, this mechanism enables the energies and finances of the private sector to be brought to bear alongside the civic aspirations of the city as a whole. The city has tried to champion partnerships in development control, so as to deal with developers before plans are formulated, and to a great extent, this has been successful. The results are now obvious in a city that consistently builds to reinforce the local characteristics of its built form.

In order to ensure that all private development contributes to the quality, vitality, containment and activity within the public realm, in particular in the city streets, the City has put in place development control plans based upon the following principles:

- The need for governments to articulate clearly the long-term vision and character of the city's public realm.
- Streets are the main contributors to the city's public realm and need to be the beneficiaries of any new development; thus, it is the streets and not individual private buildings which must become the primary built form structure of the city.
- Cities need to contain the pressures to commercialize or privatize public spaces. If the city is to remain democratic, sky bridges and tunnels over major streets should be avoided.

- Future requirements to make cities sustainable need to ensure that owners of individual sites have equal rights to light and sunshine.
- Cities need to be 24/7 cities. Mixed use should be encouraged over monocultures.
- Building frontages should have a minimum 75 per cent of active frontages such as doors and windows, to ensure that the occupants may become the passive police or the eyes of our cities.
- Heritage buildings need to be retained.

STREETSCAPE PLANS

Streetscapes are often put forward as the main component of urban design, but in reality they are only one element of a city's design. As with its master planning, Melbourne has looked strategically at areas as precincts, and has planned the overall streetscaping of these areas. Its major achievement has been in tree-planting and traffic-calming. Over the period of the last twenty years approximately 10 000 trees have been planted and 35 ha of road and parking space removed. The consistent use of stone paving and street furniture has also given the city a feeling of uniformity that is now widely applauded.

TECHNICAL NOTES

Technical notes were produced to ensure consistency of treatment in many of the day-to-day details used throughout the city. These cover such things as street furniture, kerbs and paving details. The early development of these details has allowed a consistent approach on all projects and the easy dissemination of information to developers and the community. It has also allowed the city to generate an income from the street furniture through the registration of its design and their use by other municipalities.

three
PRIVATE–PUBLIC PARTNERSHIPS

Governments cannot always afford the luxury of waiting for the private sector to intervene in key areas of city change. It is becoming increasingly necessary for governments to be proactive in stimulating particular areas of their cities. One of the most effective ways of doing this is through private–public partnerships. The City of Melbourne has, for the last fifteen years, increasingly used this approach with great success, leveraging hundreds of projects, from the stone paving of the central city streets to the $600 million Queen Victoria project. The city developed a city projects division capable of negotiating, designing and project-managing the delivery of private–public partnerships. The division was then able to identify key sites and opportunities for private–public partnerships. In the case of the Queen Victoria Building, this required the purchase of a central city block and the establishment of a public–private partnership to improve the quality, value and diversity of that part of the city's public realm. Many 'black hole sites', such as the Queen Victoria, Federation Square and City Square have been redeveloped into vibrant city sites contributing both vitality and rates back to the city. In most cases the cost benefit ratio to the council exceeded a 1:2 ratio and in some cases, such as the Queen Victoria Building, the council received over $10 million in profit for a private sector investment of $600 million. Public utilities such as vents to telecommunication ducts and micro cells have been incorporated into artwork and information kiosks, in most cases, at no cost to the city. In all cases, local issues such as a shortage of parking, poor amenities or the barrier effect of rail infrastructure have been overcome while at the same time knitting the fabric of the city together.

case study
QUEEN VICTORIA BUILDING

Purpose. Through a public–private partnership, to ensure that this key central city site was developed in a way that would provide a turn-around strategy for the diminishing retail core of the city, while illustrating how new commercial development can use the traditional form of the city to produce a twenty-first century urbanism.

Issues. In order to secure it, the city needed to purchase the site for $40 million. State government approval was needed for the city to get involved in a public–private partnership arrangement and the city needed to manage successfully the financial planning and political risks associated with a project of this size. Private developers needed to have confidence in the city as a partner and, in turn, the city needed to have the confidence in its own skills in picking the market cycle to ensure the required mix-use outcomes and, in particular, the additional 45 000 m² of retail required to turn around the slow erosion of central city retailing.

Delivery strategy. The city purchased the site and then, through its in-house project management team, packaged up the site to attract the interest of the private sector. The conditions of sale, secured through legal contracts, required the developer to deliver:

- Twenty per cent public open space with twenty-four-hour access.
- 2000 parking spaces, 1100 of which were to be short term.
- A mixed-use development with a significant retail component that would not unduly compete with existing retail within the central city.
- A built form that reflected the lanes and arcades of the city.
- The use of six individual architects to ensure the final form of the development did not become monolithic.
- The developer was to provide a financial return to council equal to one and half times the current bank rate on the $40 million down payment.
- The development was to be of a quality greater than the retail in Chapel Street, one of Melbourne's leading retail streets.
- The buildings needed to exceed a four-star environmental rating.
- The developed was to provide a childcare centre with a minimum of seventy places.

63

Outcomes. Almost all the above have been achieved and, even with the project still partially under construction, it is exceeding expectations in retailing. Swanston Street and the surrounding areas are already benefiting from increased patronage to the rejuvenated site.

CONCLUSION

Many modern cities have joined the ever-increasing club of forgettable cities. Overrun by an international style of mainly high-rise architecture, with poorly defined public realms, subservient to the motor vehicle and trapped in a suffocating cloud of pollution, they are becoming places to leave rather than visit or live in. Melbourne in the early 1980s was on the waiting list of this ignominious club. Twenty years later, it is fast becoming an exemplar of the twenty-first century city. There is still much change needed, especially in the areas of sustainability, but the city has at least started to control its growth and reinhabit its cores. In doing this, Melbourne has been increasingly willing to look to its own characteristics for design solutions. Unlike many other cities that benefit from dramatic natural settings, Melbourne is first and foremost a product of design. The strong political support for design-led solutions, and ambitious public-private partnerships, have, by 2004, seen the city step back from the edge to contemplate a better future.

REFERENCE

Lampard, E. E. (1973). The urbanising world. In *The Victorian City*, vol 1. (H.J. Dayis and M. Wolff, eds.), Routledge & Kegan Paul.

Part Two

CENTRE VS. THE PERIPHERY

#04

JERUSALEM: LESSONS FROM A SHARED CITY

Arie Rahamimoff

for Anna Orgel

This article, 'Lessons from a shared city', was prepared in the year 2000, almost four years ago. While preparing for this comparative discussion on the theme of 'Centre vs. Periphery', I contemplated the inside-outside nature of Jerusalem – is it a shared city or a divided one? Due to my sentiments about the city and my natural optimism, I preferred the name *shared* over the name *divided*. My feeling was that what is unique about living in Jerusalem is the experience of sharing a common place with a variety of individuals and communities of different cultural backgrounds. The public lecture (from which this article was written) was delivered on 28 September 2000, in Melbourne. On the same evening in Israel, the second *Intifada* started. This violent event, which is still continuing, transformed the Middle East, once again.

Urban concepts are closely connected and affected by the political and social environment. The outburst of the second *Intifada* certainly changed the perception of urban, regional and international planning in the Middle East. There was a time when borders seemed to dissipate and the walls that divided people seemed lower. All this had suddenly changed – and edges in the Middle East had to be, once again, redefined. Extremity and disconnection replaced integration and co-operation. When asked to contribute to this book, I therefore had mixed feelings as to how to approach the task. I felt it was impossible to leave the written version of the lecture unchanged, in view of everything that had occurred since then. On the other hand, I also thought it would be incorrect to rewrite it entirely, as if everything had changed in light of the changed political climate.

As I had been asked to introduce some case studies and critical analysis, I felt that this gave me an opportunity to review and revise the original material and introduce some new thoughts and observations on the subject. Therefore, the first part is to a great extent the original lecture, while in the second part I have attempted to review our work in view of the changed conditions of the past four years. The 'CityEdge: contemporary discourses on urbanism' lecture series is an excellent platform for continuously reviewing and updating thinking and observations on our professional milieu and can serve as an excellent tool for the evolving understanding of the dynamics of urbanism in the near future. Within this context, evaluation can play a major role in understanding twenty-first century urbanism in a world of major and abrupt changes.

one
INTRODUCTION

The centrality of Jerusalem in the Orient was never related to its size. When the city was confined within its wall, the division between quarters was created and the souks, churches, mosques, synagogues and public institutions created the natural boundaries and connections between them. With the expansion of the city the dividing lines and connecting zones also expanded. This expansion and separation is a continuous and ever-growing process. The division within the Old City one hundred years ago is mirrored to a great extent by the regional expansion of different communities. There are Jewish and Arab quarters and neighbourhoods which are in many cases disconnected from each other, and which reflect the division that occurred originally in the Old City. The pluralistic nature of the socially divided city creates the urban separation between communities, based on differences in their history, social background and religion. Most cities are divided and mixed. These divisions can be political, socioeconomic, religious or historical. In some cases, the mixture within the city is achieved by the dynamics of common interests shared by different groups. Despite different and even polarized attitudes, cities develop frameworks of sharing.

Jerusalem is a unique example of a divided, mixed, yet shared city. It is divided by a wall and by polarized political aspirations. It is populated by two peoples, and by a variety of religious and ethnic groups. Nevertheless, it is shared by all. The common domain is shared by populations from various historic, political and religious backgrounds. It is also shared by tourists, pilgrims and, in fact, by the entire world. In the past, policymakers, urban planners, designers and architects have played an important role in enhancing the sharing of the city. They will continue to do so in the future, by preserving and further developing an urban structure that has suitably located open spaces, commercial and social facilities, as well as cultural institutions that encourage usage by all. The preservation of existing visual links to monuments of religious and cultural value and the creation of new links, supports the composite image of a well-balanced shared city. This is essential in order to strengthen the spiritual as well as the urban, spatial and visual heritage of the city. Thus, urban respect can be restored and sustained. Jerusalem is unique. However, the lessons of developing a shared city can be relevant universally.

two
URBAN EDGES

Edges are formed by cultural, historical, political, social and environmental events. Their physical implications have a tremendous effect on architectural, urban and regional form. The concept 'edge' evokes terms like margin, frontier, utmost limit, extremity – and a feeling of something risky, alert, yet also vulnerable. It can be a threshold, an entrance and a beginning, as well as an end. The highest quality of performance can also be defined as an 'edge' In the urban context, 'edge' can be interpreted as a 'periphery', but also as a 'forefront' – a starting point. When the ancient Greeks felt that they had reached the edge of a city – its limits – they did not expand the periphery of the existing city, but went on to build a new one. When deeming that they had reached the edge of their country, they settled in Asia Minor, thus acquiring more space to build new cities. Edge development is crucial in countries of immigration like Israel. Exploring and developing regions on the edge of populated areas is universal – in Australia, the USA, Canada, Africa and South America, as well as, of course, in the Middle East. Discoveries have always occurred along edges – whether they are edges of knowledge or edges of our physical world. Greeks and Romans explored the edges of the Mediterranean. The Vikings, Vasco da Gama, Columbus and Magellan discovered the edges of the Atlantic. Other courageous travellers explored the Pacific Rim.

The context of my professional involvement is Jerusalem – widening out to Israel, Palestine, the Middle East, the Mediterranean. For us, and for many others, Jerusalem has always been in the centre as a focal point of attention. However, our region has always been at an edge – the edge of Arabia, of the Roman Empire, of Egypt, of the Ottoman Empire, of Napoleon's kingdom and of the British Empire. The reciprocity of being both at the edge and in the centre shapes the quality of a place. As globalization and localization occur simultaneously in every point on earth, it is the proportion between these two that defines the unique quality of a place. Due to economic, cultural, demographic and social changes, most cities are undergoing a process of constant change that creates new edges, thus ever-changing situations of sharing and division. The edges of a city define its uniqueness. I believe that the role of architects and planners is to explore the edges and combine them in the urban planning and, through this combination, emphasize the city's uniqueness. Over the years, Jerusalem's uniqueness has acquired unusual dimensions. Jerusalem provides an opportunity to explore and contemplate a city on the edge which is united, divided, mixed and shared – all these occurring simultaneously.

three
THE EDGES OF JERUSALEM

GEOGRAPHIC DIVIDE

Jerusalem is situated on the national watershed line, facing both the Mediterranean and the desert. Dense forestation and terraced orchards on the sloping hills characterize the Mediterranean landscape. The desert landscape, on the other hand, is barren and eroded, with very little vegetation. Thus, the geographic divide serves as the generator of urban and architectural forms that respond to the topographic and climatic conditions. Organic growth and the need for natural ventilation make urban settlements in the Mediterranean more open. In contrast, buildings in the desert are usually more confined and protected, defining a clear edge between the built form and the harsh conditions of the desert.

HUMAN MATRIX

The human matrix of Jerusalem is unique but it can certainly serve as a reference to many other cities undergoing a process of cultural and social diversification. Indeed, most cities are being transformed into multicultural human contexts through immigration, international commerce, tourism and pilgrimage. The human matrix of Jerusalem has been composed over the millennia. Throughout the ages more than seventy groups of different ethnic origins have considered Jerusalem their home. The richness of the cultural diversity can be observed in daily life, in architecture, food, music and so on. The mixture and the interaction between the different groups have created an infinite number of diverse human conditions.

TIME FACTOR

Time is measured in different cycles – daily, weekly and yearly. It also can be measured by a millennial clock. In our city we can trace major changes that have occurred over more than three millennia. The continuous and long-term diversification of the city is an amazing phenomenon. Layers of past cultures – one replacing another, one on top of the other – seep into the juxtaposing cultures of today, creating a uniquely complex and rich human texture. Past and present cultures thrive in a city built only in stone. The stone, in an attempt to touch eternity, endows the city with the visual quality of permanence and stability. In everyday life, the time dimension, differently perceived by each of the cultures sharing Jerusalem, creates different perceptions of the city. Friday, Saturday, and Sunday are holy days and the sacredness of the holy day of one community is interwoven with the everyday life of the other community in the same space. The high holidays of the Moslems, the Christians and the Jews occur at the same, or nearly the same time, and are simultaneously celebrated by the different communities, each observing its own rituals. The daily rhythm is different in different sections of the city. The more rural communities organize their lives according to the rhythm of sunlight and sunset, while the westernized populations live around the clock. This creates a synchronic contradiction and complexity in the city.

THREE RELIGIONS

Jerusalem is sacred to the three monotheistic religions. Within a distance of less than 300 m from each other lie the Holy Sepulchre – Jesus' Tomb, the Dome of the Rock and the El-Aqsa Mosque – the sacred sites for Islam, and the Wailing Wall – the most revered site of the Jewish people. Human movement towards the sacred sites defines the character of the shared city throughout the day and the week and through the high holidays of each religion. This phenomenon of the three monotheistic religions sharing the same urban space is unique. Yet to define Jerusalem as divided into three religions only – Jewish, Christian and Moslem – is somewhat superficial. The city is much more fragmented than this. A variety of denominations, religious groups and sects, as well as many secular communities, share the city. Each religious group has different faiths and has its own pantheon of mythical figures such as the forefathers and the prophets. They also use the city spaces for different social and religious purposes. They perform different rituals in the same sites as those that are sacred to other sects for different reasons. The same places have different names which bear traces of the cultural and historical layers inscribed in them by various occupiers of the region. The points towards which prayers are directed also vary: Jews pray facing the Temple Mount, Christians pray towards the east, while Moslems turn to Mecca in their prayer – facing south east. The azimuth of prayer shapes the multi-directionality of the city and its position in the universe.

NATIONALISTIC EDGE

The Old City of Jerusalem is divided into many quarters – the Moslem, Jewish, Christian and Armenian quarters, the Greek compound and the Ethiopian compound, among many others. Each quarter has its own architectural style. Within the walls of the Old City, Jews and Arabs consider the same urban place as the embodiment of their nationalistic aspirations. Beyond religious differences lies a nationalism that is of dominant importance in the process of shaping the future of the city. This creates an intimate animosity. No separation or division is possible in the physical sense. These people have to learn to live together – even if walls, fences and barriers are built between them from time to time.

Prior to 1967, before the unification of Jerusalem, when the city was not shared but clearly divided, life was much simpler. Each nationality occupied its own autonomous space. The moment the city was 'united' (a figure of speech used by the Israeli authorities) the sharing process began. The obliteration of divisions started the painful process of learning how to share the city. The urban locations which serve as places of sharing are common open spaces, markets, shopping centres, cultural institutions, public facilities, health institutions, and so on. The places which emphasize the division and the disparity are the residential areas, the religious institutions and the separate educational systems, as well as many other urban systems.

BETWEEN LIFE AND DEATH

To die in the Holy City was considered, throughout history, a special privilege. People came to Jerusalem to conclude their lives. Jerusalem the necropolis was, in fact, much bigger than the living city. Some of the most dominant structures were actually built over tombs or cemeteries. The transition from life to death and back has formed the relations between Jerusalem and its inhabitants. Resurrection and the afterlife have always been at least as important as life itself. Jerusalem has thus also been shaped by the continuous tension between segments of the city of the living and the sections devoted to the dead.

THE REAL AND THE HEAVENLY

In the minds of creative people all around the world Jerusalem is both a symbol and a real place. Images of the heavenly Jerusalem are completely separate from the real, living city. Jerusalem has been conceived as the central place between Europe, Asia, and Africa, not only in the geographic sense but mainly because of its dominant position in the myths of western civilization.

CITADEL OF LEARNING

Jerusalem has always been a city of learning. The wisdom of the biblical kings and prophets was shaped in these landscapes. The spirits of Abraham, King David, King

figure 4.1
CHRONOLOGY OF JERUSALEM MUNICIPAL BORDERS. BASED ON MAPS FROM 1. HOSHEN (2001)
2. YOUNAN (2003)

Solomon, Jeremiah, Jesus and the Apostles and Mohammed can be felt in the landscape of the city by the sensitive observer. The tradition of learning is deeply rooted in the city structure. Moslem *madrassas*, Christian monasteries and Orthodox Jewish yeshivas are all theological schools scattered around the city. Learning serves both as an integrating and as a segregating factor. Universities in Jerusalem play an ambivalent role. They sometimes enhance the disparity while at other times emphasize the unity. Some universities are shared by all while others exclusively serve specific religious or nationalistic interests. Therefore, some universities become citadels of universal and humanistic knowledge while others concentrate on sectarian learning.

four

CONSTANT TURMOIL

The historic background of the city and the dynamics of present day changes as well as the dynamics of demographic prospects create a tension and animosity between the partners

figure 4.2
WALLS DEFINE SPACE AND DIVIDE. THEY ARE CONTINUOUSLY BEING BUILT, AND
OCCASIONALLY DISMANTLED. STAGES IN THE PERPETUAL INCOMPLETENESS OF JERUSALEM.
PHOTO COURTESY OF BIMKOM, PLANNERS FOR PLANNERS RIGHTS, JERUSALEM, ISRAEL

who share the city, a tension that is most likely to continue. The demography of change will probably increase the percentage of Arab citizens in the city. In 2000 I observed that there was a steady growth of the religious population (from all religions), and an overall growth of the total number of the population. I anticipated that negotiations for peace would increase tourism and pilgrimage and many international organizations and companies would seek to establish their presence in Jerusalem. However, during the four years since 2000 Jerusalem has experienced a dramatic reduction in tourism and related economic activity. All these trends are likely to enlarge the population of Jerusalem and increase the tension within it. We may hope that these dynamics can be diverted into constructive directions, producing collaboration for the benefit of all. Academics and politi-

figure 4.3
SCHOLARS IN JERUSALEM HAVE MANY FACES. MILNER AND SALOMON, (1993)

cal leaders from all political parties are constantly searching for new guidelines for municipal and regional management in order to create institutional frameworks that can contain these changes. However, the process of learning how to share the city is long and difficult, and if it is achieved, dramatic changes in the whole region will be seen.

five
CASE STUDIES

The above observations served as a basis for the formation of the following projects, which were developed over the last twenty-five years.

THE MOUNT OF OLIVES AND KIDRON RIVER – THE HOLY BASIN

Context
The Mount of Olives and the Kidron Valley form the Holy Basin east of the Old City. The dramatic views from the top of the mountain reveal the Temple Mount – Harem e-Sherif and

the Old City. It is a sacred mountain for the three main religions. Jesus ascended to heaven from this mountain, and it is from here that the Church of the Holy Sepulchre can be viewed at the end of the pilgrims' path through the Via Dolorosa. The Prophet Mohammed, on his flight from Mecca and Medina, also ascended to heaven from here. The dramatic vistas from the Mount of Olives take in the site where Abraham prepared to sacrifice Isaac, and it is on this site that the Jewish temples were built. The most sacred cemetery for Judaism lies on the Mount of Olives. Walking around the mountain is like travelling in time through history.

The Mount of Olives is the *alter ego* of the Old City which it overlooks. The contrast between the two accentuates the mass and the void. The Old City of Jerusalem is one of the most compact and continuously built-up urban forms in the world. The Temple Mount is a clearly defined open space with freestanding edifices and the Mount of Olives is open to the natural landscape and provides views to the distant city and beyond. The interaction between them highlights the contrasts between them and signifies the unique content of each.

The Holy Basin is a place of many uses and meanings, of complexities and extremities. It serves for prayer, for burial and for living. It is a site shared by millions of pilgrims, tourists and visitors who come here for religious and cultural purposes and for tourism, but it is also the scene of everyday urban activity of various types. It houses three universities, three hospitals and three cemeteries (Jewish, Moslem and Christian) as well as being the home village for a few hundred Arab families, of whom some have lived here for generations. Over the last fifteen years, the Israeli Ministry of Tourism, the Israeli Government Tourism Corporation, the Municipality of Jerusalem and the East Jerusalem Development Company have been developing an intensive project with the aim of creating a series of belvederes, promenades, meeting places and piazzas in the most revered places. In 1989 our office was commissioned to prepare the plan for the Mount of Olives and the Holy Basin. Architects Dorothy Dyer, Alex Krantz and Eilon Bernhard participated in the preparation of the plan for the Mount of Olives.

six
PLANNING STRATEGIES

The Mount of Olives Comprehensive Plan included preservation and restoration of the site together with guidelines for development. The plan suggested building form and mass for time indefinite, restoration of the beautiful Kidron Valley and creation of a walking path, a new information centre to help orient the millions of visitors who come to the hill each year, the reduction of traffic along the lower border of the site, new parking solutions for tourist coaches, connections to the Arab village, A-Tur, at the top, walking paths that transverse the site, a panoramic observation point and the restoration of the Jewish cemetery.

Several principles guided us in the process of developing this project:

1. The preservation of the Biblical landscape by maintaining open views to all directions, preserving historical walking paths, preserving major existing land uses such as open

spaces, cemeteries, and sacred sites and preserving the skyline by minimizing the development of new buildings on the site. When planning and intervening in a site of such great historic and religious importance, small-scale interventions may not be noticed in the short term, but their long-term accumulative effect can change the character of a place dramatically. Looking back at the changes that the Mount of Olives has undergone in the past 150 years, it is not difficult to imagine how this unique and important place might continue to change dramatically and, unless treated with the greatest care, lose its sacred religious and cultural value within the hundred years. It is therefore of the utmost importance to create, via sensitive and responsible planning and through regulations and guidelines, a consensus and a normative approach to this site – inducing a sense of multigenerational responsibility.

2. Creating visual and physical links that provide access to local residents, pilgrims, and tourists alike, as well as to all the other citizens of Jerusalem. It was important for us to make sure all the potential users of the site, without any preference towards any one social or religious group, have clear and easy access to all parts and components of the site, without compromising the preservation values and principles discussed above.

3. Establishing many observation points from which the historic and cultural landscape can be experienced and viewed. The main promenade, 4.5 km long, was designed to include many smaller viewpoints and seven major observation points, each serving as a starting point for the various walking trails leading to the Mount's important sites, including the entrance to the Old City and the Via Dolorosa. The promenade extends the walk through the Holy Basin and with its many different viewpoints and vistas, creating a long and fuller experience. It organizes space and creates a sense of harmony, enabling people to move through the Holy Basin and experience it without altering it.

4. Maintaining neutrality within the multicultural space. Avoiding sectarianism was a main guideline in the planning process. There has been absolutely no preference of any one social or religious group over any other. Furthermore, visual exposure from the observation points of the monuments sacred to the three religions maintains absolute impartiality. This was achieved by bypassing the main routes through neutral and historic areas and an equal dispersal of observation points. There is no single visual focus or axis but rather multidirectional exposure. The open space serves as the connector between the different religions and cultures. The Holy Basin is thus a cultural and religious open space that is relevant to all.

5. Respect for both the sacred and the profane. Planning for the many visitors (over a million a year) as well as for the local residents (several thousands). Taking both groups into equal consideration in terms of roads, entrances, infrastructure and commercial activity and so on.

EVALUATION

The Mount of Olives is a unique place, thousands of years old, central to the cultural development of the world, and one of the epicentres of the Israeli–Palestinian conflict. From a historical point of view, fifteen years is a very short time for an honest evaluation

figure 4.4
THE MANY FACETS OF THE MOUNT OF OLIVES AND THE HOLY BASIN

of such a project. Nevertheless, it can be said that within the constant change of a sacred living open area (as opposed to a closed and regulated site), our plan has managed to lay out the foundations for the long-term preservation and protection of the area, and for maintaining the fragile consensus under possible future change. I feel that the plan, in its essence, is beyond conflict. The principle that this important site belongs equally to all has been sustained through the dramatic events of these years.

seven

THE CENTRE FOR JEWISH STUDIES, THE HEBREW UNIVERSITY OF JERUSALEM

The Centre for Jewish Studies, designed by me with my wife, architect Salme Rahamimoff, is part of the Hebrew University of Jerusalem at Mount Scopus. The Hebrew University of Jerusalem has been a central cultural institution for higher education of over seventy-five years and is the academic home of over 15 000 students and several thousand academic scholars and workers from all the sectors, religions and nationalities of our society. Mount Scopus is located at the edge of the city, facing the Mediterranean coast of Israel on the west and the Judean Desert and the Jordan Valley on the east. The university complex is surrounded by Arab and Jewish neighbourhoods and is in immediate proximity to an area of long-lasting territorial dispute. In 1997 our office won an architectural competition for planning the Centre for Jewish Studies, one of the most important institutions for Jewish research in the world. The building is located on the slope of Mount Scopus, facing the breathtaking view of three countries – Israel, the Palestinian Authority and, in the distance, Jordan. In the nearer vicinity, it faces Jewish institutions and neighbourhoods as well as the Arab village of Al' Isawiya. The building houses a research centre which is currently preparing extensive research programmes on Judaism. The three main components of the building are the stepped volume of the Research Centre facing the desert and the Arab village; the internal space which connects, in a holistic way, all the major functions of the building and the library, which dominates the contour of the building, symbolizing the dominance of the book in Jewish life.

PLANNING STRATEGIES

The Centre for Jewish Studies building embodies the duality of being both on the edge and in the centre. Its location and function are an urban challenge for any planner. They present a rare opportunity to redefine a central academic institution's role and function within the city and its political and cultural realm. The specific surroundings raise questions on more pragmatic planning issues. Should the building be closed and well defined on its site, or should it be open to many directions? Should its three-dimensional composition be integrated into its surroundings or differentiated from them? We decided upon two major planning strategies.

1. *Open accessibility*. The building is accessible from two directions; from inside the university campus, on the southern side – and from the outside, from the circumference road, the village of Al' Isawiya and entire city of Jerusalem. These two entrances create a means of access from the surrounding area into the campus and vice versa. The building serves as a 'bridge' and connector. The entrances are located on different levels so that on passing through it one can experience its activities and functions.
2. *Structural dichotomy* – unity and fragmentation. The building has two main facades of different natures and composition. The façade facing the university campus is formal, classical and monumental, while the sloping façade facing the village and the Jordan Valley is terraced and fragmented, as a gesture to the more organic changing landscape of the village below and the Judean Desert.

EVALUATION

An important question this building raises, within the context of 'edges', is whether a cultural institution located at the interface between opposed communities can serve as a bridge and mediator, as a neutral platform for dialogue and research. The architecture of the building is ready to function as it was planned. However, at present the Jewish, Israeli and Palestinian sides are at the centre of a violent conflict. High fences have been built between the centre and the nearby village and the university and surrounding neighbourhoods communicate only through gates and well-protected entrances. Only the future will tell if a building of cultural content in Jerusalem, located on the edge, can achieve its goal of being a bridge.

eight
THE JERUSALEM LIGHT RAIL TRAIN – LRT

Jerusalem is undergoing a major conceptual change *vis-à-vis* public transportation. A new system of light rail trains will connect various parts of the city from the periphery to the centre. While there is nothing new about using transportation as a major strategy for

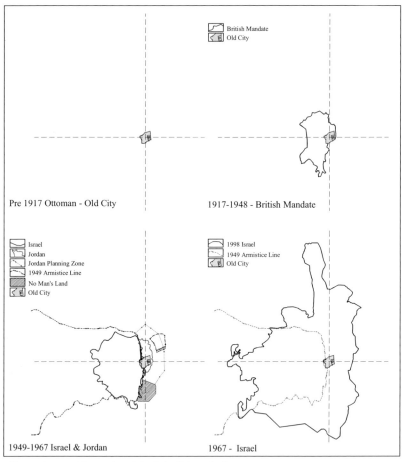

Chronology of Jerusalem Municipal Boundaries

figure 4.5
UNIVERSITY CAMPUS FACING THE JORDAN VALLEY AND THE ARAB VILLAGE OF AL'ISAWIYA —
INSTITUTIONAL AND VERNACULAR ARCHITECTURE ON BOTH SIDES OF THE EDGE

urban transformation, what is important in this case is that the light rail train (LRT) will not only connect the periphery with the centre, but will also connect the various and sometimes conflicting populations of this fragmented city. Our office is currently preparing the plan for one of the four major stations along the main LRT route. This station will operate not only as an urban (physical) connection for different modes of transportation – private cars, buses and light rail trains – but also as a focal point for interaction between different sections of the population. Train stations, like markets, public institutions and recreational areas, are natural urban connectors of diverse groups. Even if communities are segregated in many cases and live in separate neighbourhoods, as is the case in Jerusalem, the LRT station can become an excellent urban focal point for meeting and interaction.

The station will include a major square which is accessed by boulevards and roads and is connected via a green public open space, to the Judean Desert. In a divided city, transportation is a form of connection. As the LRT route will run through different parts of the city and different communities, Jewish and Arab, religious and secular, it can and, we hope, will, act as a social integrator.

KIDRON VALLEY

The Kidron Valley is located between the Old City of Jerusalem and the Mount of Olives. It connects the Old City and the Temple Mount with the Dead Sea – 20 km to the east and 1200 m below, crossing the political borders between Israel and the Palestinian Authority. The Kidron Valley is the Holy Basin and at the same time it is a conduit for drainage and sewage. At present, raw sewage from both the Jewish and Arab neighbourhoods runs down the valley, crossing political borders and artificial separating walls. The ecological ramifications of such a shameful environmental situation can thus become the catalyst for a multinational effort at solving it. Recently we have been involved, along with our Palestinian colleagues, in discussions concerning a possible joint project for the reclamation of the Kidron River Basin. As Palestinian, Israeli and European and American institutions are willing to collaborate in order to remedy ecological hazards, it appears that environmental concerns can triumph over political controversies and joint projects, with international support, can become the vehicle through which edges become permeable and collaboration emerges.

AFTERTHOUGHTS

These four case studies and over 30 years of practicing architecture in Jerusalem have brought me to the following observations, conclusions and recognition:

- History acts as a major planning factor in shaping the future of a city.
- The public domain within the city – that is, its public institutions and open spaces – preserves the identity of the city.
- The pluralistic centrality of a shared city acts as a major factor in the dynamics of the development of the city.
- Planning within a 'loaded' context is at the same time the cause and the effect of urban change. Utmost sensitivity must be expressed when planning the urban dynamics within a shared city.

nine
EPILOGUE: SHARING AND URBAN RESPECT

Unification, sharing and *division* are three modes of the urban condition. The oscillation of the urban situation between these three is continuous. I have good reason to believe that the condition of *sharing* is the normal and natural mode for urban form. In unique traumatic events and situations, however, cities are temporarily divided.

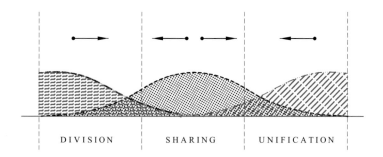

DIVISION   SHARING   UNIFICATION

figure 4.6
CONTINUOUS SHIFT ALONG THE AXIS OF DIVISION-SHARING-UNIFICATION IN THE
LIFE OF THE CITY

Recent history has taught us that the 'melting pot', a concept developed and adopted by countries of immigration when shaping the physical and sociological aspects of their land, is a false aspiration. Melting is term that conveys the opposite of respect for the unique, the different, the edge. The role of planners is to find the physical frameworks which will express respect for difference. The challenge we are facing in multicultural cities is to create a balance between urban respect and urban diversity in the context of a shared place. Urban respect derives from the recognition that every fragment of the city and the region is unique, both in physical and in social terms. This urban respect can be achieved by providing a sense of sharing, a sense that recognizes the differences that shape the city, which, whether they are social, cultural, or physical, can be expressed in many and varied lifestyles. Respect can be achieved by providing visual and physical accessibility to significant sites which are meaningful to people with different cultures and religions who reside in the city. Jerusalem is a city shared not only by the Israelis and Palestinians; by Jews, Christians and Moslems, but also between the religious and the secular, the various denominations within each religion, the natives and the newcomers; just as many other cities are today.

My observation is that the general trend in Jerusalem, in recent years and in the near future, is away from unification, and towards division. Borders are formed, then they change their meaning, and in some cases they dissolve. Nevertheless, I believe that Jerusalem will develop from the frontier of conflict that it is today, into an arena for sharing, co-operation and partnership tomorrow.

ACKNOWLEDGEMENTS

Thanks to architect Liad Kirma for editing this article.

Anna Orgel collaborated with me on the preparation of the original lecture in 2000. As a dear friend and an active participant in the Jerusalem cultural milieu, she contributed significantly to the ideas presented in this article. On the 11 June, 2003 Anna Orgel was killed in a suicide bombing attack on a bus in the centre of Jerusalem.

REFERENCES

Hoshen M. (2001). *Jerusalem on the Map*. Jerusalem Institute for Israel Studies.

Younan M. (2003). In *Envisioning the Future of Jerusalem*, (R. Brooks, ed.) The International Peace and Co-operation Center, Al Manar Modern Press.

Milner, M. and Salomon, Y. (1993). *Jerusalem of the Heavens, the Eternal City in Bird's Eye View*. Alfa Communication Ltd.

#05

DUBLIN, SHEFFIELD, MANCHESTER AND ADELAIDE: CULTURAL QUARTERS AS MECHANISMS FOR URBAN REGENERATION

John Montgomery

one

INTRODUCTION

This chapter considers the experience of former light industrial and warehousing districts, which have been revitalized as cultural quarters within cities. Such areas are classic 'zones of transition', in that a decline in economic activity has been followed by protracted periods of disinvestment and disrepair. Whilst property market activity has tended to favour the central business district or green-field city-edge locations, most of the emerging cultural quarters have required public investment and planning. Their success has demonstrated that a combination of new cultural activity, new residences and the adherence to urban design principles creates successful places, even in formerly peripheral locations. We consider two major case studies – Temple Bar in Dublin and the Sheffield Cultural Industries Quarter. Reference is also made to two other cultural quarters: Manchester Northern Quarter and the West End of Adelaide.

My argument is that successful cultural quarters tend to share the attributes of good urban places in general, offering beneficial and self-sustaining combinations of activity, form and meaning. They will, moreover, be dynamic and significant places where new work is available and where culture is produced and consumed. Where they are successful, cultural quarters should stimulate new ideas and become places where new products and new opportunities can be explored, discussed, tried and tested. Cities also provide the flow of people and the markets necessary to support viable cultural activity locally, that is in cinemas, galleries, theatres and music clubs. This activity can help reinvigorate the city economy and also provide opportunities for bright young people to set up in business. Put crudely, culture can put you on the map and make the city more interesting. This is therefore more than a question of locating new cultural venues, important though that is – it is also an issue of place-making and economic development.

Urban trends, as we have understood them for most of the post-war period, have tended towards greater decentralization and suburbanization – promoting low-rise residences, commuting by car, the use of private cars, the development of shopping malls along edges, new commercial and industrial zones, and so on. Yet more recent economic and social trends point to an altogether different set of preferences of locations and places. Many businesses today need less, rather than more, space; small businesses networks work best through face-to-face contact and people in generally are more aware of the choices available and are more sophisticated, placing greater emphasis on quality in their everyday environment. These trends have underscored the re-centring of older city districts, whether they are parts of the central business district, older residential neighbourhoods or old industrial districts.

Urban peripheries are not a single type of place and we have choices about the sort of places we wish to make. This should be governed by the relationship of any given site to the wider urban structure, the balance of uses that have already been established across the urban area and the need to improve the networks of movement. This approach to 'place characterization' allows us to see what types of place we are dealing with and to establish patterns of norms to work towards. Let us take the case of cultural quarters as an example.

two

FOUR CASE STUDY EXAMPLES

TEMPLE BAR, DUBLIN

Temple Bar is a 36 ha urban quarter, sandwiched between O'Connell Bridge to the east, Dame Street to the south and the River Liffey to the north, in central Dublin. The area was largely developed and built in the seventeenth and eighteenth centuries, and still retains the street pattern and tight urban grain from that time. There are many layers of building here, which tell a tale of trade and commerce, Georgian elegance and a gradual slide into poverty and decline. Temple Bar is in fact one of the oldest parts of Dublin, dating back to 1259 when an Augustinian monastery was built there. In the seventeenth century William Temple, secretary to the Earl of Essex and a Provost of Trinity College, built his home here and gave the area its name. A bar was the name for a walkway by the river. The area as we see it today dates largely from the eighteenth century when cargo was loaded and unloaded on ships docking at the quays on the south side of the Liffey. The network of narrow streets became a hive of buying and selling, with merchants, craftsmen, artisans and shipping companies plying their trades. There were also a large number of *bagnios* or brothels. Later, printers, publishers and instrument makers moved into the area, together with bookbinders, stationers and stockbrokers. With the building of a new Custom House in the nineteenth century, the old Essex Quay at Temple Bar fell into disuse and the area became a centre for the clothing trade such as tailors, drapers, cap makers, furriers and woollen merchants. In 1816, a metal toll bridge was erected – the Ha'penny Bridge – to enable Dubliners to cross the Liffey to visit the music hall in Crow Street (Temple Bar Properties, 1991).

The future of Temple Bar was in doubt for many years, not least because the state bus company (CIE) proposed to redevelop most of it as a new transportation centre, linking bus and rail. CIE began to buy up property in 1981, paving the way for demolition and redevelopment. Paradoxically, the fall in property and rental values which resulted triggered off a process of revitalization. Business activities which could afford only low rents on short licences – or no rent at all – moved into the area. These included artists' studios, galleries, recording and rehearsal studios, pubs and cafes and restaurants, secondhand and young designer clothes shops, books and record stores, as well as a number of centres for a range of 'third sector' organizations. They added an exciting mix of ingredients to those remaining existing businesses that had had not yet been bought out or evicted by the CIE – the printers, cutlery shops and seedy hotels. During the mid 1980s, networks of small and medium sized enterprises became established, feeding off each other and larger cultural players such as the Project Arts Centre and the Olympia Theatre. This was a rare example of planning blight breathing life into an urban area through low-rent arts activities.

By 1990, Temple Bar had many disused industrial buildings, gap sites, problems of poor east–west permeability, a residue of entrepreneurial activity and many buildings which were simply falling down. Paradoxically, Temple Bar also had a reputation as a place of discovery, vitality and a wide range of social and economic exchange. It was frequently referred to as 'Dublin's Left Bank', on account of its relatively high density, a mixture of architectural styles, its close proximity to the quay, its narrow streets and a lively atmosphere deriving mainly from its youth culture – recording studios, video companies, artists' studios, theatres and pubs, cafés and restaurants.

It was important that this alternative culture should not be lost by wholesale redevelopment of the area or by adopting a property value-led approach to urban renewal. There were many lessons to be learned from British cities where property value-led redevelopment had pushed up rents and effectively driven out the small shops, artists' studios and cultural businesses which created the buzz and made localized areas – such as Covent Garden – attractive to developers in the first place. Much needed to be done in Temple Bar, not least to prevent the building stock falling into greater disrepair. But great care had to be taken not to destroy the sense of place that had already been created by the mix of activities that were based there. Thus businesses and arts organizations in the area organized themselves to form the Temple Bar Development Council as early as 1989, and began to lobby for the area to be regenerated as a cultural quarter.

The strategy which was adopted to achieve this was, accordingly, a combination of culturally-led urban renewal, physical renewal and urban husbandry and local enterprise development, particularly in connection with the cultural industries and the evening economy. An early strategic development framework for the area was prepared by Urban Cultures Ltd in 1990–1991. This recommended:

- Adopting a stewardship ethos and management approach to knitting back together the urban area;
- Adopting twelve cultural projects to act as urban 'chess pieces', that is, localized strategic interventions to create activity and interest. These include a film house, a sculpture gallery, a photography gallery, music venues and the old Olympia Theatre;

- Providing business grants and loans to help young cultural and other entrepreneurs set up in business. This strategy was accompanied by a survey of existing businesses in the area;
- Training the various cultural industries in business skills, but also in catering and venue operation;
- Promoting and stimulating an evening economy;
- A major initiative to improve permeability and the pedestrian flow through the area, involving the creation of two new public spaces, outdoor venues, niche gardens, corners to sit in and watch the world go by, culminating in the design of two new public squares;
- A major programme of public art and cultural animation, designed to reclaim and give meaning to the area's public realm;
- An overall approach to property management and upgrading, based on balancing the need to improve the area's environment with the need to retain existing activity;
- Introducing vertical zoning linked to the provision of grants and tax relief status;
- Designing new buildings by young Irish architects, with the accent on modern design within the context of the historic street pattern;
- A major marketing and information campaign using good modern design.

This strategy, in the form of a flexible framework plan (Development Programme for Temple Bar, 1992) was implemented largely by Temple Bar Properties Limited (TBPL), a state-owned development company established in 1991. Temple Bar Properties engaged in acquiring properties, renewing them and negotiating rents with occupiers and in undertaking development schemes on its own volition or in joint ventures with private owners and developers. To do this, it was granted an initial £4 million from the EC and given leave to borrow £25 million privately, but with a state guarantee. Monies generated from rental income are ploughed back into the property renewal programme and further environmental action, and used to cross-subsidize cultural projects. In the final analysis, the total of the public funding for Temple Bar was some IR£40.6 million, the bulk of which (£37 million) was spent on the Cultural Development Programme 1991–2001. A further £60 million has been borrowed and repaid through TBPL's commercial programme. Over 1991–2001, the private sector is estimated to have invested over £100 million in the area.

TBPL was established as a small company with a limited shelf life initially of only five years (later extended to seven, and then ten). Its role was to ensure that the future development of Temple Bar corresponded to the set of cultural planning, urban stewardship, mixed-use planning and urban design principles discussed earlier. After Temple Bar Properties has completed its work, the area is intended to have its own life. Most of the physical development programme for the area was completed by 2001. Since then, Temple Bar Properties has continued to manage certain key property holdings as well as putting on various events. In addition, Temple Bar Properties and Dublin Corporation adopted a set of urban management principles for improving city diversity and mixed use, and building on the Corporation's own Temple Bar Action Plan for urban renewal, produced in 1990. With adjustments for the unique identity of individual urban places, these principles form the backdrop for street-by-street and block-by-block design guidance and development schemes.

Over its first seven years of existence, Temple Bar Properties, amongst other things, commissioned a high-profile architectural framework and urban design competition; devised an economic development strategy to encourage and support entrepreneurship and the cultural industries; created two new urban squares and an east–west route through the area; adopted mixed-use zoning to achieve diversity and to stimulate the evening economy, urban culture and street life and initiated a major area marketing and information campaign.

In 1992 there were twenty-seven restaurants, a hundred shops, half a dozen arts buildings (some of them falling down), sixteen public houses, two hotels, 200 residents, seventy cultural industry businesses and seventy other businesses in Temple Bar. By 1996, when most of TBPL's own development schemes had been completed, there were five hotels, 200 shops, forty restaurants, twelve cultural centres and a resident population of 2000 people. During the construction phase, some 5000 yearly FTE equivalent jobs had been created in the building industry (most of sub-contracted to Dublin companies). By the end of 1996, an estimated 2000 people were employed in Temple Bar, an increase of 300 per cent. The final major commercial development to be undertaken by Temple Bar Properties was the Old City, designed to create a significant retail and residential cluster in the area between Parliament Street and Fishamble Street at the western end of Temple Bar. Situated around a new pedestrian street, Cow's Lane, the development consists of 191 apartments, twenty-four retail units, a crèche and landscaped gardens.

Temple Bar Properties Ltd was effectively wound up as a property development company in 2001. By that time, Temple Bar was home to some 3000 residents, some 450 businesses

figure 5.1
TIGHT URBAN STREETSCAPE
IN TEMPLE BAR, DUBLIN

employing close on 2500 and twelve high-quality cultural venues. The whole area had become a showcase for urban design, architecture, design and style. Temple Bar Properties today (2002) retains responsibility for managing various matters across the area. A Green Plan is in preparation, including a waste management plan for the area, additional street cleaning and the ongoing maintenance and security of Meeting House Square and Temple Bar Square. TBPL continues to programme outdoor cultural events and markets, all of which are provided free of charge to the public. A traders' group (Traders in the Area Supporting the Cultural Centre) has been formed to co-ordinate the marketing of the area and to provide additional street cleaning. TBPL is also responsible for managing three writer's studios and an international visiting artists' apartment.

Success, however, brings its own problems. By the mid-1990s, Temple Bar had developed a reputation as the 'stag night' capital of Europe. Research commissioned by Temple Bar Properties at that time revealed that these visitors – largely groups of young women and men from England – were beginning to cause other visitors to stay away. This problem was addressed by a co-ordinated management response by landlords and hoteliers in the area, essentially by refusing accommodation to large same-sex groups. Cultural writers acknowledge the importance of Temple Bar as an example of using creativity and design to re-establish an area's economy and sense of place. Florida, for example, writing in 2002, refers to Temple Bar as a 'clever and far-reaching strategy of levering authentic cultural assets to attract people and spur economic revitalisation' (2002, p. 302).

SHEFFIELD CULTURAL INDUSTRIES QUARTER

The area of the Sheffield Cultural Industries Quarter (SCIQ), as defined in Sheffield City Council's CIQ *Area Action Plan*, extends to some 30 ha and is located just to the south east of the city's administrative, retail and commercial core. The area is roughly triangular in shape, and is bounded by Arundel Gate and Eyre Street to the north, St Mary's Road to the west, Suffolk Road to the south and Sheaf Square and Howard Street to the east. Sheffield Hallam University occupies much of the area to the immediate north. Parts of its estate are included within the SCIQ itself, including a new Business Studies School, the Northern Media College and the proposed School of Cultural Studies at Porter Brook. The SCIQ is within a 10-minute walk of Sheffield City Centre, the mainline Midland Station is a few hundred yards away, and access to the trunk and motorway networks is good.

For a period of some fifteen years, the SCIQ has been undergoing a transformation. By the mid-1980s, the SCIQ had become a classic zone of transition: a marginal area of the city centre which was once a thriving industrial and workshop centre, but had become characterized by vacant and derelict buildings and gap sites. Slowly at first, but with a marked quickening in the pace of development from the mid 1990s, the SCIQ is now recognized as a centre for a wide range of cultural production. This includes the fine arts, photography, film-making, music recording and graphic and product design. Important initiatives within this spectrum include the Yorkshire Arts Space Studios, the Audio

Visual Enterprise Centre, the Leadmill night club, Red Tape Studios, the Sheffield Science Park, the Site Photography Gallery, the Workstation managed workspace and the Showroom Cinema complex. The Quarter is also home to Yorkshire Art Space Society, the Untitled Photographic (now the Site) Gallery, and a cluster of some 300 small businesses related to film, music and TV, design and computers. Important links have been established between the Cultural Industries Quarter and the adjacent Science Park, particularly with regard to the development of new technology in film, photography and recording, while there are now proposals to develop a culture campus in the area which would house Sheffield Hallam University's fine art, media studies and design departments.

In the early 1980s the City Council started to develop a cultural industry policy aimed at supporting these activities and assisting the economic regeneration of a former car showroom. Two resultant building-based projects – the Workstation and the Showroom – are seen as central to the development of the SCIQ. The buildings are owned by Sheffield City Council and were developed by a specially formed registered charity, Sheffield Media & Exhibition Centre Limited (SMEC). The charity set up a development subsidiary, Paternoster Limited, that took a 125 year lease on the building. Paternoster Limited run the Workstation as a purely commercial enterprise charged with operating the building for the benefit of its tenants, and covenant profits to the parent charity (SMEC) for the benefit of the Showroom Cinema operation. The Showroom also receives revenue grant support from Sheffield Arts Department, the British Film Institute and Yorkshire and Humberside Arts.

By 1997, despite the impressive growth of new organizations, facilities and venues, the SCIQ lacked a strong sense of place. There were very few shops in the area, and few bars, other than traditional pubs catering for students of Hallam University. An important strand of both the 1998 SCIQ Vision and Development Strategy and the Action Plan for the SCIQ was to encourage secondary mixed-use, particularly along the ground floor frontages. This was to include small shops, alternative retail, cafes, bars and restaurants. The Sheffield CIQ Strategic Vision and Development Study of 1998 (EDAW and Urban Cultures Ltd.) represents the current thinking on the next phase of development within the SCIQ. It incorporates the results of consultation, research and discussions with the local and wider communities of public and private interests. It should also be read in tandem with Sheffield City Council's Area Action Plan for the CIQ, which provides more detailed planning and urban design guidance, and details of individual sites for development.

In early 1999 the SCIQ Agency was established to promote and implement an agreed development strategy for the SCIQ over a five-year period. The agency's mission is further to develop the SCIQ, building on the successes and, importantly, the broad character and nature of the SCIQ as a cultural production centre and as an urban place. The aim is to create a thriving cultural production zone with large numbers of small and medium enterprises, a centre for excellence in knowledge creation and creativity, a destination for visitors and a largely mixed-use area with various complementary activities throughout the area, generating pedestrian flow throughout the day and into the evening, including residences. The agency is composed of a non-executive board with members being drawn from local businesses, Sheffield Hallam University, the Science Park and Sheffield City Council. The board is supported by a small, full-time management team.

The Agency's five year strategy (to 2004) has the following targets:

- To have in place fifty active exporting firms in the cultural industries and an overall doubling of the businesses base within the area;
- To provide an additional 350 000 sq ft of workspace for cultural industries;
- To provide 4200 jobs (3000 of which will be direct, and 1200 indirect), of which 2500 will be net additional jobs;
- To support the opening of fifty new retail, catering and entertainment outlets provided by private investment;
- To provide for 500 additional permanent residents;
- To complete a new urban culture campus for Sheffield Hallam University;
- To complete a number of cultural projects, including a Photography Gallery, a Fine Art Gallery and a Centre for Performing Arts;
- To continue a two-pronged training and education strategy aimed at both enterprise development and providing community access to new technologies and the cultural industries;
- To upgrade considerably the urban public realm in order to provide a more pedestrian-friendly environment, including established access points and routeways and two new urban squares.

Since 1998, substantial private sector investment has been attracted into the area in the form of bars, nightclubs, restaurants and student apartments. A major visitor attraction, the National Centre for Popular Music, opened in 1999, although this has not succeeded in attracting the visitor numbers predicted. Despite the Centre's difficulties, the SCIQ as a whole continues to grow. A new 1000-capacity bar and live music venue opened in the summer of 2000; Red Tape Studios is launching a new Internet School; Modal's National Music Convention has been attracted to the Quarter and so has the International Documentary Film Festival. Yorkshire Artspace developed a new building; Radio Sheffield are opening a new headquarters in the SCIQ; the old Roberts and Belk cutlery factory is being developed as a managed workspace with a ground floor cafe bar and the former Leadmill Bus Garage is being redeveloped for six cafe bars, offices and apartments. Estimates by the SCIQ Agency (2002) reveal that the SCIQ was then home to some 270 businesses and organizations, including film, TV, radio, science and technology, new media, training and education, live performance, music, arts, crafts, metalworking and a range of support producer and consumer services.

figure 5.2
MEETING HOUSE SQUARE
AND THE NATIONAL
PHOTOGRAPHY GALLERY,
TEMPLE BAR, DUBLIN

HINDLEY STREET, ADELAIDE

Hindley Street – or the West End, as it is also referred to – is Adelaide's naughty, often seedy and sometimes dangerous night-time area, although it is also a shopping street during the day. The area tends to be dominated by strip clubs, tattoo parlours, 'pokies' (game machine arcades), twenty-four-hour drinking bars and other, less savoury, activities. In 1999 Adelaide City Council launched its West End Arts-led Urban Renewal Programme supported by Arts South Australia and the state government. The aim was to work with artists and arts organizations to develop arts and creative industry projects and programmes within the area, thereby providing the West End and Hindley Street with a more diverse identity and character. Early projects included the relocation of the Adelaide Festival Office to a shopfront on Hindley Street, Shop@rt – a programme of exhibitions in vacant shop windows, an arts market and the FestWest street festival. An annual event – West End Open House – is now held where all the venues and a number of shops, restaurants and offices hold open exhibitions along the length of Hindley Street and throughout the West End. Projects completed before 2002 include a new $30 million (about £12 million) centre for performing and visual arts on Light Square, an arts cafe on Hindley Street, and a relocation of the Adelaide Symphony Orchestra. In addition, a tenancy plan is being implemented which aims to effect a reduction in the numbers of tattoo parlours, motorcycle-related shops (most of which are run by Hells Angels) and pinball parlours. Meanwhile, a number of streets are being enhanced (with new lighting and shop-front improvements), notably Leigh Street. A number of apartment blocks have been or are in the process of being refurbished. Since 2002 when a state Labor Government was elected – progress in the area has floundered, two major proposals for cultural industry workspaces have been shelved and there are now signs that the artists are being priced out of the area by increases in rent levels.

MANCHESTER'S NORTHERN QUARTER (MNQ)

Manchester's northern quarter (MNQ) lies just to the north and east of the main shopping area around Market Street and the former Arndale Centre. For many years its major streets – notably Oldham Street – were the most fashionable of all shopping streets in the city. As with many other city centre districts, the area began to lose vitality and meaning from the late 1940s onwards. Initially, two processes were at work: firstly, the decline in the textiles industry meant that parts of the area and – equally important – in Ancoats to the east, began to experience reduced economic activity and lose businesses and jobs. This had a knock-on effect on the economy of Oldham Street and environs. Secondly, the wholesale slum clearance of the northern quadrant of the area and much of Ancoats and other adjacent areas effectively removed the resident population that had sustained many businesses in the area. As if this were not bad enough, Smithfields Market was relocated to the outskirt of Manchester in the 1970s, at about which time the Arndale Centre was built. The effect was to tear the remaining life out of what had been one of the most vibrant quarters within the city. Many businesses closed or moved away, and few people remained living locally.

By the late 1980s, the area had few businesses left. These were mainly fashion wholesalers, some specialist shops (selling prams, pets and pianos) and a few drinking and transvestite clubs. Manchester City Council became concerned that the area was not regenerating as other parts of the city were at that time, notably Castlefield and the Whitworth Street Corridor. This was despite the fact that the area had been granted commercial improvement area status, allowing landlords and shopkeepers to apply for shop-front improvement grants. By 1993, 27 per cent of the floor space in the area was vacant, many gap sites had appeared and a large proportion of the building stock was in serious disrepair. By 1991 only 345 people were living in the area.

Yet during the late 1980s, a number of new businesses moved into Oldam Street in particular, including the Afflecks Palace (a fashion emporium), the Dry Bar and PJ's Jazz Club among others, while some of the other clubs and venues had remained in the area, including Band on the Wall. These businesses formed the Eastside Association in the early 1990s to lobby for improvements in the area. In late 1993 a development strategy for the area was commissioned jointly by the Eastside Association and Manchester City Council (undertaken by Urbanistics and Urban Cultures Ltd.). Their main recommendations were to retain the existing rag trade but also to grow new businesses in creative activities, alternative shopping and the evening economy. In addition, a major programme of the conversion of residential upper floors was advocated. In analysing property ownership in the area, the consultants advised that the implementation vehicle for the area should be an alliance of landowners, developers and the City Council, with a much better resourced Eastside Association (renamed the Northern Quarter Association) that would have a prominent role in crafting development schemes for the area. A system of sticks and carrots was put in place to help convince developers and property owners to engage with the overall area master plan. These included a series of small and large grants and the sophisticated application of planning controls, up to and including detailed design briefs for key sites and properties. The problem, as the consultants had diagnosed, was that the whole area suffered from market failure: the trick was to encourage people to start investing again.

One problem with this approach is that although various new venues have been proposed within this area over the years, such new venues as have been built have tended to locate in adjacent areas such as Ancoats or Piccadilly Gardens. A number of small privately-owned clubs and bars – Dry Bar, Café Pop – remain and operate as regular small-scale venues, but the lack of venues arguably undermines the Manchester's northern quarter status as a cultural quarter. That said, a small events programme organized by the Northern Quarter Association includes the Northern Quarter Street Festival, an annual one-day open-air free event. The overall development of the area is expected to include workspace provision, particularly on upper floors, both for refurbishments and new builds. An example is the Smithfield site, on which Manchester City Council are encouraging redevelopment for a mixture of commercial, retail and leisure uses in new and renovated buildings.

The MNQ development strategy is aimed at encouraging business start-ups and growth in the creative industries, largely as market-based enterprises. In 2000, the Cultural Industries Development Service was formed to help develop sustainable cultural and creative enterprises in Manchester's metropolitan core, including the MNQ and Ancoats (see Blanchard, 1999). The area strategy has been in place for some nine years, but only now can it be said to have been a success. Indeed, many of the larger projects – such as the redevelopment of Smithfield market – are only just getting under way. Even so, many new schemes have been successfully completed, including several mixed-use retail and residential schemes along Oldham Street and individual four- and five-storey buildings throughout the area. By 2002, the northern quarter was home to over 550 businesses and organizations, although a good proportion of these were already trading in the area before 1995. It is a place for shopping, music, food and drink, entertainment, fashion, living and working. The mix includes one hundred clothing and fashion outlets; seventy cafes, pubs, bars, restaurants and clubs; fifty voluntary organizations; forty arts, crafts and jewellery shops; twenty vinyl, tape and CD shops; ten hairdressers and barbers; seven newsagents; and more than another 200 unique specialist shops, services and suppliers.

Today, the MNQ is as much a fashionable residential neighbourhood as a cultural industries or night-life quarter, and that is no bad thing.

three
EVALUATION

The bottom line is that one cannot really have a cultural quarter without cultural activity. The analysis of the success of these different projects is given below under the various key headings.

Small medium and large-scale cultural venues. Our analysis reveals the development and maintenance of cultural venues has been most ambitious and consistent in Temple Bar, but with some successes also in Sheffield and Adelaide. The weakest performer is Manchester MNQ, where no new venues that are open to the public for viewings, screening or performances, have been established.

Festivals and events. Temple Bar offers a varied, year-long programme of indoor and outdoor activities. The Northern Quarter Festival in Manchester operates for only three weeks of the year. The Festival and Fringe Festival in Adelaide are very successful, and are organized on a city-wide basis. Sheffield Cultural Industries Quarters has a poor programme of cultural animation.

The availability of workspaces for artists and low-cost cultural producers. The most impressive achievements in this field have been in the Sheffield Cultural Industries Quarter (with recording studios, artists' studios and a film companies centre) which has to date deliberately focused on cultural production more than on venues. With the Jam Factory, Adelaide also has an impressive work-based, though largely training, resource for cultural producers, in this case ceramicists, glassblowers and furniture makers. With the exception of Temple Bar Gallery and Studios, the approach in Dublin has favoured cultural venues over workspaces, while Manchester MNQ has largely failed to make any low-cost spaces available for artists and craft-workers. In Manchester there has also been very little public sector involvement in developing managed workspaces for micro and small studio and office-based businesses. This contrasts markedly with the approach in Sheffield, with the development of the Workstation and other developments that are in the pipeline. There are proposals in Adelaide to establish a business incubator space for contemporary design and crafts, but these have stalled following the election of a Labor Government. Adelaide needs to provide more workspaces for young cultural producers.

Managed workspaces for office and studio users and the economic development of small firms in the cultural sectors. Of the quarters, only in Sheffield and Manchester has there been an active programme of arts and cultural-industry business development, and in the case of MNQ this is effectively the cultural programme for the area.

The location of arts development agencies and companies. Only in Adelaide has there been a deliberate policy of relocating publicly funded organizations into the cultural precinct. In some ways, a *de facto* policy has operated in Temple Bar with many of the new venues (the Irish Film Centre, for example) doubling up as premises for the industry sub-sector development agencies. What most, if not all, the cultural quarters have in common is the presence either within the quarter, or very close to it, of a major arts education or training institution, such as the Northern Media School in Sheffield and the Visual and Performing Arts Centre in Adelaide. Temple Bar is adjacent to Trinity College, and the Manchester Institute for Popular Culture has an office in the MNQ. In the cases of Sheffield and Adelaide this outcome was quite deliberate, and both are seeking to strengthen the links between formal education and enterprise development. More such agencies, following the example of BBC Radio Sheffield, are needed. In Manchester no specific initiative of a comparable nature exists.

Arts and media training and education. All the quarters researched have a public art policy and a programme for securing new work, although not always by direct commission. Although this is to some extent a subjective judgement, the public art programmes in Adelaide and Dublin are the most impressive of the case studies described here.

Art in the environment and community arts development initiatives. The extent to which the various cultural quarters actively promote community arts development is also patchy. As in other matters, the approach in Temple Bar is to build the responsibility for community development into the overall remit for several of the cultural venues, particularly in the case of the Ark. Sheffield CIQ takes a more direct approach to this issue, with a cross-programme emphasis on access and participation. Manchester MNQ is weak on this indicator.

Complementary day-time and evening uses. As far as complementary day and evening activities are concerned, policy in Temple Bar from the outset was to encourage as fine-grained a mix of uses as possible, especially as far as including fashion and other alternative shops, cafes, restaurants and galleries. This has included maintaining low rent levels for certain types of uses. The early aspiration to become a '24-hour city' was toned down and new residential developments in the Old City are sited away from bars and pubs, in particular. One of the problems in Sheffield CIQ is a lack of street life, largely because of a lack of good, active street frontages. This problem was addressed by the SCIQ Vision and Development Study, and also by the SCIQ Action Plan, and reasonable progress is being made. The problem in Hindley Street in Adelaide is that the night-time uses are arguably too energetic, and may be driving out good day-time uses such as book-stores and boutiques. Manchester's MNQ has more complementary activities – both day and night – than cultural activity *per se*. In the MNQ, the aspiration to develop an evening economy and greater mixed use remains largely just that, an aspiration. With only a few exceptions, most of the new property investment in the area in the past five years has been for mainstream offices.

Stable arts funding. The most powerful approach of these projects has been that of Temple Bar, where the Irish Arts Council played a prominent role in devising and funding the overall cultural development programme. Such a level of commitment is currently not evident in Adelaide and has been largely lacking from MNQ. In Sheffield CIQ, major projects have come forward either sequentially or on a case-by-case basis, so that each project is subject to an independent feasibility process and has its own funding package, usually comprised of arts board funding, city council inputs, lottery funding and European money. In Adelaide, one concern may be that as so many of the new arts venues and relocating organizations are housed in properties leased from private landlords, there is no complete guarantee that they will not have to move on when rent reviews fall due.

four
CONCLUSION AND DISCUSSION

All this reveals that, although there are many similarities between the cultural quarters in terms of their overall cultural and regeneration aims, there are also many differences between them, particularly and most importantly as regards how the cultural programmes have been set up and implemented. These differences partly reflect different cultures or ways of working, and partly the set of circumstances in each place before and during the development of the quarter. It is therefore difficult to argue, as some may be tempted to do, that all cultural quarters are essentially the same and these days formulaic to boot: no more than a response to urban decline and economic restructuring together with an attempt to promote new economic activity in post-industrial cities. But beyond this, it is unwise to draw too many conclusions, or set down too many prescriptions. Good cultural quarters will only succeed if they offer a distinctive and varied cultural programme.

All of the cultural quarters researched here have good *urban place characteristics*. That is to say, they are relatively compact and walkable urban districts, are more intensely developed than suburban neighbourhoods and have a stock of adaptable buildings that are of varying ages, highly permeable, easy to read and range in scale from two-storey to at least five-storeys. This is true even of Hindley Street in Adelaide, even although Australian cities are generally laid out to more generous space standards (mainly road widths) and tend to have lower building heights (excluding the very tallest buildings) than what is found in the UK and Ireland. Hindley Street itself is a 20 m wide main street, but is no less interesting for that. Side streets such as Leigh, Peel and Victoria offer secondary permeability, although they are less often used by pedestrians.

The Sheffield CIQ has more gap sites awaiting development than the other cultural quarters. However, new schemes are being proposed almost daily in an area which no longer suffers from property market failure. The main route remains Paternoster Row, yet good pedestrian traffic is found on Howard Street and Charles Street. The Manchester MNQ offers perhaps the grandest stock of buildings of all the quarters researched. Oldham Street remains the main thoroughfare, although Tib Street has become a more prominent location for design businesses. Temple Bar remains the cultural quarter where the most effort has been invested in improving permeability, to the extent of creating at least one new street and a new pedestrian bridge, while traditional street patterns and build-to lines have been respected and adhered to.

Temple Bar is also the only quarter to have invested positively and quite deliberately in *new public spaces*, Temple Bar Square and Meeting House Square, even where some demolition of existing properties was required. In Sheffield, there are admittedly two new squares, one adjoining the National Centre for Popular Music (NCPM) and the other at the top of Howard Street adjacent to Hallam University. The former was underfunded and is poorly realized; the latter, named Hallam Square, has arguably more to do with the university calling attention to itself than representing a strategic intervention in the public realm. The latest proposal is for a major plaza connecting Midland railway station to

figure 5.3
THE WORKSTATION, SHEFFIELD CIQ,
ENGLAND

the SCIQ at the bottom of Paternoster Row. This is really a city centre project, rather than one specifically to do with the cultural quarter. The Manchester MNQ has seen little in the way of new public space, and even the long-mooted redesign of Stevenson Square has remained nothing more that a paper proposal. What new public space there is has usually been an adjunct or planning gain from a commercial office or residential development permission. There is no real strategic approach to new public space in the MNQ and neither has there been one in the West End of Adelaide, where there are no proposals as yet for new public spaces.

Successful cultural quarters exist in the mind as well as physically. That is to say, people form and retain impressions of them before and after visiting. They carry an *image of place* about with them. This is partly a reflection of the activities and sense of place one finds there, partly an issue of marketing and image-making, and partly a question of style. The most successful cultural quarter in terms of image and identity is Temple Bar which has an international reputation. Temple Bar has pursued and continues to pursue an imaginative marketing campaign and cultural programme (such as events, festivals), and has very deliberately appointed young modern architects to work on new signature buildings. Sheffield, too, has embraced modern design, but not to the same degree, while to date the SCIQ marketing has not been especially penetrating. Manchester MNQ has also encouraged modern design, albeit on the edges of MNQ, notably the new Urbis Museum. The MNQ retains its reputation as one of the cool areas in town in which to hang out, but is largely unknown outside Manchester. The West End of Adelaide is something of a paradox in this regard. Although at one point on the verge of being fashionable, the area is still viewed by the city planners as a heritage precinct to be retained, since many of the buildings are over 100 years old. Good new architecture can be found, but this is mainly in relation to conversion work (the exception to this general rule is the Embassy Hotel, which has recently been voted one of the world's best hotels). This is perhaps understandable, but Adelaide as a whole remains a city which seems unwilling or afraid to encourage greater innovation in building design. Meanwhile, the marketing of the West End is modest stuff, aimed mainly at locals, as opposed to interstate and overseas visitors.

URBAN POLICY, MARKET FORCES AND MANAGEMENT MECHANISMS

There are clearly some major differences between the various case study examples discussed above, not just between the places themselves but also in terms of the *types of intervention* (physical, planning, economic development and cultural) pursued by public agencies, and in the level of public funding. Temple Bar is clearly a direct intervention model where a bespoke, state-owned, development company was established, with a strong cultural remit, to drive forward the area regeneration. The result includes twelve new or fully refurbished cultural venues in the middle of the city. If anything, Temple Bar attracts criticism for having succeeded too well, although such an outcome was not guaranteed, certainly in the early years. Progress in the Sheffield Cultural Industries Quarter has been less spectacular (and has taken place over a longer period) but has also been impressive. Here the early emphasis was on the economic development of cultural industries supported by access, training and education programmes: a strategy for increasing cultural production. This has been achieved through a more selective programme of property acquisition and development, notably of the Showroom and Workstation, but also the Audio-Visual Enterprise Centre and Yorkshire Artspace Society. In later years, attention has extended to cultural consumption in the form of encouraging the private sector to invest in retail units, bars and clubs, and also residential accommodation. The commitment to small firm development, however, has not been diluted.

The example of Manchester's MNQ reveals that where property market failure can be shown to be temporary (1993 was, after all, a year marked by the depths of a property crash and economic slump) area regeneration can proceed by a process of plan and development brief-led development, backed by some area branding, public art and an events programme. Progress in the MNQ has been much slower than in Temple Bar and SCIQ, certainly as regards the development of cultural facilities and venues. Rather, efforts have been focused on micro and small-firm development of the creative and media businesses across Manchester. Development in the MNQ has progressed, although some of the larger schemes have taken a long time to get started. MNQ is arguably more successful as a city centre residential and retail neighbourhood than as a cultural quarter *per se*.

The West End of Adelaide is worthy of further study, to allow the effects of the strategy to be evaluated, but progress in the area appears already to have stalled. Although some major investments in arts venues have been made over the years (the Jam Factory, the Lion Arts Centre and now the Centre for Performing and Visual Arts) much of the current activity is the result of there being a precinct management plan, agreed with a variety of private property owners. On this basis, buildings have been guaranteed tenants, leases have been signed and rent levels negotiated. This includes even the refurbishment of a former cinema as a rehearsal and concert hall for the Adelaide Symphony Orchestra. The state government and Adelaide City Council have supported this process directly by relocating their own arts agencies to shop units along Hindley Street. However, proposals to develop incubator spaces for young designers and artists have been axed. The main doubt over the West End Arts Precinct is the fact that a large number of organizations occupy properties owned by private individuals and companies. Most of the leases being signed are for 10–20 years. There can be no guarantee that market forces will not in the end encourage landlords to increase rents significantly or look for higher spending tenants.

The overall conclusion is that all of these examples have been strategic in nature. Whether directly intervening in the property market, or opting to self-build particular strategic projects; whether directing the property market through development briefs and planning permissions, or employing a property leasing plan – all have had the vision and strategic goal of becoming a cultural quarter. The type of cultural quarter may have varied (being mostly consumption-led in Temple Bar, production-led in Sheffield, fairly institutional in Adelaide and design- and fashion-led in Manchester) but all four places explored the relationships between regeneration, creativity and the cultural economy. Yet all, too, face the problems of their success, notably in the form of land value colonization and gentrification.

DO CULTURAL QUARTERS REPRESENT SUCCESSFUL URBAN REGENERATION?

This raises some wider questions as to the validity and applicability of cultural quarters being designated in other towns and cities. The first question is whether arts-led urban regeneration works. The evidence of these four areas that it does is compelling, even if we allow for other factors such as spectacular economic growth, such as that in Ireland from about 1995, or a general property market recovery, as in the case of Manchester. The Sheffield and Adelaide examples show that success can be achieved against a backdrop of market failure and fear of crime. Culturally-led urban regeneration works in inner urban areas, depending on the skill of policymakers.

Secondly, is it possible to plan a cultural quarter? Again, the answer to this must be yes, particularly given the strategic planning that went into Temple Bar, MNQ and SCIQ. In all these cases, the objective was to deliver key cultural projects, but also to address property market failure and attract private sector investment. The balance varies from quarter to quarter. The most market-oriented example, MNQ, is probably the least successful culturally. The most interventionist initiative was Temple Bar, yet curiously this also seems the most organic and natural. Both the SCIQ and Hindley Street have some way to go in achieving greater diversity, although private sector investment is now proceeding at unprecedented levels, at least in recent years. It is possible to plan a cultural quarter, but resources will also need to be committed to a cultural programme, low-cost studios and business space and improvements in the public realm.

As to the wider debate on the urban structure, urban development and regeneration, it can be seen that urban intensification is possible, certainly in transitional areas whose economies have become peripheral and in need of revitalization. Not only this, but mixed-use development is not only desirable but is also achievable.

Furthermore if, as it seems likely, it will always be necessary, in all cities, to recreate or re-energize neighbourhoods and city districts from time to time, then the important thing is to recognize what type of place we are dealing with, and what type of place it could become. Geographically and economically, peripheral locations may be developed to low or to higher densities and mixes. This is a question of choice and what is appropriate for the overall urban structure. It is possible to apply urban design principles on place-making to a range of place types, and even in new locations.

Finally, it must be stressed that not every urban area can or should be a cultural quarter – this is not some trick rabbit to be pulled out of a hat. Cultural quarters work only where there are venues and workplaces for cultural producers and working artists. There is little doubt in this writer's mind that cultural activity, the urban characteristics of place and a little style add greatly to the urban and economic mix. More than this, cities which do not offer space to lively small business and cultural districts will be left behind.

REFERENCES

Blanchard, S. (1999). *The Northern Quarter Network: a Case Study of Internet-Based Cultural Business Support*. Manchester Institute for Popular Culture.

Florida, R. (2002). *The Rise of the Creative Class*. Basic Books.

Temple Bar Properties Ltd. (1991). *Temple Bar Lives, a Record of the Architectural Framework*, Temple Bar Properties Ltd.

Temple Bar Properties Ltd. (1992). *Development Programme For Temple Bar*. Temple Bar Properties Ltd.

#06
FROM CENTRE TO PERIPHERY:
THE AESTHETICS OF MOBILITY

Francine Houben

In 1976, in his book *The Joyless Economy*, the economist and welfare theorist Tibor Skitovsky predicted that an excess of standard goods would lead to increasing social dissatisfaction, because these goods are devoid of real sensory stimulation for human beings. Scitovsky's predictions that a cheerless and tasteless economy would leave deep traces throughout Europe are directly borne out in the physical planning, urban development and architecture of the last few decades. The mobility axes illustrate this clearly. Add to that more than 400 km of noise-protection barriers and you have a model of the bad taste inherent in the most visited public space in the Netherlands: the motorway.

In my book *Composition, Contrast, Complexity* (2001) I suggest that architecture cannot be put into words. The book describes twenty projects. Ten statements – on thin, fragile Japanese paper – encapsulate the views upon which I base this proposition. Or to put it a better way, perhaps, they clarify what I am seeking. The fifth statement is on the aesthetics of mobility. The twentieth project describes a room with a view. I will now attempt to explain why the architect of the library and the master plan of the Technical University of Delft is introducing this subject: the aesthetics of mobility.

one

DECEMBER 1998 VROM COUNCIL (COUNCIL FOR HOUSING, PHYSICAL PLANNING AND THE ENVIRONMENT)

As a member of the VROM council, I become involved in the political discussion about the future layout of the Netherlands. One of the topics is corridor development – I oppose this. Mobility is part of modern society; it is a daily pursuit, just like housing, work and recreation. Mobility is not just about traffic jams, asphalt, delays and tollgates, but also about people deriving a sensory experience from their everyday mobility. Every day, travelling along roads and railways, millions of people experience the changes of the city and countryside. For them, the train and the car are also 'a room with a view'.

One might wonder whether the traditional methods of urban planners, in the form of future scenarios depicted statically in maps coloured red, blue, yellow and green, are truly appropriate. These maps are not merely static – they are two-dimensional. The third dimension is missing, as are the dynamics of motion. One might be well-advised to view the Netherlands from the moving perspective of the everyday mobile person. Perhaps it is the combination of mobility, city and countryside that has given rise to the population's increasing sense of saturation.

figure 6.1
MOTORWAY AS CORRIDOR

On the VROM council, which is beautifully put together when it comes to disciplines, I find I am the only architect. To me, an architect's task is to imagine, to be a visionary, to propose and disseminate ideas, to inspire – not to fixate on that which is wrong or ugly, but to go in search of what is in fact possible. That is the moment the adventure begins.

FEBRUARY 1999: THE ART OF INTEGRAL ENGINEERING AND THE AESTHETICS OF MOBILITY

At the invitation of the Minister for Transport, Public Works and Water Management, I give a lecture entitled 'the art of integral engineering and the aesthetics of mobility'

103

figure 6.2
MOTORWAY AS ROUTE

(Duivesteijn, 1999; Houben, 1999). Before an audience composed almost entirely of engineers and administrators, I propose viewing the motorway as a design brief; a brief that requires both a cultural turnaround and a new set of instruments. This is because existing urban development practice is not up to the task.

To give the aesthetics of mobility some form, I introduce six typologies that can deal with the alternation from the scale of the city to that of the countryside. Three relate to the countryside: the panoramic landscape, the eco-viaduct and the Bali model. The other three relate to the city: the Ruhr area, Las Vegas and La Défense. They form a series running from utmost rural to urban in the extreme. As a symbol for the cultural turnaround needed, the roads may be seen as routes and given names, such as the Louis Couperus Route, the Erasmus Route, the Rembrandt Route and the Zuiderzee Route. The routes need not just vision and direction, but more importantly, a client to commission them. In the period that follows, administrators in the Netherlands seem to rise to the challenge and accept the responsibility of taking on the role of client in commissioning the great mobility axes. To me, this illustrates the unique architectural climate in the Netherlands, so admired abroad.

JUNE 1999: LOUIS COUPERUS ROUTE

Eight municipalities jointly request advice about a fragment of the Louis Couperus Route (Bestuurs Regio Utrecht, 1999). At issue is accommodating the eastern section of the High Speed Rail Line (HSL) between Utrecht and Maarn in conjunction with the widening of the A12 motorway. At the meeting, I suggest to the mayors that they take their seats according to the order in which their municipalities lie along the route. They do not find this comfortable. One can sense they are tense and ill at ease. Administrators are not accustomed to peering over one another's borders. But water systems, infrastructure, belvedere areas, ecological structures, cultural landscapes, housing construction and economics do not stop at provincial and municipal boundaries; on the contrary, they cross them. The intensive labour involved in drawing up plans, coming up with alternatives and consulting with the engineers of Transport, Public Works and Water Management, in addition to the give-and-take required among the desires of the various municipalities, reminds me of the urban renewal process of the 1970s. A lot of discussion but little vision of the whole – this cannot yield a good result.

OCTOBER 1999: ZUIDERZEE ROUTE

Four provincial authorities request advice about the Zuiderzee Route from Amsterdam to Groningen (Flevoland, Friesland, Groningen and Drenthe 1992–2000). For the meetings, we have devised a special table, 6 m by 6 m, topped by a huge land map of the area, with the Zuiderzee line shown as a snaking tube of fluorescent orange. The meeting table symbolizes and stimulates a new form of co-operation and communication among provinces and municipalities. Collages graphically depict the influence of motion on the city and the countryside. The high-speed train accelerates in the countryside, shortening both travel time and the time in which the landscape is perceived. In the cities the train slows down, extending the perception of the urban area along the journey. The combination of motion with the actual expansion of the cities and the actual shrinking of the countryside produces an exponential effect on the traveller's perception.

A characteristic of the route to the north is the interplay of infrastructure lines – motorway, railway, power lines, waterways and dikes. A conspicuous feature of the polder landscape is that the motorway network runs not quite parallel to the other lines. The railway, the motorway and the power lines play a sort of game, attracting and repelling one another. As you ride along, at times you see them all and at times they suddenly disappear. The variations in height of the magnetic suspension track – we introduce five heights: mole high, knee high, cow high, tree high and mast high – allow even greater possibilities for composition.

Research into the future development and identity of various landscapes and seven cities (Amsterdam, Almere, Lelystad, Emmeloord, Heerenveen, Drachten and Groningen) situated along the Zuiderzee Route provides dramatic evidence of the much more extensive use of space in the northern provinces, compared to the Randstad, the densely built urban conglomeration in the west of the Netherlands. Our advice is to use the construction of a rapid-transit Zuiderzee Route to bring about the change from extensive to more intensive land use.

Land is a valuable possession. The Netherlands is known for its scarcity of space. Yet land in the Netherlands is squandered because the price of land is far too low, which obviates the need for

intelligent solutions, such as dual land use, inventive combinations of, and with, infrastructure.
This is the first statement in my book, cited above.

JULY 2000: PANORAMAS AND PERFORATIONS

In this study we researched the route from Delft to Leiden, Amsterdam, Utrecht, Gouda, Rotterdam and back to Delft – the Randstad Circuit – in terms of the relationship between the ecology and the infrastructure (National Physical Planning Agency, 2000). On a map, hand-coloured symbols indicate where zones of transition and communication between the different ecosystems are needed. The motorway blocks ecological exchange between areas on either side of the road. In this way the Randstad Circuit creates a large area flourish for flora and fauna to breed. By raising the road somewhat in places, we can perforate it with ecological passages that re-establish contact between the two sides of the road in this watery area.

Another map shows the panoramas seen by motorists along the Randstad Circuit. The minimum measure of a panorama is set at one km. The longest panorama, 8.5 km, lies in the Haarlemmermeer polder. Travelling at a speed of 100 km per hour, one sees it for five minutes. We call the series of panoramas the Hollandse Meesters (Dutch Masters), after Jacob van Ruisdael, Jan van Goyen and Aelbert Cuyp, landscape painters from our Golden Age. The analysis shows that the panoramas and perforations can often share the same locations. There are building commissions to advise on cityscapes and the appearance of villages, but there is no one to keep an eye on the appearance of entire motorways. A coherent administrative policy designed to protect and maintain these panoramas could make the locations of these ecological passages instantly visible to the traveller.

NOVEMBER 2000: DESIGN OF THE MAGNETIC SUSPENSION TRACK

The magnetic suspension track that will take people from Amsterdam to Groningen at a speed of 500 km per hour will give the traveller the sensation of being in a glider flying low above the ground. (The design for this was commissioned by the consortium Siemens Nederland N.V., Ballast Nedam, ABN AMRO Bank and Hollandse Beton Groep, 2000). Nearby residents and politicians fear the magnetic suspension track will become a hulking structure with a concrete trough on fat concrete pylons, at an exorbitant cost. The old discussion about horizon pollution, typical of the Netherlands, resurfaces. This is really odd, as though infrastructure were something shameful, something to be camouflaged. But why not show it off with pride, design it just as the polder landscape was designed? Set the magnetic suspension track on a steel and concrete structure, under which the landscape flows. A fast line, a slow landscape – these can interrelate quite beautifully.

NOVEMBER 2000: DUTCH MOUNTAINS

The Netherlands has long been an urban country. Relatively small cities are set at short distances from one another. The Randstad, most of it below sea level, is a delta metropolis

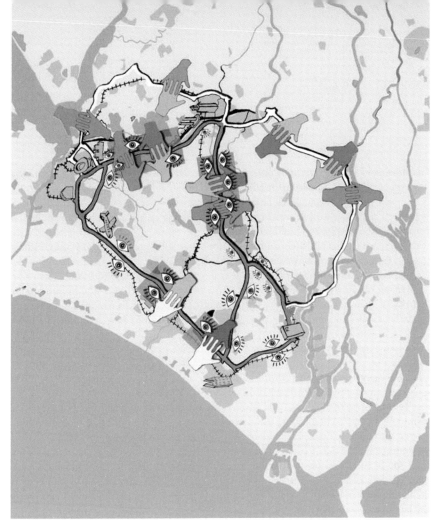

figure 6.3
PANORAMAS AND PERFORATIONS

of some 5 million inhabitants. Our highest point, the Vaalserberg, which is 322 m high, is at the southern-most point of the country. We share our highest point with Belgium and Germany. Next in line is the Posbank, on the Veluwe near Arnhem, at a height of 100 m.

A study into high-rise building policy in the delta metropolis opens with the premise that high-rise building is a relative concept (Minister of VROM, 2001). An overview of all the towers around the world lists by name, year and height, buildings such as the Hong Kong & Shanghai Bank in Hong Kong (1985, 179 m), the Empire State Building in New York (1931, 381 m), the Sears Tower in Chicago (1974, 442 m) and the Petronas Towers in Kuala Lumpur (1998, 452 m). Rotterdam's high-rise buildings are projected among them, showing what height is, in Dutch terms. Mecanoo's Montevideo, commissioned by ING Real Estate, at the head of the Wilhelmina pier, at 151.5 m, will for a short time be the tallest building in Rotterdam and thus in the Netherlands (ING Real Estate, 2003). The National Physical Planning Agency asks us to consult on a high-rise building policy for the entire delta metropolis for buildings up to 300 m high. I use terms from my book *Composition, Contrast, Complexity.*

Composition. North American cities such as Chicago and Toronto consist largely of a huge sea of suburban houses surrounding a composition of high-rise buildings, where public transport is also concentrated. The city's identity, its logo, is the skyline. Even the city of New York has two clearly identifiable high-rise building clusters: Lower Manhattan and Midtown. Contemporary Dutch cities increasingly consist of suburban neighbourhoods, with dwellings that stand barely higher than the top of a full-grown tree. This is in contrast to such European cities as Berlin, Paris or Madrid. In general, high-rise buildings in the Netherlands are set down as if incidental, as if it they were no more than church towers. They stand staring out in solitude and, whether beautiful or ugly, they add nothing to the identity of their city. Rotterdam has successfully pursued a high-rise policy for its city centre for many years, and the residents of Rotterdam are proud of their expanding skyline.

Contrast. The effect of a high-rise building on the Netherlands skyline is ruthless. It has an impact on the landscape for miles around. How does high-rise construction in the city relate to the exodus from the city to the country, in search of peace and quiet? Rotterdam is the case study. From the urban side of the Kralingse Plas (Lake), one can sense how one might escape, via the lake and the River Rotte, to the Groene Hart (Green Heart), the protected rural area encircled by the cities and roadways of the Randstad. From the rural side of the lake one can see the Rotterdam skyline. A collage shows Rotterdam's skyline expanding over the next ten years. This skyline grows steadily more beautiful and does not spoil the escape-from-the-city feeling. Beauty in architecture, urban planning and landscape design is partly defined through proportions. This drawing shows the heights increasing from a starting point at the Kralingse Plas right up to the high-rise buildings in the city centre – a range from 0 to 320 m.

Complexity. The heights of the Kralingse Plas model are projected on to the Green Heart within the delta metropolis and the contours of the Dutch Mountains emerge. The panoramas and perforations form the valleys. Of course some local-level fine-tuning will be needed. Flags indicate where intensive public transport is to be provided in the delta metropolis in years to come. Logically, high-rise buildings and intensive land use are found where good public transport brings them together. They form the peaks in the landscape of the Dutch Mountains. Each city can choose its own height, befitting its own identity. And naturally Rotterdam is the Mount Everest of the Dutch Mountains.

This can give high-rise buildings, in the form of the Dutch Mountains, visual significance within the mobility landscape and turn them into the link between motoring and public transport. Imagine that you are driving along the Randstad Circuit. At Utrecht, you see the Domtoren (Dom Tower), the highest peak at 112 m. The buildings that vault the A2 between the old town and the new Leidsche Rijn area form Utrecht's hillcrest. In Amsterdam, you drive between the Mountains of the Zuidas, with its development plans around the World Trade Centre metro station. This might become a tunnel at some point. You see The Hague lying in the distance. The skyline is evolving above the Utrechtse Baan motorway into the city and around the Central Station. Delft proudly shows off its University of Technology, and rightly considers the height of its historic inner city untouchable.

figure 6.4
DUTCH MOUNTAINS — ROTTERDAM'S SKYLINE 2002

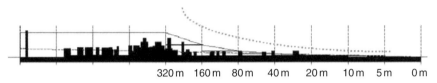

320 m   160 m   80 m   40 m   20 m   10 m   5 m   0 m

figure 6.5
DUTCH MOUNTAINS — ROTTERDAM'S SKYLINE 2010

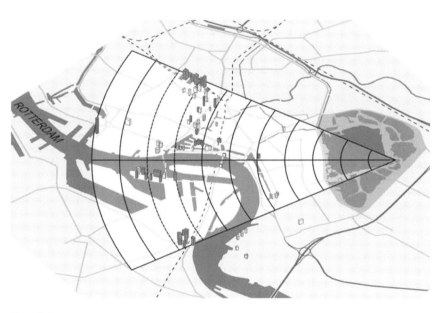

figure 6.6
DUTCH MOUNTAINS AND THE GREEN HEART

From Delft, you can already see Rotterdam looming on the horizon. Right in the curve of the Kleinpolderplein the Mount Everest of the Dutch Mountains stands majestically.

MAY 2001: HOLLAND AVENUE

The task of the study *De Leuke Weg* (The Fun Road) commissioned by the Directorate-General of Public Works and Water Management – the Roads of the Future – is to

109

research the point of view of the daily road-user (Ministry of Transport, Public Works and Water Management, 2003). The Randstad Circuit, as the most intensively visited public space in the Netherlands, becomes the case study. This is explicitly not a design brief, but an exercise in reflection on the future of the roads. The Mecanoo team is composed of English, Belgian, New Zealand and Dutch architects and landscape designers. The operational language is English, in debate and in writing. We define the concepts in English as well. Often they cannot be literally translated into Dutch. That is actually a good thing, for is it not in fact, crucial that we define words and concepts for an international audience of professionals? The team's variety of cultural backgrounds makes clear that appreciation for the infrastructure and the landscape of the Randstad varies. Apparently there is such a thing as 'Dutch genes', rooted in Dutch clay.

'Hardware', facts and figures are collected, relating to past, present and future: engineering preconditions, ownership, responsibility and commissioning of the roads. The rise in car ownership, the cost of cars and petrol, the most popular car. Increases in mobility in terms of mode, motivations for travel and average distances. Speed, traffic jams, traffic density, environmental pollution and safety. All these facts help us to understand our task. The facts stand unadorned, side by side. The facts and figures make it perfectly clear that a rich society is a mobile society. Car ownership is much cheaper, in relative terms, than it was 20 years ago. Fuel-efficient cars, in spite of the rise in petrol prices, have considerably lowered the cost of travelling per kilometre.

The Dutch network of motorways is – in contrast with other countries – mostly an upgrading of former provincial roads. The motorways are also the only routes between the cities. Even in a country like the Netherlands, with reasonable public transport, the car remains by far the most common means of transport. The most important motivation for motoring is not commuting to and from work, but rather private use. Most distances covered are less than 5 km, a distance that could be also be covered by bicycle.

'Software' is collected. On 12 July 2001, four cameras are installed in a car at the driver's eye-level. The tapes of 105 minutes of film for each camera are used to analyse 153 kms of motorway. Data are included such as:

- The number of lanes and the speed limit – Overschie has since become an 80 km-per-hour zone.
- The tempo of the exits – an average of one exit per 2.8 km. Is that a lot or a few?
- The petrol stations – there is one every 15 km. What will happen to these stations in the future?
- Overpasses and viaducts – there are seventy of them over 153 km of motorway.
- The programme. In architecture, we are used to analysing programmes. We make a stab at it for the motorway – noise barriers, noise embankments, business areas, greenhouses, housing, parking areas, grass and crops, planting, tunnels. We differentiate between what one can see to the left and to the right. If the Green Heart lies in the

middle of the Randstad, and the cities lie along its edge, then we should be able to read that from the programme. This is not borne out by analysis.

- Depth of field. Openness is a characteristic of the Randstad. Where and how far can you see? We work with six categories from 0 to 2000 m. As a motorist, do you experience the Green Heart?
- Once the petrol stations are projected onto the depth of field diagram, most of them turn out to be within our panorama areas. What does this entail for the design of future petrol stations?
- Landmarks. We recorded as landmarks striking infrastructural works, noteworthy buildings and properties and urban panoramas. The Randstad Circuit proves not very expressive. When you roll the film, it is actually very boring. Of the seven cities, only Rotterdam displays a strong panorama when viewed from the road.

In each case – as notes on the actual analyses – points of interest for future design specifications are defined. The hardware and software are published in the research road atlas. 'Visioware' (visionary design) is proposed. The design atlas attempts to develop a design approach to the motorway from the point of view of the road user. The design atlas is compiled as a catalogue, with the suggestion that – as with any catalogue – it may be partly extended and superseded. The structure is built around three concepts, three spatial domains – the road, the verge and the field – which together form the perspective of the road user. Sometimes the domains intersect one another. This is an attempt to develop a conceptual language to help a designer with the brief.

THE ROAD

This is the slab of asphalt or concrete on which one drives. The road surface itself is a subject of study in terms of engineering and communication. At issue is the form of the road, but also the road that becomes a building and the building that becomes a road, under-the-road programmes, above-the-road programmes, stacked roads and tunnel roads.

THE VERGE

This is not only the shoulder that runs from the edge of the asphalt to the drainage ditch, but also the entire area within the sphere of influence of the road. It looks like a piece of no man's land; you experience it as a non-place. Parts of it are owned by the Directorate-General of Public Works and Water Management and other parts by third parties. With the slogan 'purge the verge' we suggest abolishing this no man's land. Let the rural landscape or the landscape of buildings connect directly to the road. With the slogan 'identify the verge' we suggest giving this non-place an identity of its own by adding a programme, or by turning it into a specifically designed landscape. Petrol stations could be placed on or under the road, for example, or as large green hills alongside; or noise barriers could be equipped with digital information displays. And of course we should not overlook any of the possibilities offered by landscape architecture.

THE FIELD

This is the area that stretches to the horizon, the area that influences your field of vision. This is the area of the panoramas of the Dutch Masters and the Dutch Mountains. It lies outside the sphere of influence of the motorway, outside the purview of the Directorate-General of Public Works and Water Management. Great measures are at issue here, both in height and in depth.

THE SEQUENCE

All the design proposals for road, verge and field together to form a route – a route which reveals the Randstad: cities, countryside and ecology, economics and development, know-how and culture, recreation and amusement. The comic strip, *De avonturen van de Leuke Weg* (Adventures on the fun road) shows the roads of the future. Our study, originally given the working title 'De Leuke Weg' by the Directorate-General of Public Works and Water Management evolves into a mature 'Holland Avenue'. And during the final preparations for the Rotterdam Architecture Biennale the study gets an international sequel.

two
FEBRUARY 2002: ROTTERDAM INTERNATIONAL ARCHITECTURE BIENNALE

Requests for lectures and interviews about the aesthetics of mobility are coming in from all over the world. I go to Italy, for instance, and Ireland, Norway, Canada, the United States, Malaysia, Australia and Mexico to talk about mobility aesthetics. It amazes me. The studies are typically Dutch – what use are they to them? The international interest allows me to travel with new eyes. I photograph and film the cities from taxis, cars, trains and buses, and I talk about them with local architects and universities. The cultural differences among the various countries on how to deal with mobility are significant. In Tokyo, I behold the literal expression of my idea of the Dutch Mountains. From my hotel room I can see, towering above Shibuya train station like a huge mountain, the next great train station, Shinyuku. It pleases me to see how completely train and car are absorbed in Tokyo into the mobility landscape of this cosmopolitan village. Buildings stand atop and under stations, atop and under railways. The most beautiful buildings stand right next to the city motorway, which almost seems to go through the buildings.

In late February 2002, I am asked to direct the first International Architecture Biennale in Rotterdam, with mobility as the theme. In consultation with the Technical University of Delft, I decide to accept and to do it under the aegis of the Chair of Aesthetics of Mobility. The next day I leave for Mexico, for lectures and workshops. On the way from Mexico City to Queretaro, I drive past the artwork of five coloured towers by the architect Luis Barragán, who, together with artist Mathias Goeritz, created the artwork *Torres Satelite* (1957) in Queretaro, Mexico. It stands midway between the motorways – in Mexico they set their great works of art and monuments right where everyone can see them.

figure 6.7
VERGE — FIELD — ROAD

figure 6.8
IDENTIFYING THE VERGE

During my visit to Monterey Tec University, the idea emerges to invite other large cities from around the world, with their universities, each to do a study – like Holland Avenue – of a route of about 100 km long. Los Angeles, Tokyo, Beijing, Hong Kong and the Pearl River Delta, Jakarta, Beirut, Budapest, the Ruhr area and, of course, Mexico City and the Randstad are selected – ten cities with totally divergent cultural and economic backgrounds, problems and perspectives on the future. In June 2002 all the cities come to

Rotterdam and Delft, meet and present their cities with their specific problems, and exchange information. All of them receive the same round wooden platform on which the four cameras are to be mounted, as well as detailed instructions on how to carry out and record the research. They will further supplement the research in their own ways and define their own design briefs.

three
VOYAGE AROUND THE WORLD

In August 2002 we travel around the world in twenty and a half days. In Los Angeles – at the beginning of the automobile era – motorways were once laid out as 'scenic parkways', to allow full enjoyment of the city and landscape. These days you can tell which part of the city you're driving through only by the graffiti on the numerous noise barriers made out of the same concrete blocks. The radio is on, and the station you pick defines the world in which you imagine yourself.

Nowhere is the motorway landscape as breathtaking as in Tokyo. The roads snake through the city on two, three and sometimes even five levels, skirting the most beautiful of buildings. Yet Tokyo is actually a train town, in which you can tell you've reached your destination when you hear the tune specific to the station. Around the stations, you see multiple uses of space in their ultimate form.

Upon arrival in Beijing we discover that the myth of the bicycle metropolis is almost extinct. Each year car ownership rises by 20 per cent, and when you know that 70 per cent of China's population still lives in the countryside, you realize that this rapidly sprawling urban wasteland is merely poised on the eve of a virtually unfathomable flood tide of automobile traffic. Hong Kong. A greater contrast with Beijing is hardly conceivable. City and mobility have been lumped together on this island into one gigantic and compact edifice with a view out onto a breathtaking natural harbour. From Hong Kong we cross the border – like 90 million people every year – into China. In the border city of Shenzen you feel and see the bubbling energy of China. We take the Gungzhou Shenzen Superhighway, a 100-km private road on pillars, high above the swarming urban sprawl that alternates with rice paddies. We are surrounded exclusively by lorry traffic. This road is in fact the conveyor belt of the Pearl River Delta – the area that produces 90 per cent of everything that is 'made in China'. No torrents of commuters speeding back and forth between home and employer are to be seen, for this motorway itself is simultaneously a dormitory town and a working town. From the road you can see the factories flanked by the dormitories for the young women who work in them.

In Jakarta we slice through a thick layer of brown smog as we come in to land. The roads are gorgeous, but mobility has nearly ground to a halt here. Rich or poor, everyone wages a daily struggle to reach his destination. It is not rare to take three hours to get to work and another three hours to get home in the evening. In the tropics, this means a life spent in darkness for many.

MEXICO CITY, BEIRUT, BUDAPEST AND THE RUHR AREA

We visit the other Biennale cities individually. In Mexico City, in an effort to reduce air pollution, the motorways have been transformed into park-like ribbons. And they are used that way, here and there proudly decorated with artwork and feats of architecture. And always there is a forest of advertising along the access roads. In Beirut there aren't even footpaths. Everyone in this thousands of years old and surprisingly cosmopolitan city, is dependent on the car. On fine days the populace cruises in an endless line of cars along the Corniche, an esplanade along the beach. For Beirut residents the car is part of the ego.

Back in Europe we see how Budapest, despite its good public transport system, is in danger of suffocating in its severely swollen automobile traffic, an upheaval this city on the border between east and west had not counted on. Freedom and economic growth mean cars. Residents are beginning to move further away from the city and the city is not able to address this problem. A parallel to what happened to European cities in the 1960s and 1970s is easily drawn. You can drive forever in the Ruhr area without noticing that you are in one of the most densely populated areas of the world. In the Ruhr area you can't see the city for the trees. Since the dismantling of the old mining industry, nature has taken possession of this diffuse metropolis.

MOBILITY LABORATORY

During the Rotterdam Architecture Biennale we are holding a mobility laboratory (Mob_Lab) for architects, engineers and artists from all over the world, to exhibit their ideas about mobility, with themes such as architecture, public transport, urban planning, environment and health, technological innovations, cars and transport systems, art and mobility. An international selection is to be exhibited, showing an overview of the new ideas thriving around the world in architecture and design in relation to mobility.

HOLLAND AVENUE DESIGN TASK

Twelve international architecture schools will also present their vision and design proposals for Holland Avenue, namely the section between Delft and Overschie. There will be documentaries on culture and mobility made in association with the public broadcasting network. During the Biennale, the academic world and the architecture profession will present their worldwide research into the topic of mobility simultaneously.

four
THE FUTURE

In the last twenty-five years, mobility and automobility have shown explosive growth. The motorways have a culture of their own, a trend that Reyner Banham describes as early as 1971 in his book *Los Angeles, the Architecture of Four Ecologies*. The design discipline, along with administrators, seems to have shut its eyes to the issue throughout this twenty-five-year period. The topic of automobility and the motorist is politically incorrect.

115

Designers must see to it that everyone make use of public transport. My generation was brought up on this attitude, which incorporates a noble motive – that the environment, the landscape, the public space of cities and villages would suffer because of the car. However correct in itself this observation may be, it just leads to stalemates. The task for the future is to develop the environment, the economy and technology fully and in the right balance. This means the architects' task is to come up with solutions that break new ground – to produce designs that answer the steadily growing demand for mobility. This demand should not be resisted, but rather channelled along the right lines. It is vital that work be done on public transport and motorways, as well as on bike, skates and footpaths. Wonderful transfer junctions between the train, the metro, buses, cars and bicycles must be designed. The landscape angle must be combined with an awareness that mobility routes are public spaces with a culture, a code of conduct and an aesthetics of their own. Research and design must lead to the development of a new set of instruments. I have shown you the opening gambit.

And this is of course possible in the Netherlands, where we create buildings as landscape and landscape as buildings. We add to this inspiration from Tokyo, the cosmopolitan village that has fully absorbed the train and the car into its urban mobility landscape, and a touch of Mexican culture, such as the splendid artwork by Barragán. We set off to explore the world in search of more inspiration, so that the aesthetics of mobility may conquer the negative influence of the 'joyless economy'.

REFERENCES

Banham, R. (1971). *Los Angeles, The Architecture of Four Ecologies*. University of California Press.

Bestuurs Regio Utrecht (1999). HSL-oost. A study commissioned by Bestuurs Regio Utrecht regional administration.

Duivesteijn, A. (1999). A paper presented the opening of the exhibition 'Mecanoo architecten. 1:20 – 1:200 – 1:200.000. Stoel, Schuur, Streek' in the ABC architecture centre in Haarlem, 20 May.

Flevoland, Friesland, Groningen and Drenthe (1999–2000). *De Zuiderzeeroute*. A study commissioned by the provinces of Flevoland, Friesland, Groningen and Drenthe.

Houben, F. (1999). *Mobiliteitsesthetiek en ingenieurskunst. Architectuur en de openbare ruimte, De dynamische delta 2*, Uitg. Ministerie van Verkeer en Waterstaat/Mecanoo architecten, p. 20–41.

Houben, F. (2001). *Composition, Contrast, Complexity*. Birkhäuser Verlag.

Ministerie van VROM, (2001). Dutch Mountains. A study commissioned by the National Physical Planning Agency which, under the title of 'Box: Hoogbouw in de Deltametropool', is included in *Ruimte Maken, Ruimte Delen, Vijfde Nota over De Ruimtelijke Ordening 2000/2020*, pp. 232–3.

Ministry of Transport, Public Works and Water Management/DWW/Delft (2003). *De Leuke Weg*. A study commissioned by the Directorate-General of Public Works and Water Management 'Roads to the Future' and published under the title 'Holland Avenue, a research road atlas; Holland Avenue, design road atlas'.

National Physical Planning Agency (2001). Panoramas and perforations. A study commissioned by the National Physical Planning Agency, which, under the title 'Box: Panorama's en perforaties', is included in *Ruimte Maken, Ruimte Delen, Vijfde Nota over De Ruimtelijke Ordening 2000/2020*, (Fifth Report on Physical Planning 2000/2020), The Hague, 2001, pp. 168–9.

Skitovsky, T. (1976). *The Joyless Economy; an Inquiry into Human Satisfaction and Consumer Dissatisfaction*. Oxford University Press.

Part Three

CITIES ON THE EDGE

#07

REBUILDING KABUL

Ajmal Maiwandi and Anthony Fontenot

Fifteen years after the collapse of the Soviet Union in 1989, the devastating reverberations of the Cold War continue to infect the globe. The past few decades have witnessed major political upheavals marked by the shifts from communism to capitalism, the realignment of alliances, and renegotiations and impositions of regional and global power. This has resulted in a series of localized civil wars along with pre-emptive wars of occupation in new struggles for power. The resultant shattering of civil society and the demolition of cities, which are a natural focal point of conflicts, has brought on a strange new urban phenomenon – an epoch of continuous destruction and reconstruction that generates specialized global and local industries that thrive off the process.

This new milieu of post-war reconstruction in cities as widely spaced as Berlin, Beirut, Kosovo, Sarajevo, Mostar, Kabul and Baghdad, is giving birth to a new culture in which many experiences are shared, such as extreme violence, destruction, separation, forced displacement, exile and migration. In fact, it has come to define, for an increasing number of people, an alternative to contemporary global urban life. People in this network of commonality have experienced a long list of similar side effects following war, such as social trauma and cultural amnesia. The demolition of monuments and the changing of street names illustrate efforts to repress past histories, which has become a common theme in cities making transitions from communism to capitalism. While many aspects of this new layer of identity offer similar experiences for diverse people ranging from Europe to Middle East to Central Asia, there are also distinct differences characterized by each group's unique response to their situation. The colossal reconstruction of Beirut, supported by a unified vision imposed by Solidere, employed extreme tactics of *tabula rasa* whereby the entire downtown central district was to be scraped clean to its surface in preparation for a brand new city. Berlin became a spectacular European showcase city in the 1990s, while the massive scale of the Hausmann-like urban redevelopment process itself became a major tourist attraction. In this series of post-war reconstructions, global practices become more evident as they absorb new ways of investments, finance and construction. The reconstruction of Kabul, on the other hand, has taken its own path in respect to this milieu. With no large-scale development, spotty investment and no significant plan, Kabul's reconstruction remains largely invisible to the world. Unlike many of the other large-scale post-war urban reconstruction projects, Kabul is being stitched together bit by bit. As yet, Kabul has defied the grand gestures of big business reconstruction, allowing multiple-scale projects to unfold simultaneously and slowly transform the city.

More than anything else, cities caught in this milieu of construction, destruction and reconstruction are dependent on massive capital investments. The reconstruction of these cities relies on gigantic, complex capital investments, which are among the largest urban contracts and projects under way today. This reconstruction economy, having gained new ground in the recent past, now uses its experiences with various places of conflict to organize itself on the basis of common principles, ideas and techniques in creating systematic formulas for achieving successful reconstruction. While coalition forces, the UN, the World Bank, non-governmental organizations and various large and small companies make up a bewildering collaboration in the effort to assist a devastated people, post-war reconstruction for many international implementers is a purely financial venture based on immense profits.

Where Kabul is concerned, approximately $25 billion has been spent on destroying the city and maintaining the current military operations. Only $600 million of the pledged billions has been spent so far, constituting a sort of international warm-up (or trial run) for the inevitable negotiations, bids and contracts that will follow. Since the invasion of Afghanistan by US forces in October 2001, nearly $8 billion in money and assistance has been pledged by the international community in support of its stabilization and reconstruction. Of the $4.4 billion pledged in Berlin in 2004, for this year alone, 25 per cent is channelled through the government, 15–20 per cent through non-governmental organizations, 45 per cent through the UN and the remainder through smaller organizations. While there is ample cash currently flowing into Afghanistan to support the reconstruction, the problem, it seems, is deciding who is to get it, how and when it will be spent and who will make the decisions on these matters. The local and international gatekeepers of this flow of cash wage a war of attrition based on a lack of trust and transparency and the schedules of international and national politics in their individual drive towards deciding on how best to spend the funds. Headline needs, such as education, elections and the formation of a national army are at the top of the list, yet other requirements, such as the close protection team for the President, also siphon off a large chunk of the aid, estimated to be at nearly $45 million for this year alone. Schools are being built and children, at the latest estimate numbering nearly 4 million, are being enrolled in these schools, but what is often lacking from such statistics is a qualitative description of the conditions of the educational environment. Most of the schools in Kabul operate on three shifts a day, which means that the average student gets one and a half hours of schooling per day, in cramped and often unbearable spaces, without schoolbooks or paper on which to write, yet the numbers still impress the politicians. Afghanistan resembles a stage set, upon which the favourite plays of the international donors are continuously re-enacted, especially the now classic headline-grabbing, heart rending, election-winning dramas concerning schoolchildren and women's rights issues – without achieving much progress in either.

Although the rebuilding of Afghanistan should ideally include the construction of institutions, laws and regulations, systems of social and economic welfare, together with the infrastructure of cultural identity. All too often, however, the expectations of reconstruction are expressed purely in terms of physical reconstruction. That being said, and with all the resources available there is still a dearth of large-scale reconstruction in the city. Apart from the highway projects, which were actually implemented to provide easy access for military quick-response teams, and the millions being spent on new facilities by the coalition forces in Bagram and NATO in Darluman, there is scant infrastructural or large-scale urban reconstruction that is a direct result of institutional or international intervention. On the contrary, as some have predicted, the real drive in the construction business that is changing the face of the city are the activities of the private sector, in its rush to build in the current lawless situation. In this context where anything goes, development is haphazard, unregulated and without control or interference from the state. Therefore, as long as there is enough money and enough connections (whether legal or, as is all too often the case, illegal) to support the process, the development of real estate continues in this unplanned and uncontrolled manner, accommodating those who can afford it or those with the strength to bypass rules and regulations. The construction industry in Afghanistan currently thrives in four main sectors: major military-related projects subcontracted to foreign companies (which are seen as safe in the current climate of distrust); small-scale government projects usually subcontracted to relatives or for hefty kickbacks; the dramatically growing private sector that is funding large-scale development, with funds that are sometimes dubious and sometimes legitimate; and small-scale developments in retail and residential premises. The lion's share of the construction is contracted out to foreign companies, which are mostly Turkish but are also Indian, Chinese and Central Asian in origin. These organizations, while channelling money out of the country, also exacerbate the inefficient technical skills of local companies that are struggling for the leftovers. This lends itself to the increase of illegal contracting procedures locally and the further anger of local contractors.

It could be argued that the hype of reconstruction has had more of a real impact on Kabul than the process of reconstruction itself. The myth of a reconstructed Kabul has caused a mass influx of Afghans returning from Iran, Pakistan and other countries which had absorbed the diaspora. This inrush has overwhelmed the city. People returning and expecting to find programmes and assistance to help re-establish them in Kabul all too often find themselves abandoned with no support beyond their own means. As a result, makeshift container and tent settlements have emerged throughout the city, creating instant ghettos. Even before the outbreak of twenty-three years of war, the city of Kabul had already become swollen to its maximum capacity. The current in-migration of returnees and refugees has drastically increased the burden on an already overpopulated and devastated city. It is estimated that of the 3.7 million people currently living in Kabul, 58 per cent live in informal settlements with very limited, if any, services available. In 2003–2004, an estimated 500 000–1 million returnees have arrived in Kabul alone. With nearly 40 per cent of its buildings destroyed in the war, barely existent sewerage systems, sub-standard streets and roads, Kabul is in desperate need of a new urban infrastructure as well as the thorough upgrading of that which does exist. In response to these overwhelming conditions, a certain progressive technocratic wing of the Afghan government is pushing for the creation of a new satellite city on the fringes of Kabul. The plans for this development, which are intended to address the mass influx of people arriving in the city, have been rendered useless by the realities on the ground that range from obstacles such as armed men shooting at survey teams to the lack of underground water sources to ensure its sustainability.

figure 7.1
ONE OF THE MANY CAMPS SPREAD ACROSS KABUL, HOUSING TENS OF THOUSANDS OF RETURNEES
AND INTERNALLY DISPLACED PEOPLE, MANY OF WHOM WERE RETURNED TO THE COUNTRY UNDER
THE UN'S REPATRIATION PROGRAMME, BUT ARE NOW LEFT WITHOUT A HOME OR THE MEANS TO
SUPPORT THEMSELVES

The complexity of overlapping intentions and often conflicting desires of the diverse
participants of Kabul's urban development, such as the local government, military forces, warlords, criminals, squatters, international donors and locals, has created a three-dimensional
matrix of uncertainty and chaos imposed on the political, ethnic and geographic landscape
of the city. This confusion produces a city in constant flux, changing and rearranging itself
by the minute, often in opposing directions. Daily movements through the city are experienced as a series of random blockages, road closures, security barriers and new temporary
constructions, causing vendors to rearrange themselves constantly along the changing
streets – manipulations that can ultimately result in alienating the public from its urban
environment. Kabul has become a maze of confusion, experienced as wild juxtapositions of
diverse and often conflicting programmes. Large areas of the city become unrecognizable
from one day to the next. While these changes sometimes reveal the potential to see the city
anew, it also can have enormous negative consequences on the psyche of the population,
who increasingly feel like alienated outsiders in their own home city.

In post-conflict environments (or, more specifically, those that experience less conflict
than before) like Kabul, there is a lack of such basic amenities as stability, security, established governing institutions, the availability of materials, technical construction knowledge, reliable transportation and the lack of a strong central control mechanism. All this
raise the question of how cities may actually get reconstructed under such circumstances.
The answers are critical for establishing an apparatus for the development and co-ordination
of the private sector who are the major players in the redevelopment of the city. The complex specificity of intricate local networks and knowledge, which changes from day to day,
are essential for ensuring the future growth of a city that reproduces itself without any
direction. In such scenarios, mass discrepancies emerge between an ideal vision of an
organized plan for moving into the future and the stark reality of what is possible within
the chaos of the city. The everyday life of people struggling to exist and move forward,
forced to the margins of an unpredictable economy and its effects on the urban condition,

is all too often littered with stumbling blocks that are developed to help advance the rich and powerful while ignoring and undermining the efforts of the disenfranchized. Yet in a year of elections and political wrangling that needs, at least for the sake of appearances, to look legitimate, the power of public opinion has given the local poor an unexpected weapon.

Kabul is a city of fragments held together by an invisible collective web, spun by divergent groups ranging from warlords to non-governmental organizations to government officials to destitute widows with children. Occupying the blurry periphery of the faint planned vision of the city's future, in an attempt to make sense of the overwhelming void of economy, normality, security and health, occupants of the city fluctuate between euphoric moments of inventive entrepreneurship and hopelessness. This spectrum of rapid juxta-positions of highs and lows is indicative of many processes currently at work in the city. The differences between how the reconstruction of a city should develop through planned organization and the reality of how a city actually develops through various complex, frag-mentary, contradictory and incoherent individual acts establishes the possibilities of its urban potential.

Currently there are no master plans to debate, no large-scale initiatives to critique. What emerges from this void are fragments of urban schemes, independently pursued, which make up Kabul's current reality. This process inhabits a space where anything goes, where a variety of every scenario imaginable occurs. In Kabul, the city centre has become a wild-west zone filled with ministries, compound blocks, free-for-all markets, restaurants, fac-tories, uncontrolled waste collection and security barricades. We experience unchecked or illegal high-end commercial development next to illegal squatter developments, the hell of barbed wire and AK47s, traffic jams of up to an hour per kilometre, lorries, carts, dogs, cats. Wholesale businesses use the rooftops for mass storage, multi-storeyed blocks are filled with recycling materials, naked children bathe in the polluted and waste-infested river, people are wasted on opium in all kinds of weird places with all kinds of smells and tastes, ditches are filled with shit and the rank smell of stale and dried piss. This mael-strom of urbanity in decline is the context within which the reconstruction of everyday life unfolds.

While ranging from the ideas of powerful individual personalities to the institutional impo-tence that guides the process of reconstruction in the city, the complex scenarios which have emerged and the characters who are responsible for both the deterioration and the rapid growth in the urban environment are the products of a new culture – a culture that was both imposed and home-grown – a culture that is simultaneously foreign and Afghan.

one

THE WARLORD

A former warlord, who has now metamorphosed into a businessman or politician with (military) power and money and an institutional position or having the connections that facilitate his desires, is in a key position to pursue development in the city. His private militia is still intact and carrying out his orders. Having diversified and expanded his traditional power base to include dealings in the trafficking of narcotics and stolen artefacts; in the construction and real-estate market the Warlord has secured a major role in shaping the future of the city, no matter what guise he takes on in the course of his life. Using the powers still available to him, he takes or buys public or private land, and manifests in built form the physical equivalent of his gross, barbaric, political and military power. To mark the city as his own – the spoils he feels he has won through waging war – he uses buildings the way an animal uses its excrement to mark the boundaries of its territory. He builds overbearing and vulgar buildings in concrete with outrageously coloured glass, signifying his presence and reminding the people of the city of his authoritarian control over them. When formerly they used to fear his rockets and tanks, today they fear his buildings. They could not forget him and his power even if they wanted to and each day, as they pass his monuments to plunder, it reminds them of their subordination to the powerful thugs that still control Afghanistan. His buildings, while lacking sensitivity to their surroundings, also lack any identity further than brutally scarring and occupying the city fabric.

His armed militias litter the sidewalks outside his official residence and places of visitations – and along with the brightly coloured sheds used as guardhouses in every street of the city – mark his dubious trail. As long as he can proceed unchecked, his influence

figure 7.2
OPEN PUBLIC LANDS, SOME IN THE CENTRE OF THE CITY, BUT MOSTLY IN THE SURROUNDING AREA, LIKE THIS ONE NEAR DEH SABZ, ARE CONSIDERED BY THE POWERFUL AND ARMED AS AN INHERITANCE FROM THE DECADES OF SACRIFICE DURING THE *JIHAD*. THE LANDS, WHICH WERE ILLEGALLY OCCUPIED THROUGH THE SACRIFICE OF BLOOD, HAVE NOW BECOME ONE OF THE MOST LUCRATIVE BUSINESSES IN THE COUNTRY. THE SELLING, DEVELOPMENT AND RESALE OF THESE LANDS HAS EARNED PEOPLE MILLIONS AND THE GOVERNMENT IS UNABLE, POLITICALLY OR PHYSICALLY, TO STOP THIS CONFISCATION

figure 7.3

MANY OF THESE AREAS REMAIN UNDEVELOPED FOR MONTHS AND MAY BE LIKE THIS FOR YEARS INTO THE FUTURE, YET THE LAND IS DEMARCATED FROM THE START BY THE BUILDING OF A PERIMETER WALL

shrouds the city with fear and silent indignation. But he builds frantically, because he feels in his bones that things might change, and soon. In the event that one day he may be dispossessed of his military and political powers, he wants to ensure that he has something for old age – but he forgets that a nation like Afghanistan has a transgenerational memory and that wrongs that go unresolved today or tomorrow will be set straight years down the line, for better or worse. Yet, for the moment, nothing stands in his way. With the help of his handpicked staff and allies that occupy positions in other ministries, he continues to surf through the weak links of a newborn administration, satiating his appetite and those of his cronies. Vast tracts of government land on the edges of the city are occupied and divided between himself and his friends and sold off wholesale to dealers, who then subdivide the land and sell it off again for an immense profit. Like explorers on the moon staking flags to claim their territory, public land is confiscated and marked by the building of perimeter walls.

two

THE RICH RETURNEE

A rich returnee with money, contacts and an empire built during the *Jihad* years in combination with the profits of business dealings in the west, is primed for investing in Kabul. Armed with money, a good family name, and an already vast list of assets in the country, he hires a Pakistani architect to design the building of his dreams. The problem is that he has been daydreaming in Dubai for far too long, and his dream buildings from abroad look like nightmares impositions from within. As a result of both legal and shady dealings, he has now obtained prime land at a major intersection in the centre of the city and is proceeding to build a twelve-storey building with a market on the ground floor and flats above, in an area of two- or three-storey buildings. He doesn't care that his building looks like Noah's Ark in a sea of low-rise development. Green reflective glass, imported concrete from Pakistan, and steel fabricated in the former Soviet Union make up his new vocabulary of built urban form. The local market, struggling to get off its feet with outdated machinery, unskilled labour and expensive materials doesn't fit into his equation and he could not care less. He can hardly be blamed for this, as his market sells goods of which 90 per cent are imported from the neighbouring countries at inflated prices aimed at the foreigners or other rich returnees like himself. Where a thriving local market once existed, now people rely on long lines of lorries entering the country and flooding the local markets with foreign goods ranging from Pakistani bottled water and fruit to Turkish toilet paper. The labour used to construct the building is foreign as well. Turkish, Pakistani and Central Asian construction labourers build most of the major buildings in the city, importing their own ideas and construction practices while exporting monetary resources. His interests are well secured, as the property he owns in the best parts of town is now occupied by foreign organizations who deposit enormous rents directly into his offshore accounts. By not declaring the full amount he earns to the tax office, he cheats the local government in order to gain greater profits. His business dealings in the city add to the desperate lack of funds in the government coffers. He is ingenious, constantly inventing new ways to avoid paying proper taxes such as by signing multiple contracts, one for the actual rent and the other for a nominal rent, used for official purposes and to avoid paying the 20 per cent property rent tax imposed. He returns to a changed land, imagining it to be the same as the one he left it decades ago, blinding himself to the differences between the city of his memories and the disorderly city of today.

three

THE DRUG BARON

A warlord who has become a drug baron with money, power, and bad taste, can now take by force what his money cannot buy. As Kabul is the symbolic centre of international support and local status, he builds a vacation home here to stay in when he visits the corridors of power for more aid to his local constituency. As his imagination is fuelled by imported models of living, he begins to build his multi-storey villa of concrete, clad with coloured tiles and reflective glass on confiscated or illegal land adjacent to the Presidential palace. His business empire ranges from planting illegal narcotics to the trafficking and sale of the final product across international boundaries into foreign markets. This enables him to pursue acquisitions such as illegal property, which he buys wholesale from corrupt politicians and warlords, and sells again at high premiums. At the same time he helps to facilitate the expeditions and operations of coalition forces in the country, and this buys him the immunity and support he needs to continue to develop his trade in relative safety and to weaken his competitors. Unwitting non-governmental organizations and donors help his narcotics trade by paying for and implementing irrigation and infrastructural projects in the regions of his business, thus facilitating the harvesting and distribution of his crop.

four

THE LOCAL BUSINESSMAN

A local businessman with a little extra cash and family assets who wants to invest in real estate, engages in a process known as the *hawala* debt system. This traditional system allows him to borrow enough money to build, for example, a market. The *hawala* debt system is the equivalent of a start-up bank loan, but is actually far more flexible. As long as one's family is well known and has reasonable assets, one is assured of getting a loan without much difficulty or collateral. In the long list of the standard but unofficial processes of land acquisition and construction of the market, of course, one must bribe dozens of government workers, firstly to acquire the land and then for the permits to build. State employees at all levels accept bribes and facilitate the illegal selling and buying of public and private land as a way of supplementing the salaries that the administration is unable to pay them. Considering that the average weekly salary of a governmental worker is anywhere between 1500–2500 Afghanis ($30–$50), even when paychecks are delivered this is barely enough to survive on. As temporary permits are easier to acquire, many people file for temporary permits but build permanent buildings, knowing full well that the authorities will not tear down the illegal construction at any time in the near future, if ever. As each floor is constructed, the funds are enlarged by selling off space to local vendors who are eager to purchase any available space in the overcrowded city. Thus as long as the start-up capital exists, the success of the venture is guaranteed. As cash increases, so do the number of floors, but without adjusting the structural capacity of the building. The columns of the last floor are left unfinished in the hope of adding even more floors in the future, which gives the impression that the building is still incomplete, although the lower floors are occupied and functioning. This image of incompleteness creates an atmosphere that the city is in constant transformation or is permanently unfinished.

five
THE POOR LOCAL

If one happens to be a poor 'nobody', without money or power, at least one has the enormous advantage of being among thousands of others in the same condition who all want similar things. *En masse*, one achieves what one cannot as an individual, both politically and in terms of establishing a livelihood. The Nobody joins a squatter settlement on public land and starts a successful small business houses in a container, or other makeshift structure. Eventually, he builds himself a mud-brick house on the mountainside or in another less desirable area of the city. As mud is free and a surplus of unskilled labour is available to mix it, he proceeds to construct a house based on a general knowledge of traditional mud-brick construction. He begins by digging a hole near the area where he wants to build, piling the soil that has been excavated next to the hole. His labourers, comprised of friends and relatives, assist in the construction. Once the walls are up, he spans the distance between different rooms with wood logs placed closely together, then covers this with a layer of straw. On top of this layer, he then spreads mud across the surface – constructing a roof membrane approximately 50 cm thick.

After completing the construction of this two-roomed structure, in which he and eight members of his family will live, he eventually adds a bathroom. Adjacent to the closest wall adjoining the street, he digs a hole in the ground with an access slot from the street. His toilet, as well as all the toilets in the settlement, are serviced by the local 'shit collector' who periodically maintains the toilets by shovelling the excrement from the access hole near the street onto his cart, then carrying it off. Lacking any garbage service in the area, the hole that was dug out for making mud, eventually gets filled with his rubbish where it collects until the rancid fumes forces the city to respond by collecting the rubbish. Once the Nobody has established a roof over his head, a place to stay dry in the rain and warm in the winter, he then pursues access to water and electricity. Because the city considers this settlement illegal, it refuses to provide him with even the most basic amenities and intentionally stops individuals or companies who attempt to do so.

Since the government hopes to demolish these informal settlements in the future, they refuse to accept that these developments are legally assets for the city. Thus the poor local Nobody is forced to buy a donkey and send his children and wife out for approximately three hours a day to carry water up from the nearest well located at the bottom of the mountain. As for the gas to fuel the stove for cooking, which used to be done on open fires fuelled by wood collected nearby, or from tearing down trees in other areas of the city, he now purchases butane tanks. Because electricity is scarce in even the richer areas of the city and his unplanned house has no chance of getting an official electricity connection, he teams up with his neighbours and, by pooling their resources and working

figure 7.4
VILLAS LIKE THIS ONE ARE POPPING UP ACROSS THE CITY, WHERE THE ARCHITECTURE IS FOREIGN TO THE TRADITIONAL TYPOLOGY OR EVEN PREVIOUS MODERN PHASES OF HOUSING, AND COPIES MIDDLE-EASTERN OR PAKISTANI TYPOLOGIES AND TASTES. THE LUXURIOUS WALLED COMPOUND PRESENTS A STARK CONTRAST TO THE PHYSICAL ENVIRONMENT OF THE MAJORITY OF THE PEOPLE WHO LIVE IN POVERTY, AND REPRESENTS THE FRUIT OF OFTEN ILLEGAL ACTIVITIES AND THE FORMATION OF A NEW CLASS OF ELITE, GAINING ITS WEALTH THROUGH BUSINESS VENTURES, PRODUCING AND SELLING DRUGS, REAL-ESTATE AND LAND-GRABBING SCANDALS AND COUNTLESS OTHER ENTERPRISES, SOME OF WHICH ARE LEGAL BUT WHICH ARE MOSTLY ILLEGAL

together, he runs an illegal electric line up to the settlement from the nearest electricity pole. If he or his neighbour is not electrocuted in the process, he has secured two or three hours of electricity for his family per day. As land becomes scarce in the lower areas of the city and densities begin to increase, some of the settlers who aspire to elevate themselves to a higher social status by refusing to build in mud, begin constructing houses using concrete blocks and baked bricks. The lively competition among these neighbours creates a constant transformation of the area where each family rivals the next by updating, incorporating new materials and painting their houses in bright pastel colours, providing contrast in an otherwise colourless city.

six

THE INTERNATIONAL DONOR

Certain international donors believe that, simply because their organization works in Afghanistan, they have the right to do anything they choose, in any way they want, and within any time frame that they decide on. While undertaking highly visible projects, for which the donor government has allocated funding, such as a school in the poorest and most historic quarter of the city, foreign contractors are employed to work fast within the tight deadlines that are established for the funding. For most of these projects, the time frame is usually a year from the point of allocation to the completion of the project. Since there are no building codes or regulations in the city, contractors operate with impunity and to standards that cannot be verified or controlled. For that matter, neither the donor nor the contractor can be held accountable for any unforeseen disaster resulting from substandard workmanship.

The unspoken attitude that 'beggars can't be choosers' lingers on and around these projects. As the international donor's feet never touch the ground long enough to recognize the local context, they keep their distance from the people they are there to help. Similar to volunteer workers in a leper colony, they do not fraternize with the locals, almost as though they believe that the helplessness of the locals might be contagious. Surrounded by a close protection unit, a lightning quick visit from the donor country's foreign minister, who paints the air with talk of friendship and the poor conditions of the country before they arrived, is immediately followed by another lavish lunch at the embassy. Compared to the tight budget with which they undertake projects, their lavish guesthouses and offices provide a stark contrast to their stinginess with the locals, revealing the double standards by which they operate.

seven

NON-GOVERNMENTAL ORGANIZATIONS

Well meaning non-governmental organizations who want to help the Afghan people often arrive in the country with their highly paid foreign staff, embarking on endeavours such as building cheap schools and hospitals and cleaning up the local sewage. A construction project, which may have been budgeted at $20 000, may ultimately cost

$60 000 after an additional $40 000 is spent to pay and house foreign staff. In this way, resources that could have been allocated for other potential projects are diverted from actual gains on the ground. Because donors are detached from their constituency and are not required to follow up or maintain continual support for a project, non-governmental organizations are regulated by a similar process and when their funding runs dry, they move on to the next highly funded project, initiating the same process without looking back.

Working in Afghanistan is not easy and sometimes non-governmental organizations are tricked by clever Afghans in remote communities to help them rehabilitate their irrigation systems or provide fertilizer to nurture the crops and secure their livelihoods. In reality, non-governmental organizations often unwittingly contribute to the illegal trade in the cultivation and distribution of poppy plants, resulting in the consolidation of the narcotic industry in the region.

At other times, in the non-governmental organizations' eagerness to help local communities, schools are set up and services are provided in areas that have been occupied forcefully, not by the poor or helpless in the country, but by the rich in Afghanistan or those who are armed. In this way, the unsuspecting non-governmental organizations help to legitimize the illegal practice of land-grabbing.

eight
THE UN

As a multinational institution caught up in its own bureaucracy, the various departments of the UN working on projects throughout the world can sometimes get sidetracked in studies and investigations which result in seemingly absurd outcomes, such as questionnaires that were distributed to the local population of Kabul, in which they were asked, 'does the municipality collect stray dogs in your area?' or 'can you find a shop in your area that sells door hinges?' In light of the severity of immediate needs and issues to be addressed, such activities are seen by the locals as a vast waste of resources, time and money.

Other misguided studies, assumptions, or political manoeuvrings promoted by the UN can have serious consequences, affecting huge disenfranchised populations. For example, the UN's policy of the forced repatriation of millions of Afghan refugees has further overwhelmed Kabul by forcing a large population with limited resources into an already overcrowded city. Concurrently, the UN unwittingly facilitates global and regional political agendas, as the repatriation programme moves forward through the bribes and intimidation of the host governments of the region. Agreeing to remove large numbers of refugees from areas of relative safety and comfort and send them back to a country that daily grows less stable where they have no guarantee of work or a place to live adds enormous pressure on the current urban condition, leading to a further deterioration of the already poor urban environment. In addition, this UN repatriation policy also undermines legitimate asylum claims from hundreds of Afghan asylum-seekers across the globe. This applies particularly to the United Kingdom and other countries committed to distributing and publicizing a positive image of Afghanistan as a liberated country representing a model of democracy and post-war success. The only way to reinforce this image is to claim that people are happily and of their own accord returning to Afghanistan. This is in stark contrast to the reality. Kabul is filled with UNHCR tents housing thousands of people who live in desperate poverty, adding to the sense of insecurity in the city and placing an unbearable burden on the fragile and often inadequate institutions.

nine
THE FOREIGN POWERS

The various foreign powers positioned in Kabul often act as though they have the right to intervene and must be given permission from the government to build whatever and wherever they please. Unfortunately, the local government and its institutions are so blindly grateful for this kind of investment that they do not calculate the side effects of these acts, such as the destruction of cultural heritage or the lack of convergence of this investment with their own plans for their country. Sites and projects are selected without knowing the local context or consulting the people. The normal chain of command is avoided for the sake of expedience, relying on the politicians and their official powers instead of planners and architects. All this activity adds to the lack of capacity in planning and architectural institutions and further fuels chaos in the country. Many foreign governments working in Afghanistan do not understand that Afghans, especially the poor, consider it discourteous to say no or refuse a request. They rely instead on their guests not asking of them things that will put them in a precarious position. This in turn places the burden of thought, responsibility and accountability on the often incompetent shoulders of the locals, resulting in messy situations that cannot be resolved.

ten
ISAF OR COALITION FORCES

The coalition forces, whose mandate it is to keep the peace, take large chunks of central and peripheral land to build bases and headquarters. As security for the coalition forces is of paramount importance, whole streets are blocked off and they are also able to commandeer adjacent sites or structures, altering the flow of traffic and the shape of the city. While living under heavy security in imported air-conditioned containers, these hermetic compounds are fortresses of concrete and barbed wire, equipped with armed men peering out of perimeter posts under threat of constant attack, while the coalition governments maintain the position that Afghanistan is a safer place. In a constant state of paranoia, ISAF forces travel about in heavily armed convoys, further adding to the feeling of instability in the city. Meanwhile enormous funds equivalent to $1000 a day per soldier are spent on support, logistics and the construction of bases. Contracts for building these structures are usually issued to foreign contractors, because they do not trust the locals who are interchangeably classified as terrorists, when attacked, or helpless, when aided.

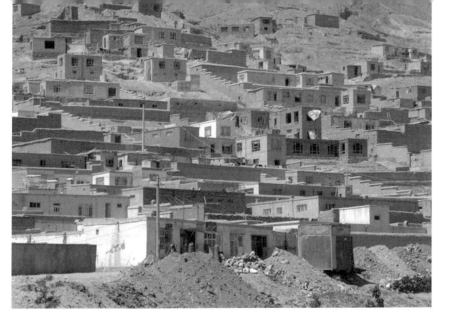

figure 7.5
THE OPEN LAND SHOWN IN THE PREVIOUS IMAGES IS THEN SOLD OFF IN LARGE CHUNKS EITHER
TO PEOPLE WHO DEVELOP IT AND RESELL IT FOR PROFIT OR TO FAMILIES WHO LIVE ON IT
AFTERWARDS. AT THIS STAGE OF DEVELOPMENT IT IS VERY DIFFICULT TO CONFISCATE LAND
AS THE PAPERWORK HAS CHANGED HANDS SEVERAL TIMES AND THE NUMBER OF PEOPLE
INVOLVED HAS INCREASED DRAMATICALLY

figure 7.6
KABUL IS A FORTIFIED
CITY WITH MANY
COMPOUNDS LIKE THIS
ONE SPREAD ACROSS
ITS FABRIC. IN
CONTRADICTION TO THE
OFFICIAL PROPAGANDA
ABOUT THE IMPROVEMENT
OF THE SECURITY
SITUATION, THE
REALITY CAN BE SEEN IN
THIS IMAGE. THESE
FORTIFICATIONS EMIT
THE SENSE OF FEAR AND
INSECURITY, WHICH
FILTERS FROM THE
INTERNATIONAL
COMMUNITY INTO LOCAL
GOVERNMENT AND THEN
INTO THE CITY AND ITS,
INHABITANTS WHO ARE
DAILY CONFRONTED WITH
THE REPERCUSSIONS OF
THIS PARANOIA

Buildings are built when needed, without the consideration that the structures might
remain after the forces no longer need them, and how in turn these structures will affect
the overall form of the city. The compounds are built in the shape, form and using the
materials of cities of the west, with all the trimmings of homegrown comfort, including

bars and shopping areas. The further removed soldiers are from home, the more seriously they seem to take their customs and traditions – disenchanting the locals who increasingly feel that they are imposed upon, rather that protected.

eleven

THE US FORCES

As the *de facto* rulers of Afghanistan, the US is increasingly expanding its territory in Kabul. The entire area surrounding the US Embassy has been dominated by blocking off all streets in the vicinity with concrete barriers, containers filled with sandbags and armed men. In order to extend the territory further, a massive tunnel has been dug under one of the main roads, leading to a field opposite the Embassy. Upon this site, the Marriot Kabul is in the process of being constructed. This new complex is to serve as the centre of the expatriate population in the city, who can freely consume alcohol there while enjoying themselves under the close protection of embassy security. Beyond these secured zones, helicopters and drones circle the sky over Kabul leaving buzzing echoes throughout the city centre after the outrageously low fly-bys. In this new world, home is never left far behind, as all the comforts and trimmings of their native land are imported by the Americans into this urban 'wilderness'. Refusing to follow any of the local laws and international standards, the US personnel display their disregard for the locals by refusing any opportunities for mixing – except for their wild interactions in traffic, which reminds one of monster car derbies. These soldiers posses a dangerous combination of fear of the locals and a trigger-happy instinct, travelling in packs even to buy their bread from the baker each day. The compounds resemble American gated communities, designed to keep out the savages while locking in the paranoid. The protection walls are impenetrable barriers, converting a diverse nation into a homogeneous enemy. Perimeter walls are studded with twenty-four-hour surveillance cameras and laced with barbed wire. Bright security lights peer into the dark abyss; the amoebic fluid that nurtures an enemy in flight. Out in the far away provinces, the provincial reconstruction teams follow a conflicting mandate of simultaneously building roads and bridges to befriend the locals and fighting a war with imaginary and real enemies – sometimes within the very same population as those they are trying to help. This confused doctrine of winning the hearts and minds with one hand and fighting the very same people with the other has proven to be as unsuccessful here as it was during the Vietnam War, and has resulted in increased attacks on the real aid community, now unfortunately linked with some of the same activities and motives as the US in the eyes of the locals.

twelve

THE LOCAL GOVERNMENT

Marked by scandal after scandal, the local administration is increasingly relegated to a corner from which it is forced to accept anything on the table, from wild ideas about monumental Uzbek concrete structures on historic sites to adventure theme parks with rides (à la Disneyland) on the historic fort of Balahisar. The idyllic visions and plans of the returnee politicians arriving from abroad to take up posts are brought to a violent halt by the realities of a struggling country whose institutions are handicapped by political wrangling and rampant corruption. While government officials desperately advocate prototype housing for the masses, all too often these proposals are based on outdated and complicated systems of prefabricated concrete slabs or experimental interlocking bricks from Thailand, for example, that have been tested and rejected in the 1950s. Afghanistan has become the land of re-experimenting with dysfunctional architectural technology in the hope of reviving the country. Lacking the energy and the resources necessary for creative thinking, this accumulation of fumbled projects reinforces the image of Afghanistan as an incompetent and hopeless repository for the world's leftover notions.

Careful not to unravel an already fragile political system, some in the administration look the other way when the powerful flex their muscles. Without realizing that action in these instances would help reinforce the legitimacy of the local administration with regard to its local population who are desperate for change and representation, officials remain silent and inactive. As opposed to engaging fully with the potential of the local context, the government's attention is too often directed at development in foreign lands, in the hope that Kabul can aspire to resembling a western cosmopolitan city. In this hypnotic state, politicians entertain ideas about new cities and new beginnings on the fringes of the existing chaos and destruction. But what good are new cities in a place that consists of old mentalities and old ways of life? Our political fragility and the need to unify the various groups, and thus the country as a whole, has forced the government to ignore blatant acts of corruption, human rights abuses and their own impunity.

figure 7.7
THIS IMAGE SIGNIFIES, MORE THAN ANY OTHER, THE PLIGHT OF THE COMMON INHABITANT IN THE CITY IN LIGHT OF THE CHANGES INFLICTED UPON BOTH THE URBAN ENVIRONMENT AND THE POLITICAL LANDSCAPE, WHICH HAVE RESULTED IN THE ALIENATION OF THE PEOPLE FROM THE CITY AND FROM THE RULING CLASS WHO GOVERN IN THEIR NAME

thirteen
CONCLUSION

Unlike in the past when political officials were driven by the ideologies of modernization and pushed forward new urban developments and programmes that they believed would transform society, today cities in general, and Kabul specifically, seems to be guided by the collisions of controlled accidents. Like other cities experiencing upheaval, a kind of economic laissez-faire logic drives the organization of the city. As David Harvey remarks, the city, in its current manifestation, has proven to be both 'a venerable form of human organization as well as remarkably resilient, recovering fast from devastation, sometimes in a better state then they were in before'. This acute and insightful observation allows us not only to reflect on the similarities between changes that are occurring in cities in general, but to think about its attachment to specific places. This current crisis places Kabul in the forefront of a strange, unexpected trend, as a leading example of explorations into a new kind of brutal capitalism in financing, real estate and construction advanced by the immunity of lawlessness.

The capacity for contemporary cities to overcome all manner of tribulations must in part be attributed to the fact that cities, in their capitalistic form, are hyper-active sites of 'creative destruction'. They dance to the capitalist imperative to dismantle the old and give birth to the new as expanding capital accumulation accompanied by new technologies, new forms of organization and rapid influxes of population (now drawn from all corners of the earth) impose new spatial forms and stresses upon the physical and social landscape. If, in making way for and creating the new, some of the old must first be destroyed, then why does it matter if this destruction is carried out by the wrecker's ball or inflicted by some contingent act of violence?

Harvey captures all too well the many unsettling scenes of Kabul. In this new context, lacking any real master plan, urban development seems to have formed an unholy alliance with the random forces that allow the scars of war itself to act as urban planner. The long years of brutal warfare have staked out and cleared its own territories, opening areas for new construction.

Kabul, a city on the edge of legality, stability and success, moves forward with criminal black market investments on the one hand and courageous acts by many common people in fighting poverty and hopelessness on the other. While ignored by headline news, the efforts of committed locals to provide people with real jobs beyond the militia and drug-trade employment, and by serving on the new front lines in the battle to rebuild Afghanistan, become invaluable installments in the reconstruction of a city that seems as pliable as the mud from which it was built. Inadvertently, somehow the city seems to resist the normal big and fast development while absorbing various small and slow-paced projects. This slow development could very well prove to be immensely beneficial for the long-term reconstruction of the city. While it has become an accepted norm to assume that it is efficient and desirable to rebuild cities at a gigantic scale, there could be many advantages to a slower, piecemeal process. What are the standards by which we should gauge the rebuilding of Kabul? If reconstruction means cleaning and organizing disordered spaces, repressing illegality and imposing aesthetic 'standards' on what has become 'unsightly', then Kabul is a failure of immense magnitude. Yet the current situation in Kabul has turned the table on many conventional understandings of how cities grow, develop and are reconstructed. The long-held belief that there is a direct relationship between stability and economic growth has been successfully refuted in Kabul. Currently there is an inverse relationship between security and stability and the economic growth that is fuelled by the criminal underground. As the security situation deteriorates, regulations and controls disappear, allowing the illegal market in drugs, the black market and the construction industry to flourish. Kabul is changing daily, due to the money that is invested by the corrupt, unscrupulous and criminal elements of the society. It is changing much faster and more drastically by these means than by the financial efforts of the reconstruction process initiated by the international community. The repressed tendencies of the city have exploded onto its surface. Instead of an overall orderly master plan driving the reconstruction of the city, it seems as though a series of accidents, collisions and the side effects of various local, international, official and underground forces are actually the forces behind the reconstruction of Kabul.

The rapid daily changes occurring in Kabul are producing increasingly heterogeneous conditions that lack predictability and control. The battles being fought in the streets of the city between the poor struggling to survive, the military forces constantly seeking control, a growing, wealthy private sector pursuing real estate development and a government that is failing in its attempts to gain control can only result in the slow transformation and mutation of the city. Following the war or Berlin after the fall of the Wall, in Beirut major sectors of the central business district were reconstructed in a short period, in a unified and homogenous way. Where Beirut and Berlin accomplished in a few years what might have otherwise happened over several generations, Kabul will achieve by being built in fragments, incorporating changing technologies and trends and new desires.

Like a collage suspended in an unintentional balance between the tension of drastically opposing forces, Kabul will be a city of contradictions and collusions, of old adjacent to new, of excesses underlying simplicity, of power next to wretched poverty, and most drastically of all, between local and international agendas. Kabul is a thriving work-in-progress simultaneously representing the conflicts as well as the energetic and experimental growth of a third world city. Planning, in its traditional form and logic, cannot save Kabul; it can only stifle a city on the edge of defining new urban forms, shapes and programmes. In this atmosphere the only logical way forward is for the government to harness the current situation in the city and recognize the tremendous assets, flexibility and resource of the private sector, illegal or not. Rather than attempting to control or stop the process, government agencies might lead initiatives that provide minimal surgical insertions to guide the flow of activities along more desirable paths. At the same time, while the forces described above continue to develop in the private sector, it is critical for the administration to address immediately basic, mainly infrastructural public concerns – such as making potable water accessible to all, developing sewer systems, upgrading and building roads and providing electricity and other basic services that the private sector will not address. By employing a minimal input, maximum output strategy, the administration's limited resources could have a far greater effect for a larger number of the population. These infrastructural interventions could set the stage for more people to engage positively with the city and its institutions, thus creating the skeletal structure onto which organic growth can blossom. Such urban proposals are not meant to be taken as ends in and of themselves; but are necessary stages in a continuous reinterpretation of a dynamic process. While the city is no longer a static entity capable of succumbing to singular gestures, visions can no longer be implemented. Kabul, in it its current state, constitutes a convoluted swarm of collective visions of a society in doubt, representing the struggling and desperate gestures of a people coming out of decades of conflict while tentatively dreaming of the future.

#08

BELGRADE: DE(CON)STRUCTING URBANITY

Darko Radovic

In memoriam to Lola Stefanovic: friend, we wish you were here. (*The Age*, 2000)

> *5 October 2000, 22:23. I'd like it so much if you were here, as well as all my other friends scattered around the world, so that we can be happy together. This day makes all the suffering worthwhile. The latest news is that three military planes took off towards the south. Together with the family, we hope.* SB, Belgrade University Professor

> *5 October 2000, 23:45; I told you it will happen ….* UC, architect

> *6 October 2000, 8:57…. at last what had to happen did happen! Walking the streets of Belgrade, looking at all those young people, the elderly and the kids, I asked myself why? Why all that had to happen to us, why we had to wait so long, to wait for what is just a basic human right … Yes, the House of Parliament was on fire, and TV Serbia was on fire but I, I who cannot stand destruction of any kind, for the first time in my life did not feel any remorse. … the damage to the Parliament is not major, and on the freed TV one can, at last, hear words that make sense, news that is news … People are, simply, happy because everything is over. Literally millions of people shouted that big, larger than ever, historic ENOUGH! I wish you were here, with us.* A, architect

> *6 October 2000, 11:46. Don't worry, everything is OK – I am really not sure if you can under-stand from TV reports how unbelievably magnificent all this was. Cheers!* M, urbanist

> *6 October 2000, 17:48. At last Belgrade was exciting in a beautiful way. I hope this leads to a happy ending. No one still knows what is happening with Milosevic and his family. No one knows what is going on with the Serbian Government. But, the first step has been taken, and next steps will be easier.* S, economist

These extracts from e-mail messages I received from Belgrade during the days of Slobodan Milosevic's fall from power (*The Age*, 2000) capture the atmosphere, the magnificence, the exhilaration and the sadness of early October 2000. Those were the words of my friends who, for long ten years, never gave up hope and never accepted extremism; words from the people who were strong enough to keep their heads up. Throughout 2000 Milosevic was close to defeat. He had survived much unrest, but this time it was clear that the situation had changed. On 5 October 2000, after an unsuccessful effort to manipu-late another election result, Milosevic was deserted by the key pillars of his power – the police and the army. Several months later he found himself at The Hague facing the War Crimes Tribunal. On the day of his fall the atmosphere in the streets of Belgrade was festive. At the same time it was obvious that beneath the surface big political games were simmering. No one knew what the forthcoming weeks, even days or hours could bring. Very soon it was to became obvious that Milosevic and his family were just a tip of an iceberg of tyranny, violence and corruption. The social condition they helped establish was not going to be easily eradicated.

This essay is about that condition and the efforts towards the physical reconstruction of the damaged city. I focus on the city of Belgrade, the crisis of its urban culture and on some selected projects from the years that followed Milosevic's fall. In all countries of the former Yugoslavia the complexity of the events of the 1990s was overwhelming. The irrationality of the early 2000s in Serbia goes far beyond understanding (not only my own). The analysis of these times needs careful research and detailed elaboration. Here the discussion of these issues will be kept to the necessary minimum.

one
REGIONS OF THE UNTHOUGHT

Belgrade is a very complex place. Maria Todorova (1997) reminds us of Derrida and Kristeva, who come from similar

> *places that define the outer limits of Western European culture: Derrida in colonial Africa, where the French empire fades into the great open space of Africa; Kristeva in Bulgaria, crossing-ground of the Crusades and the historical territory of contention between Christianized Europe and the Ottoman Empire.*

Todorova emphasized that

> *in such places it is possible to live both in and beyond the West, knowing the boundaries of its language, and looking southward or eastward as if toward regions of the unthought.*

Since Roman times and the original *castrum* at the confluence of the Danube and Sava rivers, the fate of Belgrade was that of *limes*, the place that marks the outer limits of 'western culture'. That place was always familiar with tyranny, *the unthought* and resistance. The history of Belgrade is the history of perpetual destruction and rebirth. The vicious cycle continues into our times. Since the establishment of Yugoslavia in 1917, Belgrade was its capital city, a true microcosm of the nation's fascinating complexity. After World War II it was both the federal capital and the capital of one of the constitutive units of Yugoslav – the Republic of Serbia. In the 1980s, with looming economic crisis and growing Serbian nationalism, the cosmopolitan side of the capital started to erode. Belgrade has found itself, again, at the *limes* – soon to be pushed over the edge, outside the cultural space of Europe, into the realms of the unthought.

What followed was the period in which Belgrade, like the rest of former Yugoslavia, endured immeasurable social, cultural and physical damage. When Milosevic fell, the country and Belgrade itself were in desperate need of social reconstruction. But, the necessity of radical change collided with a frightening inability to move beyond the straightjacket of nationalistic dogmas and frameworks established by the criminalized elites. Continuing conflicts in all aspects of life are recorded sadly in the changes in the urban culture and physical structures of the city.

Compare cities with another marvel of civilization – the text. The city is often described as a palimpsest of interwoven messages and meanings. For Lefebvre (1996), there is even

> *the language of the city: particularities specific to each city which are expressed in discourses, gestures, clothing, in the words and use of words by the inhabitants. He speaks about urban language, language of connotations.*

There is also, of course, *the writing of the city: what is inscribed and prescribed on its walls, in the layout of places and their linkages.* The dialectics of decline and resistance of Belgrade's urbanity makes an amazing 'reading'. Here I will table some of the texts *for* the city of Belgrade – the new laws, the urban plans and projects and the stories associated with them. While reading, as Vovelle (1990) would stress, it is important to keep in mind that 'there is not, by definition, a simple or unambiguous reading of a picture or an object, reflecting a code which can be deciphered.' Deciphering the messages inscribed in those new ideas and in the streets offers ambiguous insights into the essence of the city and its troubled present. The better one knows the city, the more exciting readings become. I dare also say that the more one loves the city, the deeper and stronger the messages become.

two
RECONSTRUCTION PROJECTS

The modern history of Belgrade is strongly marked by planned urban development which dates back to the mid-nineteenth century. Planning doctrines and fashions reflect the diverse cultural influences which established a strong local culture of urbanism. The immediate post-1945 period was based on models of Soviet provenance. Since the early 1950s, Yugoslav planning practices significantly departed from those models. By the 1980s they evolved towards the coherent integration of participation, self-management and other concepts which were central to the peculiar, Yugoslav brand of socialism.

Urban planning and urban design ideas and practices of former Yugoslavia have yet to be researched. The immediate past destruction and all the violence that has happened in those spaces, together with an unfavourable global ideological climate, leave many issues for future investigation. What is important to us here is that Yugoslavia and, in particular, its capital, Belgrade, had a rich history of urban planning and design. That layered history of ideas offers many readings. An interesting part of the text begins with the 1980s, when the overall social and economic crisis became obvious and the decline of the core values that held together a complex, multiethnic society proved to be unstoppable. Everyday life begun to contradict legislation. Urban processes went beyond their legal frameworks. Historically,

Yugoslav planning suffered from political interference. It was often forced to reflect ideals, rather than reality, but its implementation always favoured public interest. An overall decline in the 1980s turned that philosophical basis upside-down, foreshadowing an imminent end of the socialist ideal and a return to the domination of capital and private interest.

three
THE NEW PLANNING AND CONSTRUCTION LAW OF SERBIA

In response to that condition, since the mid-1980s, the planning professions among others concerned with the production of space, were pushing towards the redefinition of the legal framework of their activities. But, the new law became possible only twenty years later, after Slobodan Milosevic was taken from power. Despite all the political somersaults of his disastrous political career, he seemed reluctant to abandon some of his socialist instincts. In reality, he and his corrupt clique were far from idealistic. They were aware how important for their own power was the control of land and real estate. The outdated, inflexible laws in operation at the time provided fertile grounds for their machinations and their unchecked grabbing of wealth. With the ascendance of a right-leaning and liberal opposition to power in 2000, the time for change has come. But, while the political mantras of the new elite were different – including an orientation to the free market and opening towards the west – many believe that the key agent of speedy reform was a redistribution of power and access to wealth.

The new Planning and Construction Law of Serbia was efficiently drafted and put to public discussion. Its main aim was to streamline development procedures. The general structure of Serbian urban planning remains hierarchical, with urban regulation developed through co-ordinated plans of various scope. Plans of a higher order (such as regional and master plans) provide the basis for a finer resolution in a more precise area (regulations), which contain all the necessary ingredients for planning and building permits. The government provided long-awaited, simplified legislation that covers all aspects of the construction and management of built environments. The emphasis was on simplicity, grounded in the imperative of attracting foreign and private investment at almost any cost, with specific concerns for the protection of public interest within the new, and for the majority unfamiliar, environment.

four
THE MASTER PLAN 2001–2021

At the outbreak of the civil wars, two documents regulated the urban development of Belgrade – the spatial plan (1981), and the master plan (1985). The 1985 master plan was already a compendium of amendments to an earlier plan dating from 1972. Those amendments were mainly technical, for in the 1980s there was neither the political courage nor the energy for substantial rethinking. In early 2001, the Council appointed the Institute for the Urbanism of Belgrade to produce a new master plan.

Problems emanating from its flawed information base well illustrate that producing an effective master plan was an almost impossible task. The available data dated back to the

figure 8.1
THE BELGRADE MASTER PLAN 2021 (INSTITUTE FOR URBANISM)

1971, 1981 and 1991 Census, which by now were almost irrelevant. Over the last 15 years an unknown number of refugees had descended into the city; changing beyond recognition the ethnic and social maps of the city, while the process of change was never recorded. These impoverished communities held values vastly different from those surveyed and recorded some thirty, twenty, or even only ten years ago – not to mention an almost totally destroyed industrial basis and widespread corruption and organized crime. In parallel to their planning tasks, the master plan team therefore had to reach out for and compile the basic elements required for their work.

The team, lead by experienced urbanists Macura and Ferencak, took a pragmatic approach. Aware that Belgrade desperately needed some basic patching up, along with elements of a long-term vision, they proposed some down-to-earth improvements and modest steps towards the restoration of basic livability. The master plan therefore sets the following programatic slogans for Belgrade 2021:

> *Belgrade, the city of our country; Belgrade, a European metropolis; Belgrade, the Danubian orientation; Belgrade, in accord with nature; Belgrade, sustainable city; Belgrade, an urbanized and regulated city; Belgrade, a city of complex memories; Belgrade, a city of defined vision.*

At the more practical level, the plan addresses a number of issues of strategic importance for the functioning of the city. They include the completion of the ring road, new bridges, the reuse of neglected spaces, including the centrally located historic fortress and a strategy for the War Island reserve. It also legalizes much of the illegal construction that has been built over the previous 15 years, taking the position that neither the city nor the country could afford to demolish these buildings. The master plan treats them as an undesired resource, an asset in need of improvement and to be brought into legal use. After comprehensive discussions and a significant number of amendments, the master plan was adopted by the city council in early 2003.

five
MAJOR PROJECTS – ST SAVA AND BICYCLES

During the Milosevic era, Belgrade saw a number of major planning and urban design initiatives but only few of these went beyond populist rhetoric. Many served as smokescreens for the transfer of public funds into private pockets. One of the significant projects completed in that turbulent period was the St Sava Plateau, a long overdue spatial conclusion of the central promenade of Belgrade.

The story of the St Sava Orthodox Church dates back to 1894 and a decision to build a temple where, according to legend, in 1594 the Turks had burned the remains of a Serbian saint. In 1926 Nestorovic and Deroko won a national competition of ideas and construction commenced. During the savage bombings of World War II the construction was damaged. Three competitions that followed sought ideas for the urban integration of the ruined site, but the unfavourable political climate stalled the process until 1985. It was the forth competition, organized in 1989 to coincide with the 500th anniversary of the Battle at Kosovo, which brought forward a scheme that would eventually conclude the long project. Bobic and Macura came with a proposal which confidently balanced the complex interests of an increasingly vocal church and the wider community.

Another anniversary of immense national importance was used as a catalyst for the completion of the project. The Plateau was officially opened to the public as part of commemorations which marked the 200 years since the Serbian Uprising in 1804. Compared with the original competition entry, the scheme made a number of concessions to the changed reality of an impoverished capital city. Nevertheless, the Plateau now provides a grand conclusion to the historic and functional axis of Belgrade. From the beginning, this was the project in which numbers mattered. The government Website informs us that it

figure 8.2
ST SAVA PLATEAU (BOBIC
AND MACURA)

has a surface of 60 000 m², some 25 000 of which are pedestrian areas and smaller squares; 15 000 m² of granite paths; 34 000 m² of green space; 419 trees, 2800 shrubs and 15 000 flowers; 5 km of irrigation pipes and more than 300 lights, among other things.

In the early 2000s a number of financially and symbolically less ambitious projects were build and, together with some of the often unnoticed improvements to the infrastructure, made significant contributions to the urbanity and livability of Belgrade. One of those was a new bicycle path, an gesture which helped the citizens of Belgrade discover many, until recently lost and hidden, urban spaces of high recreational value. A similar contribution to the public realm was achieved through improvements in urban management and seemingly simple technical interventions in the city centre, in particular. The introduction of a new parking regime, for instance, almost instantly generated a number of benefits, such as the pedestrian reclamation of the key urban spaces and the gradual return of the (long forgotten) urban use of cars.

six
DESIGN COMPETITIONS — THE REPUBLIC SQUARE

Throughout the years of crisis, Belgrade's culture of design competitions thrived. Local professional circles and organizations deserve praise for this form of resistance to the madness which had swamped almost all spheres of public and private life. The majority of winning schemes were condemned to remain on paper, but their contribution to the ecology of ideas and to some distant, better future of the city should not to be underestimated. Among the many competitions the Republic Square Gallery stands out for its particular significance. The main square of central Belgrade is a place with a long history, where some of the major expressions of civil disobedience and demonstrations against the Milosevic's regime also took place. In 2003 the city council announced a competition of ideas for a public gallery, which would commemorate the assassinated Prime Minister Zoran Djindjic.

Forty design teams took part in that competition, which was eventually won by the most inexperienced entrant. A final year student of architecture Bojana Puzic, and a recent graduate, Natalija Ristanovic, proposed a bold, contemporary design to house 8000 m² of a complex programme. The brave geometry of the scheme with spaces organized around an ascending ramp would, in the words of one of the winners, reach far beyond traditional exhibition spaces and bring together the weakened cultural energies of the city. Due to the subsequent political change in the country, however, the gallery is not likely to be built.

seven
AN ATMOSPHERE OF CONTROVERSY

Despite differences in character, importance and scope, all these projects have something in common. They are all associated with an air of controversy, an atmosphere which has haunted the recent history of the country and which continues to define the social condition of post-Milosevic Serbia. The overall political situation, which still includes a close association between the worlds of politics, organized crime and the post-war *nouveau riche*, does not allow a transcendence of the crisis. The culmination of this climate of corruption and violence was the assassination of Zoran Djindjic in March 2003.

The urban reconstruction of Belgrade and, all the projects described above are inevitably tainted by the overall social condition. In a highly politicized, antagonized and criminalized social fabric the 'readings' of this new text of the city and for the city provide conflicting stories, a true Balkanian *Rashomon*. The new Planning and Construction Law of Serbia does facilitate development and offer more transparent procedures and accountability. It embodies the values of an era of social transition, which is not necessarily appealing to the majority. The moderates seem to agree that the law, with all its shortcomings, does bring back the possibility of an urban order, in that it reduces the opportunities for illegal activities which degrade the urbanity of Belgrade, in particular the infamous 'free interpretations' of the city rules and guidelines. But its inauguration was met with stiff opposition.

While the master plan 2001–2021 was still at the stage of an early draft, one of my colleagues told me with resignation how the project had been initiated 'only to legalize the wealth of some of the Godfathers'. On a more optimistic note, he added that he wanted to see it as an opportunity to squeeze in a number of other ideas and measures which would be truly beneficial for the city.

The master plan is a document to be read from many angles. For instance, the stated aims offer interesting insights into the social organization of the city and the country. They expose the aspirations and the frustrations of the present. Belgrade would be both 'our own' and 'European', where term 'our own' remains only loosely defined. The text refers to 'former Yugoslavia' and 'our present country', without spelling out the name of the current social construct (which, at the time when work on the master plan began was still called Yugoslavia, soon to be renamed the Union of Serbia and Montenegro, which might be further altered and 'balkanized' into a separate Serbia and Montenegro). Reference to 'complex history', in a similar way, may be just an euphemism, a phrase which hints at, and at the same time covers up, the ugly stories from the most recent history (which Serbian politicians increasingly avoid).

Critics say that the master plan allows too much political control over urban development, and that it does not go far enough with putting regulations in place. One of interesting examples is that the still influential Department of Defence maintains ownership over many lucrative central locations. Those locations have a significant real estate value and, as they have been exempted from planning regulations, are prone to abuse. Some critics persist in mentioning the legalization of illegal developments in the same sentence as the term, 'Godfathers'.

The St Sava Plateau is a story on its own, a veritable palimpsest of texts and meanings. Interpreting the story has always been, and remains, politicized from every ideological position. This project is a big gain for the city, but also for a reinvigorated Serbian Orthodox Church, which is often associated with the extreme Serbian right. Despite its much shorter history, the Republic Square competition does not lack controversy. Dr Zoran Djindjic was the first democratically elected Prime Minister of Serbia. He was an uncompromising fighter for a future of a kind that was neither accepted, nor acceptable, to everyone. As a politician, Djindjic was both celebrated and rebuffed. Clearly associated with many of the victories of the anti-Milosevic opposition, he was therefore frequently accused of having close links with the underworld. In order to reduce this controversy, the city council decided that the Square would keep its old name, that the gallery would not be named after Mr Djindjic, and that the design would include only an appropriate commemoration of his life, in particular the ideas of progress which he so strongly advocated. The results divided not only political, but also professional circles. The President of the Institute of Architects praised the pragmatism which 'suited the times', but many objected to the possible construction of the awarded scheme. A renowned local architect, Mihajlo Mitrovic lashed out at 'incompetence of the organizer'. Referring to the youth of the winner he said that the history of architecture 'does not know *wunderkinds*', and that the competition scheme was 'hardly legible' in its use of contemporary architectural jargon and presentation techniques and so on.

All this adds to the text of the Republic Square project and Belgrade itself. How should we read the haste in which the competition was staged? How can we understand the frenzy to undermine the results? Answers to those questions cut deep into the political tissue of Serbia. Even a 'clash of architectural styles' in Belgrade is not necessarily what it seems to be on the surface. New architectural languages represent new ideas. It may be that it was these ideas, not the forms in which they were represented, that electrified some of the critics. What matters to us is that an urban and architectural design has, yet again, found itself in the eye of the storm. It has brought together all the political, ideological, professional and other debates of a divided society. Why is that so? Why cannot the post-war and the post-dictatorial times bring forward the long-dormant creative energies of Serbia? Why does the social capital of the country, and in particular that of its main city, seem all but dead?

I have discussed those themes with several colleagues from Belgrade who referred to the total decline of authority and social values during the Milosevic era, about an *ad hoc* urbanism without rules, about the rule of brutal force. In the 1990s illegal construction and illegal money from 'unknown' sources built up, and in that process severely damaged Belgrade. Dragan Zivkovic, a former long-time curator of the architecture collection in the Museum of Applied Arts in Belgrade, emphasizes the importance of social context which makes all projects end in controversy. It was in the early 1990s that he reminded readers of the relevance of Machiavelli in the planning of Belgrade (Zivkovic, 1992). We both agree that internal social destruction of Serbia and Belgrade was caused by the primitivism best described as *palanka*.

eight

THE DOMINATION OF *PALANKA*

Palanka is term used as a synonym for 'small town'. Several places in Serbia are indeed named *palanka*. But there is another, additional, more profound and sinister meaning.

Palanka denotes the state of mind which can hardly be defined in its own right. Our best definitions can only place it in opposition to *urbanity*. *Palanka* represents provincialism at its worst. In the early 1970s Yugoslav philosopher, Radomir Konstantinovic, published a profound analysis of this phenomenon. Less that 30 years after the publication of *Filosofila palanke* (Konstantinovic, n.d.) the depth and the relevance of his analysis became tragically obvious. Slobodan Milosevic in Serbia and his nationalist counterparts in other parts of former Yugoslavia took power by using the raw, destructive power of the small-town mentality. Konstantinovic wrote:

> *The universe of* palanka *exists only in spirit. The spirit of* palanka *is the only absolute* palanka, *with the reality of* palanka *always lagging behind it.* Palanka *does not possess an ideal to strive for.*

In so far as cities are citizens themselves, *palanka* is its inhabitants. Some describe them as 'in-betweeners' (Velmar-Jankovic, 1991), people in the tragic state of transition from villages and rural lifestyles (which, having abandoned, they have grown unable to comprehend) and cities (which reject them and which they reject).

> *In his essential beliefs* palancanin [DR: inhabitant of *palanka*] *is more faithful to the* palanka *than to himself. He is not an individual on a personal path; he is a sum of particular experience, of particular position, of particular style. What he guards when he defends* palanka *are exactly those position and style....* Palancanin *has an extraordinarily strong sense of style, because of his extraordinary sense of collectivity, frozen in (or represented through) that very style.* (Konstantinovic, n.d.)

That 'frozen' status is what makes *palanka* radically opposed to the dynamism of cities.

> *The spirit of traditionalism is one of the basic expressions of* palanka; *to be in the spirit of* palanka *means to exist according to its strongly stylistically determined will, in the way that ensures repetition of* palanka's *own yesterday.*

The concept of *palanka* helps explain the social destruction of Yugoslavia. One could argue that the Yugoslav wars have begun as wars of xenophobic, exclusive *palanka* against the pluralism and inclusiveness of Yugoslav cities. Once at war, *palanka* proved able to radicalize and mobilize their own tribal circles, thus 'elevating' the conflict to the level of ethnic groups and later to the levels of religion and the other cultural signifiers of Yugoslav peoples and regions.

If one follows the traces of destruction and in them seeks understanding of the origins of an never-ending post-Yugoslav crisis, we come across the phenomenon of the barbaric treatment of cities during the conflict. The assault on Yugoslav cities had begun long before the outbreak of armed conflict (Radovic, 1998). For decades, Yugoslav cities were under sustained pressure from growing Balkan nationalists and their anti-urban sentiments. By the late 1980s the crisis has gone through to the very foundations of society, undercutting basic values, which gradually gave in to aggressive, intolerant, non-urbane and anti-urban practices. Denial of 'the right to the *oeuvre* [participation] and appropriation [not to be confused with property but use value]' that is 'implied in the right to the city' (Lefebvre, 1996) was gradual. People accustomed to queues for basics like bread and milk slowly surrendered their urbanity. They were slowly conditioned towards non-participation and obedience.

The assault on the urbanity of Yugoslav cities came not only from chauvinist, retrogressive, atavistic internal reflexes. The cities embodied a pluralist, cosmopolitan and inclusive culture that ridiculed narrow particularism and the xenophobia of nationalistic exclusiveness. The Sarajevan novelist Dzevad Karahasan, in his *Exodus of the City*, claims that Sarajevo suffered 'only because there are the temples of four faiths in it' (Karahasan, 1994). The primitive nationalisms that overtook former Yugoslavia found such diversity threatening. The monocultural utopias of their shallow mythologies seemed to offer security, a timelessly enduring refuge from urban challenges, instead of the dynamism of ever-changing urbanity.

In the light of the atrocities like those committed in Vukovar, Mostar, Sarajevo or Srebrenica it is difficult even to speak about suffering of places that experienced minimal or no physical damage, where almost nobody was killed. But, we must remember that cities are *koinonia* [fellowships] (Downey, 1976), that they are in essence the relationship between citizens (which, among the many expressions of this relationship, also finds a certain physical, urban form). Many cities that escaped with less physical damage, or were even undamaged altogether, endured scars as deep as those caused by the shells and the bombs. The Yugoslav capital, Belgrade, is one of those cities. Its terrible curse had also begun long before the war, when relentless, uncompromising challenges were made to the values that stood against chauvinistic barbarism. As its urban culture weakened, latent nationalism grew into the violent, aggressive and insatiable national-socialism of Milosevic's regime. Every aspect of urbanity crumbled, even faster than the facades of the neglected city (Prodanovic, 2002).

The architecture of the Milosevic era can shed light at the character of *palanka*. One of the *nouveau riche* Karic family villas, located in a prestigious and once elegant suburb of Dedinje, offers a good example of *palanka* as architectural style. Designed by the owner himself, in size and splendour inspired by soap operas, its decoration includes nothing less than two replicas of Michelangelo's David and two replicas of the antique statue of Venus.

figure 8.4
VILLA KARIC, DEDINJE,
BELGRADE

figure 8.5
HOUSES ON TOP OF A HOUSE, CENTRAL BELGRADE

Combined wealth and taste for kitsch produced one of many monstrosities that scar both the social and the physical urban tissue of Belgrade.

Another notorious example is the addition of a top floor to a prominent, centrally located six-storey residential block. An urbanite-to-be decided to use the 'flexibility' of local authorities and invest his money in his right to add a floor to an urban block at one of the best locations in Belgrade. *Palanka* as a style leads to the most unexpected outcome. Two double-storey detached houses of the kind that adorn small towns, the real *palankas* of Serbia, have been constructed on top of a modernist building! The symbolism of that gesture is enormous. *Palanka* is there, in the best location in the city. It remains unchanged, it is uncompromised by the urban context. It came to the very centre, invaded the alien, unacceptable modernist style and, unconcernedly, now dominates the cityscape of Belgrade. *Palanka*, unable to compromise – a victorious *palanka* indeed.

Belgrade surrendered to *palanka* in the early 1990s, when it stayed silent while Milosevic's regime was crushing the other urban centres of the former Yugoslavia. Cites have more in common that nations so that when citizens remain deaf, blind and mute in the wake of aggression towards other centres of urbanity, that is the sign that their urban values have declined to an unacceptable low. The tanks of the Yugoslav Army were rolling into Slovenia, Croatia and Bosnia and Herzegovina – and Belgrade remained silent. Chauvinist pseudo-intellectuals were firing words of hatred around, and the city remained silent (Radovic, 2002). That was a clear sign that Belgrade has lost its way. History knows of many such cases. Some of the great cities of this world, including Rome, Berlin, Tokyo, Paris and Washington have had their times of shameful silence. Belgrade, too, was unacceptably silent in the late 1980s and early 1990s.

151

Palanka, as an anti-urban and an anti-urbane state of mind, is not exclusive to the Balkans, to former Yugoslavia or to Serbia. It is a global phenomenon. In *Our Abilities*, Jorges Luis Borges (1999) describes the Argentinian small-town mentality in a way that clearly corresponds to Konstantinovic's depiction of the Balkan *palanka*. In those communities the foreigner is also 'an unforgivable, always mistaken, largely unreal creature'. Borges' version of *palanka* shares the Balkan 'unrestrainable delight in failure' of the other. *Palanka* is universal. '*Palanka* is not in the world, it is in the spirit, possible everywhere' (Konstantinovic). It may take different forms, it may speak different languages but what connects the backwaters of Argentina, the non-descript, conservative Australian suburbia, the vast non-urban conglomerations of America and Konstantinovic's or Hadziprodromidis' (2000) Balkan *palanka* is that same spirit of provincial, autistic exclusiveness. Lessons from the former Yugoslavia, thus, have some universal relevance. We all now live in times when *palanka* seems to have gained the power of global reach and the disastrous repercussion are obvious.

REFERENCES

Borges, Jorges Luis (1999). *Our Abilities, Selected Non-Fiction*. Viking.
Downey, Glanville (1976). Aristotle as an expert of urban problems, *Ekistics*, **253**, 12.
Hadziprodromidis, Leonidas, (2000). Umorstvo Jugoslavije *Republika*, **234**.
Karahasan, Dzevad (1994). *Sarajevo, Exodus of a City* Kodansha International.
Konstantinovic, Radomir n.d. *Filosofija palanke*, Treci programme.
Lefebvre, Henri (1996). *Writings on Cities*. Blackwell.
Prodanovic, Mileta (2002). *Stariji i lepsi Beograd*, Stubovi kulture.
Radovic, Darko (1998). Yugoslav war and the right to the city. *Environmental Justice Conference Proceedings*. Available online at http://www.arbld.unimelb.edu.au/envjust/papers/allpapers/radovic/home.htm.
Radovic, Darko (2000). Friend, wish you were here. *The Age*, 14 October.
Radovic, Darko (2002). Urbanity and the Other, *WM globalfusion*.
Todorova, Maria, (1997). *Imagining the Balkans*, Oxford University Press.
Velmar Jankovic, Vladimir (1991). *Pogled s kalemegdana*, Biblioteka Grada Beograda.
Vovelle, Michel (1990). *Ideologies and mentalities*, Polity Press.
Zivkovic, Dragan, (1992). Otudjenje vremena i prostora, *The Post-graduate Publications*, Faculty of Architecture, Belgrade.

#09

REFRAMING JOHANNESBURG

Graeme Reid

The Johannesburg inner city lies at the heart of greater Johannesburg. Starting in the late 1960s, the inner city (including both the city centre or business district and the surrounding residential areas), has experienced a long process of decline. It continues, however, to play a vital role in the city as a whole, particularly in the process of addressing the geography of the apartheid city. This article explores the redevelopment the inner city, examining the nature and role of the city centre, as well as the processes that are used to promote its regeneration. It draws on the work and ideas developed by the many professionals, city council officials and political and business leaders who have participated in this process of reinterpreting and understanding the city centre within a context of a city that has moved rapidly from a city governed by apartheid laws of exclusion to one of democratic governance premised on ideals of economic and social inclusion; from an isolated city to one increasingly integrated into the region and one that is proud of its position as a leading African city.

In 1994, Johannesburg was made the capital of the Gauteng province of South Africa, one of nine provinces established as part of the new political dispensation. The smallest of the provinces, Gauteng is the economic engine of South Africa. It contributes 38 per cent to South Africa's GGP and 9 per cent of Africa's. Johannesburg, in turn, contributes 40 per cent to the Gauteng GGP and 16 per cent of the national GGP. But unemployment runs at over 30 per cent (although some estimates put it as high as 40 per cent) with large and increasing numbers of people surviving through employment in a growing informal sector.

Consisting of the amalgamation of thirteen local authorities which, prior to 1994, were defined along racial lines, the City of Johannesburg covers a substantial area of some 2300 km². It is home to 2.8 million of the seven million people who live in Gauteng. And while the north of Johannesburg is well serviced and developed, the legacy of apartheid is one of serious service delivery backlogs in the south. Many of its 791 000 households are housed in informal settlements and backyard shacks in the former black townships and only 96.4 per cent have piped water, 84 per cent are connected to a municipal sanitation system and 85 per cent have electricity.

one

DECENTRALIZATION

In significant ways, the development of Johannesburg's metropolitan area has followed the route of many cities in North America. The Johannesburg city centre of old was the 'capital city' – certainly in economic terms – and the central business district, often referred to as 'New York on the Highveld'. But the preconditions for decentralization were laid in the 1960s when government copied the American car-centred freeway system, providing convenient mobility for a wealthy minority living north of the Johannesburg city centre. The establishment in 1969 of Sandton, as a separate white local authority north of Johannesburg, laid the basis for the development of Johannesburg's first 'edge city', which competed with Johannesburg by offering lower rates and favourable zoning for commercial and retail developments (Rogerson and Tomlinson, 1999).

Other factors drove the process of decentralization to the north of the city centre especially the high land values and rentals there. It suffered from its own particular problems of being too big: shaped by poor planning and the location decisions of planners and investors alike, the city became spread out, with office workers 'needing a car or public transport to make a meeting' (Rogerson and Tomlinson, 1999). But there was no internal public transport system and the problem was compounded in the 1970s by city planners who, in an attempt to address traffic congestion, severely limited the number of parking bays allowed and available. Combined with a restructuring in the office market that saw demand for office parks grow, and the subsequent development of suburban shopping malls, by 1992 the city centre provided only 44 per cent of A and B grade office space in metropolitan Johannesburg.

By 1997, the figure had dropped substantially to 37 per cent. In addition, more than half the metropolitan area's retail space was located outside the city centre and in 1997 Midrand – previously outside the Johannesburg boundaries but incorporated into the metropolitan area in 1999 – had more new office developments than in any other centre in the Johannesburg/Pretoria region.

This second and more rapid phase of decentralization in the 1990s was driven by other, mostly non-economic, factors related to the fundamental changes that occurred in South Africa beginning in the early 1990s. From the signing of the Soweto Accord in 1990 (between organizations forming part of the mass democratic movement and the apartheid local government structures) local government went through a process of fundamental transition and restructuring, leading up to democratic local government elections in 1995. During this period a hiatus in decision-making occurred in the white Johannesburg City Council, which, led by the liberal Democratic Party, was keenly conscious of the fact that it was the last white-only local government. Faced with a new constituency which had not voted for it, it struggled to deal with and respond to the changes facing the city and to develop systems of management that did not rely on the exclusionary laws of apartheid.

Crime and grime became the major problems. In a 1993 report in support of the establishment of the first business improvement district in the city centre, muggings were reported as averaging twenty eight to thirty per month (Central Johannesburg Partnership, 1993). Other factors contributed to the flight of capital to the north: unregulated street trading, inadequate facilities for minibus taxis, a lack of public amenities, high commercial vacancies, badly maintained buildings and a lack of reinvestment, squatting, the illegal conversion of commercial properties to overcrowded and poorly serviced residential buildings and poorly maintained and managed public areas.

Prior to 1990, in terms of the notorious Group Areas Act and other racially based legislation, black people – Africans, 'Coloureds' and people of Indian and Asian decent – were unable to live in or own property in the city, from which they were banished at night. The city was 'in a sense, an European City within which Africa was firmly subordinated'. (Rogerson and Tomlinson, 1999). After 1990, the city experienced greater and more rapid demographic changes than probably any other city in the world. The residential population went from being almost exclusively white (excepting the domestic workers who inhabited the 'locations in the skies' – rooms built to house them at the top of high-rise apartment buildings in inner city suburbs) to almost exclusively black, and grew by 25 per cent between 1992 and 1996 (Inner City Housing Upgrade Trust, 1996) – without an increase in housing stock – to reach a still relatively low overall figure of 220 000 by 1999.

In the residential areas and the business district of the inner city, the enforcement of by-laws ceased, and building control, land-use management and other planning regulations, along with credit control, were all but abandoned. The inner city housing environment became increasingly unstable, with white landlords and the new black tenants in contestation over rentals, obligations and rights. Many landlords milked their properties and abandoned them. Banks, facing increased defaults and a breakdown in public service delivery, responded by massive redlining of most of the inner city, causing more disinvestment and fulfiling the banks' prophesy of urban decay.

In the city centre the deregulation of the taxi industry led to a massive increase in the number of people using minibus taxis. In the absence of proper facilities, taxis were ranked on the streets. Park Central/Jack Mincer, the first formal taxi rank for an industry that transports 45 per cent of the 800 000 daily commuters to the city centre, was built only in 1998 and opened in early 1999. These informal taxi ranks brought with them a myriad of problems, stifling commercial and retail activity in the buildings around them and bringing increased vacancies and the decline of these properties. Similarly, the abolition in 1991 of all local authority by-laws to regulate and manage informal street trading brought a massive influx of street traders and a resulting increase in waste management problems, congestion on the pavements, the informal control of space and further decay in the built environment. Indeed, most of the businesses that left the city in the mid-1990s cited unregulated street trading as one of the major reasons for relocating. Interestingly, the only attempt to address these issues came from business through the improvement districts, which began slowly to reduce the density of street trading and provide trading facilities for informal traders within the districts.

In many ways the forces that shaped the metropolitan area and the city centre were profoundly different from those that affected other inner cities around the world. As a consequence of the apartheid planning, Johannesburg's inner city sits positioned between the urban, dormitory sprawl of the systematically underdeveloped south, which is home to

Soweto and the large informal and semi-formal settlements housing more than 50 per cent of the city's population, and the sprawl to the north, the economic heartland. By the mid-1990s it was clear that, more than any other area of any city in South Africa, the Johannesburg inner city had become an area of contestation: among traders and taxi operators; between formal retailers and informal traders; between foreign migrants and South Africans, both seeking economic refuge in the inner city and between the diverging economic and social systems of the north (and significant aspects of the city centre's economy) linked into the global economy and a significant portion of the labour force operating either outside the formal economy or 'directly linked to the rest of Africa through migrant networks'. As Professors Rogerson and Tomlinson (1999) note:

> The appropriate image might well be one of two vastly unequal wheels turning, and the point where they grind is in the central city.

By 1995, many had written off the inner city. In 1997, a headline in *City Press,* a Johannesburg, English-language weekly with a predominant by black readership, stated: 'City in ruins. Entering a city in filth' *(City Press,* 1997). The *Business Day* reported, 'UK property firm says SA's CBDs are "finished" ' *(Business Day,* 1997). The newly elected local authority had inherited a city centre in crisis.

A new approach to thinking about the Johannesburg city of old was clearly required that no longer characterized it in the way the marketing documents of the early 1990s did, as the 'Gateway *to* Africa' (Bremner, 2002) but as an African city providing significant economic opportunities and contributing to increased growth and prosperity in Johannesburg and the region.

two

INNER CITY URBAN RENEWAL

There were a number of important factors prompting the new city government to tackle inner city urban renewal. Despite the fact that the bulk of Johannesburg's population still lives to the south of the city centre, it is in the north and to the north east that economic growth is occurring. And while the old Johannesburg central business district was no longer the centre of this growth in the metropolitan area, it was positioned in a pivotal location with regard to the formal economic hub that was being consolidated and stretched from the inner city to Midrand and Pretoria in the north and the Johannesburg International Airport in the east, or what is known as the 'Gauteng golden triangle'. As such, it is able to provide marginalized communities from the south of the inner city with an entry point into the formal economy and it remains the largest employment centre in metropolitan Johannesburg and a major economic generator and employment and service centre (City of Johannesburg, 2002).

With 800 000 people travelling into the inner city every day to work, trade, conduct government business and travel onwards, the inner city served as the largest transport hub in

Johannesburg. With 7 million m² of floor space, representing a replacement cost of built infrastructure in excess of R30 billion, housing stock worth over R1.2 billion and a sound and extensive infrastructure, it was an asset Johannesburg could not afford to let go to waste. Equally important, the Johannesburg city centre is the heart of the city, and its image, vitality, success and well-being are representative of the whole of Johannesburg. So indeed, there was, and still is, a general feeling that if you can get it right in Johannesburg, you can get it right anywhere.

In early 1996, together with business which had organized themselves as the Johannesburg Inner City Business Coalition, the Greater Johannesburg Metropolitan Council established an Inner City Development Forum. Various sectors were represented on the forum, including provincial government, business, community organizations and labour. The Forum's first task was to develop a vision for the inner city. This process, funded by business, reflected some of the suspicions that still existed between the parties. Instead of working in one process, it was agreed that each sector would develop its own vision and these would then be debated and an attempt made to draw up a consolidated vision that all sectors would be able to support. Over 150 organizations finally came together and adopted a vision for the Johannesburg inner city. To some extent the vision represents the process, as it covers a relatively extensive range of sector-specific issues. But what was remarkable, according to people who participated in the process, were the similarities of aspirations and the ease with which agreement on the vision was reached.

In July 1997, the vision for the inner city of Johannesburg was launched by President Thabo Mbeki (then Deputy President). The vision is:

The golden heartbeat of Africa. A dynamic city that works…Livable, safe, well-managed and welcoming; people-centred, accessible and celebrating cultural diversity. A vibrant 24 hour city; a city for residents, workers, tourists, entrepreneurs and learners; focused on the twenty-first century, respecting its heritage and capitalizing on its position in South Africa, Africa and the whole world. A truly global city; the trading hub of Africa thriving through participation, partnership and the spirit of UBUNTU.

Although the vision can be criticized for its broadness and its failure to articulate a distinctive identity and the competitive advantage of the inner city, the process served to create and cement a partnership for urban renewal, particularly between business and government, that had not existed before. In addition, it provided a framework for subsequent work, including the formulation of a development strategy and a programme of activities to start the process of renewal. Most important, it represented the start of new way of working that, rather than being informed by consultation on plans developed by officials and professionals, was based on participation in the planning process by stakeholders themselves.

three
DEVELOPMENT STRATEGY

The development strategy articulated six key areas of intervention. It sought to make the inner city an economic hub; a centre for cultural and sporting activities, events and conferences; a desirable residential environment; an international, national and local education centre; a place with a desirable quality of life. To enhance its centrality the public transport system was to be upgraded. What the development strategy did not do was to articulate its impact spatially, nor did it attempt to articulate what the impact of the vision and the development strategy might be on the built form of the city. In addition, the programme to support the economic objectives was based on inadequate data and a limited understanding of the role of the inner city in the metropolitan economy.

The next step in the process was to develop, on the basis of the vision and the broad-based development strategy, a spatial and economic framework which would become the guide for a programme of action for urban renewal in the inner city. A high-level project team – which included politicians, business leaders and city officials – was established to drive and direct the process, which was funded by the Greater Johannesburg Metropolitan Council, the Urban Management Programme of the United Nations and the Johannesburg Inner City Business Coalition. External consultants – researchers, economists and urban designers – were contracted to provide additional capacity to the team, and became integral members of the team as opposed to consultants to it. Numerous structured workshops with broader groupings of stakeholders were used to secure the participation and engagement of key sectors, and culminated in a city consultation with over 100 key stakeholders at which the spatial and economic framework was endorsed. (GAPP, Rogerson and Tomlinson, 1999). The approach to developing the framework was also informed by an understanding of a critical new role that the city centre had to adopt. Given the polynodal nature of the metropolitan area and the fact that it had been created by both the economic forces that drove decentralization to the north and the apartheid planning that separated the city from its underdeveloped and primarily black south, the city centre was the place where integration – racial and social – could happen. In light of this, the development of the framework was underpinned by a set of ideas which, it was believed, would promote and foster this opportunity and thus promote urban renewal.

The first of these related to the role of public space. Public space is limited in the city. The building boom of the 1970s saw much of the city centre's public open space given up by the city for office development, and today only 1.6 per cent of land is public open space. Creating attractive, well-managed public space where people would meet by design or accident would be essential. The second related to urban amenity as a key to the success of the inner city. Given the contestation between the users of the city and the importance of public space, promoting urban amenities was to be central to the urban renewal programme. Streets needed to be more than merely functional and they needed to represent an amenity for an integrated and integrating city. The vision for the inner city had clearly articulated this as a desire of all stakeholders, but its importance in economic terms was

figure 9.1
BERTHA STREET PARK LOOKING NORTH, WITH WITS UNIVERSITY ON THE LEFT

underscored in the work of the Australian Urban Futures Research Programme (Lepani, et al., 1995), and the following analysis: 'Unless our ambition is to be a low-wage "developing" nation, high urban amenity is a basic'.

Thirdly, the existing form of the city centre did not address the needs of the majority of users of the city. The fact that the city had become too spread-out had to be addressed. The approach favoured was to promote the shrinking of the core around the nodes within the city centre that continued to function well as commercial centres – the major developments housing the banks, insurance companies and the mining houses – while finding new and distinctive or defining uses for other areas. In this process specific precincts or districts where new uses had begun to emerge organically could be fostered. Thus, for example, an area that had previously housed large-scale garment manufacturers had become home to close on 1000 micro- and small garment-industry related businesses, with an emerging emphasis on African, urban fashion. The Fashion District was born and recognized in the spatial and economic framework for the inner city. The programme to promote this district sets out key objectives, such as: promoting linkages and networks, providing businesses skills and promoting the functionality of the area through urban design interventions which specifically seek to improve the ability of the garment and fashion industries to do business in the area.

Fourthly, public transport within the inner city and the promotion of pedestrian prioritized routes in the city had to be addressed to accommodate the majority of city users who relied on public transport to reach the city, as well as catering for the projected further growth in the residential population. Finally, the development of the framework was predicated on the need to include and stimulate the informal sector in the urban renewal process. For the first time, the importance of the informal sector as an economic sector to be accommodated – and not merely regulated – was recognized. Whereas before 1991, informal traders had been permitted through licenses and the payment of a fee to trade on identified street corners, the approach now adopted in developing the framework was to try to create space and facilities which would accommodate informal sector businesses and facilitate their integration into the formal economy. As a result, a network of markets linked to newly developed multi-modal transport facilities accommodating taxis, rail transport and buses was proposed and developed in an inner-city street-trading management programme. The outcome of the process was a spatial and economic framework based on twelve parallel strategies, applicable in different degrees in the different districts identified as making up the inner city.

four

PUBLIC TRANSPORT

These strategies addressed the following areas: movement connectivity, parking and traffic management, public transport, pedestrian priority areas, key installations and the natural environment, residential and community development, the building stock, service infrastructure, economic development, social investment, education, management, marketing and public relations, safety and security and upgrading the image of the inner city. What emerged then was a programme of prioritized interventions which, drawing on the above parallel strategies, could be applied in different districts according to the needs identified in each one. What did not emerge was a grand master plan, or 'the big project'. The programme for urban renewal was thus incremental, inclusive and sustainable. It is, however, management intensive and required a new way of approaching developments from professionals. This is illustrated in the development of the first major public transport facility in the city centre, the Park Central/Jack Miner development. Located some 500 m from the central railway station and serviced by a number of bus routes, it accommodates 2000 minibus taxis and is used by over 100 000 daily commuters. Prior to 1994, when the facility had been handed to taxi associations to be used for taxi holding (parking during off-peak) and ranking, Jack Mincer had been a municipal parking garage. By 1998 it was characterized as chaotic, dangerous and dirty. Waste management was nonexistent and competition over space and routes, together with street crime, made it extremely unsafe. For commuters, there were no facilities: no shelter from the weather and the few public ablution facilities that were provided were blocked and unusable.

However, standing on an adjacent building and looking down on the informal rank, it was clear that it was far from chaotic in the way in which the taxi associations managed their business. Previously, a taxi rank would be developed without much consultation with the taxi operators themselves. Why this should have occurred might be bewildering, given that no-one would approach the development of a shopping mall without engaging with the anchor tenants. It is to be explained by the fact that at that stage the informal taxi industry was mostly marginalized and was seen as – and indeed often was – violent and dangerous. A site would be identified by city planners, surveys of the number of taxis and commuters who would probably use the facility conducted and the facility designed and built. It would then be presented as a *fait accompli* to the taxi industry. Thus, for example, in 1996 a new taxi rank had been developed on 5th Street in Sandton without any input from the taxi associations. To this day, it remains unused and in mothballs.

A different process was adopted for the development of the Park Central/Jack Mincer Rank, in collaboration with the developer of a proposed adjacent retail centre. The taxi leadership was brought into the design process from the beginning. Representatives of the six associations which would ultimately use the rank were brought into the project team, engaging with urban designers, architects and traffic engineers on design and management issues. The process, although difficult and initially characterized by posturing and position-taking, allowed ultimately for the development of a facility that addresses the needs of both commuters and the industry itself. While placing new demands on the professionals, requiring them to build relationships with an industry that until then operated on the margins, the process produced a number of design innovations that were incorporated into the development, and without which the effective use of the facility by the industry undoubtedly would have been compromised. Most important, the new facility produced efficiencies in the industry that resulted, on some routes, in a reduction of travel time of up to 45 minutes, as well as increased business for taxi operators. It also produced a sense of investment and ownership on the part of taxi operators, and developed new management systems to manage the completed facility with the City.

In a very practical and obvious sense, top-down planning processes were transformed into participatory processes in which professionals become facilitators, instead of experts. For city official and professionals, it has meant learning to work with the new users of the city. It has meant understanding the way in which the new communities of the inner city live their lives and engage with the built environment. It has meant understanding how the informal systems, networks and supply chains of the informal sector work and, through engagement and innovative design, designing out the bad and reinforcing the good. Most important, it has meant building a city which can accommodate the 'diverging economic systems of the north' and a labour force operating outside formal economy.

figure 9.2
JORISSEN STREET
BUS STOP WITH
PEDESTRIAN-FRIENDLY
LIGHTING AND NEW PAVING

figure 9.3
SAPPI PARK ENTRANCE TO THE BALLET CENTRE, CIVIC THEATRE

five
BRAAMFONTEIN

This, together with the recognition of the city centre as a place of interconnected precincts or districts (GAPP and Urban Solutions, 2000), helped shape a process of urban design that began to move away from addressing merely utilitarian aspects of the environment to finding ways of articulating the identity of the precincts – and hence the city – and accommodating competing uses. As should be the case, urban design has become a tool for promoting a sense of place as well as providing opportunities for the economic growth of new sectors. This is well illustrated in the case of Braamfontein, a high-density adjunct to the Johannesburg city centre that accommodates diverse interests: local government, a large number of non-governmental organizations, educational institutions, including the University of the Witwatersrand (Wits University) large corporates as well as smaller businesses, convenience retailers, a small residential component and the city-owned Civic Theatre complex. But like the city centre, the area had suffered from blight, crime and grime, leading to a marked deterioration with the relocation of prime business and retail tenants to suburban areas with resultant high vacancy rates and a degraded public environment in Braamfontein itself.

The redevelopment of Braamfontein targeted the creation of a well-managed, vibrant and physically attractive area, with a growing evening economy, the better use of property stock and increased private sector investment that would support new economic opportunities and create the space to 'enable a multiplicity of ways of being in the city' (Johannesburg Development Agency, 2002; Sack and MMA Architects, 2002). The urban design brief was developed through a series of engagements with key stakeholders the better to understand the area and was informed by a detailed economic analysis and study of the management of the area. A multidisciplinary team was appointed to develop the urban design framework through a highly interactive design process. This involved a number of activities. Focus groups and workshops were held with a range of stakeholders, including Wits University, the major corporates, informal traders and taxi drivers, residents, small businesses and non-governmental organizations. A design workshop was held

figure 9.4
LOOKING OVER SAPPI SQUARE DOWN AMESHOF STREET TO WITS UNIVERSITY

involving students of architecture, planning, fine arts, journalism and urban geography from Wits University, working under the direction of Professor Lindsay Bremner, Head of Wits' School of Architecture, in which the students were asked to observe the area and put forward concepts for how they wanted to see the area developed. International experience and expertise was secured through the participation of Argentinian architect and urbanist, Miguel Angel Roca, in both the student design workshop and a week-long design workshop involving the participation of all stakeholders from the area.

As Monica Albonico, the lead architect and urban designer in the process puts it: 'Processes like these…, reversing roles and breaking conventional linear methodologies, produce more ideas, greater understanding and better tools to work with'. (Darroll, 2003). The result of the process was an urban design framework adopted by the City of Johannesburg in October 2002, that works

> *as an instrument for change and not a blueprint dictating a single path to success. It … is adaptable, resilient and accommodating to emerging needs and changing demands.* (Darroll, 2003)

six
STRATEGIC AREAS

Currently, the inner-city urban-renewal programme focuses on four strategic areas prioritized by and flowing from the spatial and economic framework. The first and major priority is about getting the basics right and focuses on urban management. The city's new waste-management company, Pikitup, has significantly improved the management of waste. Improvement districts and CCTV surveillance technology have significantly reduced crime and have changed perceptions of the city centre. In Newtown, the city's cultural district, which has been a focus for major public sector reinvestment since 2000, both systems operate. When the project to revitalize Newtown by creating a cultural district and a cluster of creative industries was formulated in 1999, the key message from business, cultural organizations and citizens was that, because of crime, Newtown was a no-go area. By September 2002, *The Star* was writing that 'the Newtown Cultural Precinct in Jozi was *the place* to be' (Phosa, 2002). Getting the basics right also addresses public transport and the management of street trading. Four new multi-modal transport facilities have been built so far and two more are under construction. Markets are being created and street traders increasingly trade from proper facilities rather than the streets.

The second relates to housing development. From the unstable and conflictual inner-city residential environment of 1995, 5 per cent of housing stock now falls under social housing management (which was nonexistent before 1994), and in 2001 there was an estimated investment of R30 million by the new private sector in the non-subsidized housing market in the inner city. Most importantly, Trafalgar, South Africa's largest residential property management company, re-entered the inner city in 2000 and now has just on 2000 units under management there.

The third relates to community development, and focuses on the provision of social services in the city centre. A coalition of non-governmental organizations and community-based organizations, in partnership with the local authority, have established in the heart of the high-density residential area, Joubert Park, a conservation and neighbourhood centre. It addresses community development as well as promoting sustainable urban development, home and balcony gardening, and a sense of community in an area where, less than twelve years ago, its members were not allowed to live. The city regional administration promotes integrated service delivery offering access to local government through decentralized People's Centres.

Finally, the programme addresses economic development. The targets for economic development are the creative industries, cultural tourism, growing sector-specific small and medium enterprises within the inner city and the retention of the financial services. A number of new developments have been initiated. These range from major developments such as Constitution Hill, where South Africa's new Constitutional Court is being developed and which will provide a cluster for institutions established to promote the law and the Constitution in South Africa, to smaller urban upgrades within the city centre's core.

The inner city renewal strategy has been given impetus by the Executive Mayor, Clr Amos Masondo, who in early 2001 declared inner city regeneration one of the six key priorities of his administration. *Joburg 2030*, the city's economic development strategy adopted in February 2002 (City of Johannesburg, 2002), also provides direction to and support for the regeneration of the inner city. In addressing the spatial economics of the city, it emphasizes the need to limit sprawl while recognizing and addressing for the first time in the city strategies the polynodal nature of the city. Thus *Joburg 2030* seeks to promote the effective and efficient functioning of each important business node in a manner that ensures their complementarity. Clustering industries in these nodes and promoting economies of location become important objectives in *Joburg 2030*. In this manner, the strategy builds on the notion of shrinking the core of the business district in the city centre, while at the same promoting other distinctive districts within the city centre.

seven

CONCLUSION

The urban renewal strategy is slowly beginning to turn the city around. Through the Johannesburg Development Agency, national, provincial and local government will invest over R1 billion in a three-year period in economic infrastructure and urban upgrading in the city centre. Vacancies of A grade properties are around 15 per cent, their lowest since December 1999 when vacancies topped 25 per cent. Transnet, South Africa's state-owned transport company, bought and refurbished the landmark Carton Centre and relocated their headquarters to it. ABSA opened its new inner-city head office 1999, a R450 million development. Most recently, SAPPI, South Africa's multinational paper producer, announced it would remain in Braamfontein and invest R150 million in developing their global headquarters there together with the surrounding public environment. Other major corporates in the area, including Liberty, the multinational financial services group, confirmed their commitment to the area at the same time and, with other major property owners, committed a further R20 million to urban upgrading. In the east of the city centre, former white-only nightclubs have reopened, drawing a fashionable, young and racially mixed clientele.

In this process, creating environments that support broader social and economic development objectives for the city and its users has been a priority, and rethinking the strategies, approaches and processes of, and outcomes from, the redesign and development of the built form has been fundamental. Firstly, we have emphasized that urban design is one of the (important) tools to realize our development objectives, but it is not the starting point. The urban design brief is developed on the basis of an analysis and understanding of the role of the city centre, economically as well as socially, that addresses the needs of new users, the major points of contestation and conflict, new economic opportunities and how urban management – or getting the basics right – can be enhanced. The design response is thus critical in supporting other strategies: how to design out the over-reliance on enforcement agencies to ensure that competing needs can be accommodated; how to create environments where urban amenity is enhanced while retaining the functionality required by a myriad new users of the city; how to develop the public realm so that it enhances social integration and new economic opportunities, whether they are in residential, commercial or retail development; and how to create environments which will support the formalization of the important (and for too long ignored) informal sector.

Secondly, our strategy has been to deal with and understand the inner city as a series of interrelated but differentiated districts or precincts. Urban design interventions have been used to uncover, articulate and strengthen the organic character of each area. As Neil Fraser, the Director of the Johannesburg Inner City Business Coalition likes to remind us (quoting former Philadelphia Mayor Ed Rendell), 'cities are about people, place *and pizzazz*'. Working at a precinct level, we use urban design processes to re-enforce the sense of place and identity and introduce the 'pizzazz' that will enhance an area's competitive advantage. Often this is easily done: for example, in the Fashion District, the urban design intervention was to 'stitch' the area together by introducing mosaics into the pavements designed to reflect the stitching most commonly used in garment manufacturing.

Finally, urban design strategies, while working at the local precinct level, must ensure that the whole functions in an integrated and efficient manner. Thus in developing the urban design framework for a particular precinct, we will seek to formulate development principles that allow connections to be made and the area to be integrated into the region. In doing so, we emphasis the grid, the development of a network of public open spaces and the development of landmark elements. Most important, the urban design framework must 'enable a multi-plicity of ways of being in the city' by creating opportunities for a mixture of land uses.

Two critical outcomes have been realized through this approach. Urban design frameworks now act as critical 'instruments for change' by providing platforms from which the private sector – formal, informal, big and small businesses – and citizens can creatively contribute and grow. And they provide a basis from which we are able to re-engineer constantly the renewal strategy as new challenges arise in the framing of the Johannesburg city centre as a truly global, African city.

REFERENCES

Bremner, L. (2002). Writing the global city from Johannesburg. Paper presented at the Wits Institute for Social and Economic Research, University of the Witwatersrand, 20 June.

Business Day (1997). UK property firm says SA's CBDs are finished. 5 November.

Central Johannesburg Partnership (1993). *Central Improvement District Business Plan.*

City of Johannesburg (2002). *Joburg 2030: the High Road to Growth.*

City Press (1997). City in ruins. 2 March.

Darroll, L. (2003). Empowering public space: the Braamfontein regeneration project. *Urban Green File,* **8**, 4, 26–31.

GAPP Architects and Urban Designers and Profs Rogerson, C. and Tomlinson, R. (1999). *Inner City Spatial and Economic Framework.* Greater Johannesburg Metropolitan Council.

GAPP Architects and Urban Designers and Urban Solutions Architects and Urban Designers, (2000). *City Centre Development Framework.* City of Johannesburg.

Inner City Housing Upgrade Trust (1996). *Inner City Housing Survey.*

Johannesburg Development Agency (2002). *Braamfontein Regeneration Project Business Plan.*

Lepani, B., Freed, G., Murphy, P. and McGillivray, A. (1995). *The Economic Role of Cities – Australia in the Global Economy,* Urban Futures Research Program, Australian Government Publishing Service. Available online at http://www.wapc.wa.gov.au/pub-lications/futureperth/papers/lepani.pdf.

Phosa, P. (2002). *Jozi* rocked last week. *The Star,* 5 September.

Rogerson, C. and Tomlinson, R. (1999). *Inner City Economic Development Strategy.* Greater Johannesburg Metropolitan Council.

Sack, A. and MMA Architects (2002). *Braamfontein Urban Design Framework.* City of Johannesburg.

#10

MEGACITIES AND THE URBAN CENTURY: SHRINKING WORLD, GROWING CITIES

Janice E. Perlman

Janice E. Perlman

one

GLOBAL PARADOX

It may seem paradoxical that in our ever-shrinking 'global village' where information and capital transactions zip across cyberspace in nanoseconds, we are witnessing enormous urban growth and concentration at just the time when predictions were that spacial proximity would become irrelevant and cities would implode or wither away – to be replaced by endless suburban sprawl or electronically connected estates on top of scenic mountains or ocean bluffs.

The dual explanation for this apparent contradiction is that the vast majority of the world's urban growth is occurring in the developing world, where hi-tech is not yet hegemonic; while in advanced industrial countries, top leaders in business, government, academia and the arts have found that electronic messages are no substitute for face to face meetings. The very essence of the globalized economy with its dispersed information and capital flows needs a focal point for 'command and control' as well as a locus for personal interaction where body language and facial expression can help interpret meaning across cultures. Likewise, the kind of networking and trust-building that is the glue for civil society and the prerequisite for critical decision-making is still impossible to replicate electronically. In short, the energy, synergy and creativity formed by serendipitous encounters in the heterogeneous mix of the metropolis have no parallel in virtual reality.

two

THE URBAN CENTURY AND THE FOUR TRANSFORMATIONS

The twenty-first century has been called the urban century. Over the next few years, for the first time since the rise of cities ten thousand years ago, over half the world's population will be living in urban settlements. This transformation from a predominantly rural world to a predominantly urban one forces us to rethink our most basic paradigms – not only of the urban condition – but also of the human condition. It will profoundly alter how we conduct every aspect of our lives from the household level to the international level, and determine the legacy we leave for future generations.

At the beginning of the nineteenth century, only 5 per cent of the world's population lived in urban areas; at the beginning of the twentieth century, it was close to 15 per cent; and today, as we enter the twenty-first century, close to 50 per cent of us are urbanites. Looking towards the future, the trend is even more dramatic. According to the UN, 'virtually all of the population growth expected during 2000–2030 will be concentrated in the urban areas of the world'.

From 2000 to 2030, the urban population is expected to increase by 2 billion persons; the same number that will be added to the whole population of the world. The current urban population of 2.9 billion people will swell to 4.9 billion by 2030 whereas the total world population, which is now 6.1 billion, will grow to 8.1 billion over the same time period.

The second major transformation is a total reversal in the locus of our major cities, from the highly industrialized countries of the north to the developing countries of the south, in Asia, Africa and Latin America. In 1950, only three of the world's largest cities were in poor countries; whereas, currently, only three of world's largest cities are in rich countries.

This reversal has contributed to the third transformation – from the city of the elite to the city of the masses, or from the formal sector city to the informal sector city. While cities of the first world are remaining relatively stable in population, cities in the developing countries are growing at about 2.3 per cent per year, and their low-income areas, (shanty-towns, slums and squatter settlements) are growing at twice that rate. This means that poverty is becoming urbanized, as cityward migration transforms rural peasants into urban squatters. Housing, jobs, and services, not provided through state or market mechanisms, are created by the ingenuity of the urban poor through the 'informal economy,' which accounts for .25 to .66 of the real economy of these cities.

Perhaps the most dramatic transformation of all is from cities, as we have known them, to enormous megacities with populations over 10 million each. By 2015 it is projected that there will be twenty-three of these huge metropolitan areas, six of them with over 20 million inhabitants each. The increase in the proportion of the population living in large urban agglomerations is mostly the result of a rise in the number of such agglomerations rather than of the rapid growth of the population of most of them. Thus, the number of cities with 5 million inhabitants or more will pass from forty-one in 2000 to fifty-nine in 2015. Among those cities, the number of megacities (those with 10 million inhabitants or more) will increase from nineteen in 2000 to twenty-three in 2015. Most of the large cities are located in developing countries. In 2000, only ten of the forty-one large cities were in the highly developed countries and only one more will be added by 2015 (*UN Population Division,* 1999, p. 7).

Table 10.1 shows the growth of twenty of these megacities from 1950 to 1975 to 2000 and the projected sizes and growth rates for the year 2015. They are listed in rank order by size based on 2000 figures. There is a great deal of discrepancy among the figures by various agencies on this, but most sources agree on which cities will reach 'mega' scale by 2015. The table omits Lagos, which should be included just below Los Angeles in the ranking. Despite the vast differences in history, culture, political systems and levels of

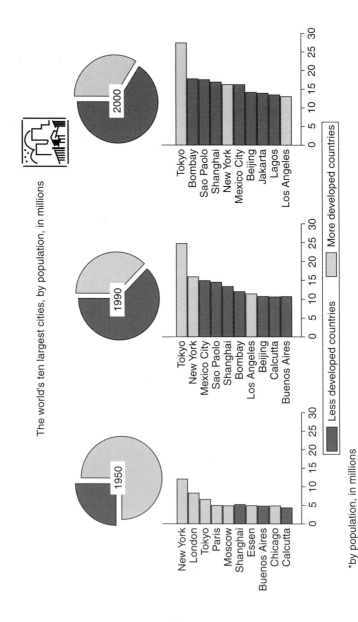

The world's ten largest cities, by population, in millions

*by population, in millions

figure 10.1
CHART SHOWING LOCATION OF THE WORLDS MEGACITIES

TABLE 10.1

POPULATION OF MEGACITIES IN 1950, 1975, 2000 AND 2015 IN MILLIONS

POPULATION BY YEAR	1950	1975	2000	2015
1 Tokyo	6.9	19.8	26.4	27.2
2 Mexico City	2.9	10.7	18	20.4
3 Sao Paolo	2.5	10.3	18	21.2
4 New York	12.4	15.6	16.7	17.9
5 Mumbai	3	7.3	16.1	22.6
6 Los Angeles	4	8.9	13.2	14.5
7 Calcutta	4.4	7.9	13.1	16.7
8 Shanghai	5.3	11.4	12.9	13.6
9 Dhaka	0.4	2.2	12.5	22.8
10 Delhi	1.4	4.4	12.4	20.9
11 Buenos Aires	5	9.1	12	13.2
12 Jakarta	1.5	4.8	11	17.3
13 Osaka	4.1	9.8	11	11
14 Beijing	3.9	8.5	10.8	11.7
15 Rio de Janeiro	3	8	10.7	11.5
16 Karachi	1	4	10	16.2
17 Metro Manila	1.5	5	10	12.6
18 Seoul	1	6.8	9.9	9.9
19 Paris	5.4	8.9	9.6	9.9
20 Cairo	2.4	6	9.6	11.5

This table was constructed using data from the UNPD World Urbanization Prospects 2001 Revisions, p. 9. The year 2000 is used instead of 2001. It lists the 20 largest megacities in order of size in the Year 2000, according to the UN Population Division's 2001 Revision of World Urbanization Prospects. It is surprising that it does not include Lagos. According to UN HABITAT's, *Cities in a Globalizing World*, (2003, p. 300), the population of Lagos for the year 2000 is 13.4 million, which would put it just ahead of Los Angeles in the top ten. Lagos, like Dhaka, is notable for its rapid growth rate at a time when growth rates in many megacities are diminishing.

development, I have argued that in many ways the megacities have more in common with each other than they do with many of the smaller towns and villages in their own countries or regions.

To begin with, the sheer size of the megacities presents a situation for which we have no collective experience. No precedent exists for feeding, sheltering or transporting so many people in so dense an area, nor for removing their waste products or providing clean drinking water. Urban managerial and physical systems based on human settlements of 50 000–100 000 may be able to stretch to 250 000 or even accommodate populations of one million, but they begin to show signs of stress at four million, and are blatantly unworkable at ten million. One area in which this has become obvious is pollution. The megacities are experiencing critical environmental degradation, pushing to the limit the

TABLE 10.2

MEGACITY RANKINGS BY YEAR 2000: POPULATION IN MILLIONS

		1950 POP.	1950–1975 RATE	1975 POP.	1975–2000 RATE	2000 POP.	2000–2015 RATE	2015 POP.
1	Tokyo	6.9	4.2	19.8	1.2	26.4	0.2	27.2
2	Mexico City	2.9	5.2	10.7	2.1	18	0.8	20.4
3	Sao Paolo	2.5	4	10.3	1.2	18	0.5	21.2
4	New York	12.4	1.7	15.6	0.4	16.7	0.5	17.9
5	Mumbai	3	3.6	7.3	3.1	16.1	2.3	22.6
6	Los Angeles	4	3.2	8.9	1.6	13.2	0.6	14.5
7	Calcutta	4.4	2.3	7.9	2	13.1	1.7	16.7
8	Shanghai	5.3	3.1	11.4	0.8	12.9	0.6	13.6
9	Dhaka	0.4	6.6	2.2	7	12.5	4	22.8
10	Delhi	1.4	4.6	4.4	4.1	12.4	3.5	20.9
11	Buenos Aires	5	2.6	9.1	1.1	12	0.6	13.2
12	Jakarta	1.5	4.8	4.8	3.3	11	2.9	17.3
13	Osaka	4.1	3.5	9.8	0.5	11		11
14	Beijing	3.9	3.1	8.5	0.1	10.8	0.5	11.7
15	Rio de Janeiro	3	4	8	1.7	10.7	0.5	11.5
16	Karachi	1	5.4	4	3.7	10	3.2	16.2
17	Metro Manila	1.5	4.7	5	2.8	10	1.6	12.6
18	Seoul	1	7.6	6.8	2	9.9		9.9
19	Paris	5.4	2	8.9	0.32	9.6	0.2	9.9
20	Cairo	2.4	3.7	6	1.8	9.6	1.3	11.5

Ranking are made for 2000 figures. Osaka and Seoul have missing information for 2000–2015 growth rates.

carrying capacity of their bio regions to sustain human life. While all urbanites are affected, the urban poor are the most vulnerable, particularly since squatter settlements are often located in the most undesirable areas of the cities such as floodplains, marshes, steep hillsides or sites bordering toxic industries.

The physical infrastructure used in cities worldwide was mostly developed in a short twelve-year period at the end of the nineteenth century, when there was little awareness of the finite nature of natural resources or the scale that cities might reach. It was in that time period that the basic designs for indoor plumbing, sewage and garbage disposal, internal combustion engines, the elevators and steel-frame construction that permits the construction of skyscrapers and so on, were all developed. Since then the major advances in science and technology have been applied primarily to military needs, space exploration and consumer products. For example, despite the worldwide scarcity of water and the plethora of water-conserving alternatives, the standard toilet copied by countries everywhere wastes 15 l of water every time it is flushed. The question now is how to find creative ways to apply the advances in both 'high' technology and 'appropriate' technology to the building and maintenance of the urban infrastructure, housing and collective consumption in service of the preservation of the environment.

In addition to making up the backlog in urban services and meeting current demands for services, megacities are faced with the prospect of ever-increasing demands in both quantity and quality – all within limited city budgets. They are all dealing with the extreme polarization between rich and poor in their cities and the problems this engenders at every level, including crime and violence. Government responses are stymied, not only by budget deficits, but also by the fragmentation of programme- and policy-initiatives, short-term thinking and the lack of strategic planning together with deep distrust among the public, private and voluntary sectors which need to collaborate if the basic problems are to be solved. Finally there is a pervasive and powerful resistance to any change in the *status quo* by those with vested interests and incentive systems which discourage risktaking.

One might imagine that given this set of challenges, international aid agencies and foundations would be readjusting their loan and grant priorities from the rural-based world of the mid-twentieth century to the new urban realities. However, despite these overwhelming urban trends, less than 10 per cent of all international assistance funding goes to cities while over 90 per cent still targets rural areas, in the misguided belief that investment in rural development will somehow stem the tide of cityward migration. Almost every country has responded to the urban explosion by trying to limit the growth of the largest cities. These efforts range from restricting in-migration and dispersing the would-be migrants (to growth poles, new capitals, smaller cities or resettlement areas), to stimulating rural development in hopes of equalizing the level of living in the countryside and the city. These efforts have been met with limited success in the developing world. Some, such as rural development, have even proved to be counterproductive, actually hastening out-migration from the countryside. Even in command and control economies which were willing to use their police force to limit the size of the city, such as China and the former USSR, or South Africa during apartheid, people managed to sneak into the cities illegally and become part of the uncounted floating populations.

three
CHALLENGES, OPPORTUNITIES AND RESPONSES

The congestion, pollution, crime and contamination in these cities are well covered by the mass media. What go unnoticed are the energy, vitality, and opportunity exerting the magnetic force that attracts the best talent and most highly motivated people. What distinguishes megacities from capital cities (capitals of nation states) and world global cities (capitals of capital and information flows) is precisely that megacities are capitals of people. People have voted with their feet, seeking a better life, more choice and wider opportunities for themselves and their children.

The very diversity and proximity of all these people confronting together the crises and contradictions of urban life are what make these megacities such fertile soil for innovation.

Their importance economically, politically, intellectually and culturally makes them the trendsetters. As Manuel Castells writes:

> *Megacities are the directional centers, the centers for technological innovation, the senders of symbolic messages, images and information, the producers of producer services, the collective factories of the new manufacturing, as well as depositories of the remnants of traditional manufacturing. Megacities are the nerve centers of our interconnected global system... they are the amplified portrait of ourselves.* (Castells, 1994)

There is no doubt that megacities are magnets for the best and the brightest and have been the centres of innovation and advances in civilization and culture throughout history. The list of historical megacities in Table 10.3 gives us inspiration and such writers as Jane Jacobs and Peter Hall have argued this point with elaborate evidence and eloquence.

TABLE 10.3

LARGEST CITIES IN THE WORLD THROUGHOUT HISTORY (POPULATIONS IN THOUSANDS)

CITIES IN HISTORY

	100 CE	1000 CE	1500 CE
1	Rome, Italy (450)	Cordova, Spain (450)	Beijing (672)
2	Luoyan, China (420)	Kaifeng, China (400)	Vijayanagar, India (500)
3	Seleucia, Iraq (250)	Constantinople, Turkey (300)	Cairo, Egypt (400)
4	Alexandria, Egypt (250)	Angkor, Cambodia (200)	Hangzhou, China (250)
5	Antioch, Turkey (150)	Kyoto, Japan (175)	Tabriz, Iran (250)
6	Anuradhapura, Sri Lanka (130)	Cairo, Eqypt (135)	Constantinople, Turkey (200)
7	Peshawar, Pakistan (120)	Baghdad, Iraq (125)	Gaur, India (200)
8	Carthage, Tunisia (100)	Nishapur, Iran (125)	Paris, France (185)
9	Suzhou, China (n/a)	Al-Hasa, Saudi Arabia (110)	Guangzhou, China (150
10	Smyrna, Turkey (90)	Patan, India (100)	Nanjing, China (147)

	1800 CE	1900 CE	1950 CE
1	Beijing, China (1100)	London, UK (6480)	New York, USA (12463)
2	London, UK (861)	New York, USA (4242)	London, UK (8860)
3	Guanzhou, China (800)	Paris, France (3330)	Tokyo, Japan (7000)
4	Tokyo, Japan (685)	Berlin, Germany (2707)	Paris, France (5900)
5	Constantinople (570)	Chicago, USA (1717)	Shanghai, China (5406)
6	Paris, France (547)	Vienna, Austria (1698)	Moscow, Russia (5100)
7	Naples, Italy (430)	Tokyo, Japan (1497)	Buenos Aires, Argentina (5000)
8	Hangzhou, China (387)	St. Petersburg, Russia (1439)	Chicago, USA (4906)
9	Osaka, Japan (383)	Manchester, UK (1435)	Ruhr, Germany (4900)
10	Kyoto, Japan (377)	Philadelphia, USA (1418)	Kolkata, India (4800)

Information compiled from Chandler, T. (1987).

Yet the problems continue to multiply. The timing is urgent. Experience has shown that there is often a twenty to twenty-five year time lag between new ideas and their incorporation into public policy. We cannot afford to await another generation for the next set of urban policy innovations to address the needs of city dwellers. Even if current birth control programmes and efforts to encourage the growth of small and intermediate-size cities are much more successful than those in the past, there will still be hundreds of millions of people living in the world's largest cities and more migrating there. Thus, it is time to turn our attention to how to make megacities work better for the people who are already there and those who are inevitably coming.

So, where can we find solutions to these problems? Conventional solutions are not the answer. Experience over the past twenty years shows that, since intelligence is not distributed along class or geographic lines, the most promising innovative approaches often come from local experience – from the people and community groups. Street level bureaucrats and small-scale enterprises are closer to coping with problems on a daily basis than policymakers at national level.

There is enough energy and creativity in the cities today to address their myriad challenges of liveability, but there are too few mechanisms to channel these forces into policy or to multiply the effects of approaches that work. Thus, there is a compelling need to discover alternative approaches that make better use of the abundant and underutilized human resources in the city and create multiplier effects with the scarce natural and financial resources at hand. To address this need, I founded the Megacities Project, a transnational non-profit network among these cities. Our immediate objective was to shorten the twenty to twenty-five year time-lag between new ideas and their implementation. Our approach was to identify, document and transfer successful urban innovations among cities, creating a 'can-do' climate for urban problem-solving. We did this by building a network of networks within and among the megacities.

Over the past seventeen years, the Megacities Project teams in twenty cities have identified hundreds of workable solutions and transferred some forty of them across geographically, culturally and politically disparate communities worldwide. After ten years of uphill struggle to promote an asset-based view of megacities and reverse the incentive system for risktaking, our approach was incorporated into official United Nations policy at the UN City Summit in Istanbul in 1996 under the rubric of urban best practices.

We are now focusing on two areas: preparing the next generation of urban leaders for the complex challenges they will face in the future and generating new knowledge through longitudinal research on the intergenerational transmission of poverty. We began developing crosscultural, cross-disciplinary and cross-sectoral urban experiences for undergraduates through the International Honors programme which is now in its seventh year. The outmoded nineteenth century model that was applied well into the twentieth century pits economic development against environmental sustainability and has led to the ever-greater disparities between rich and poor and the ever-greater squandering of natural

BOX 10.1

URBAN SUSTAINABILITY PRINCIPLES

LESSONS LEARNED FROM THE MEGACITIES PROJECT:

1. Urban environmental, social, and economic sustainability are essential for global sustainability. Concentrating the human population in cities is essential to prevent sprawl and to preserve both agricultural and wilderness areas. Circular rather than linear urban infrastructure systems are needed to turn 'waste' into 'resources', that is, outputs from one process can become inputs into other processes, rather than being discarded.

2. Alleviating urban poverty is essential to ensuring urban environmental regeneration. As the urban poor settle in the only areas available to them, they often encroach on watersheds, riverbanks, hillsides, marshes, forests, or open spaces critical for healthy cities. Without running water, sewers, cooking fuel and so on, their daily subsistence needs conflict with environmental sustainability, so that solving their housing and infrastructure needs is a priority for the eco-system.

3. Strong civil society and grassroots initiatives are essential for lasting solutions to both poverty and environmental degradation. Small is beautiful, but it is still small! While most innovations arise from local initiatives, they need help to maximize their impact.

4. To reach scale, it is essential to transform 'micro' solutions into 'macro' impacts, by either sharing what works among local leaders from place to place (via social networks, social movements and so on) or transforming public policy from the bottom up.

5. There can be no urban transformation without changing the old incentive systems and rules of the game and forming collaborative partnerships among mutually distrustful sectors linking the local to the global through a transnational non-governmental organization network, representing the interests of the third sector, independent from government and corporate interests.

6. There can be no sustainable city of the twenty-first century without social justice and political participation, as well as economic vitality and ecological regeneration.

© 2004 Janice E. Perlman

---

resources. The lessons learned from our case study series on innovations at the poverty/environment intersection are listed in the box entitled 'Lessons learned'.

There are few courses in universities that permit students to think about this matter and little research is being undertaken that is breaking new ground in this area. We are currently doing a thirty-five-year follow up on the life histories of hundreds of people interviewed by the author in 1969 in Rio's *favelas* (Perlman, 2004). This is the first in a series of such studies around the megacities. We have created a transnational independent network which can give voice to citizens in cities as the multinational corporations pursue profits and the international agencies broker geopolitical power. As Stephen Toulmin writes in Cosmopolis, we are part of

> *...the emergency of organizations and forces which are not simply international (organized by collaboration between nation states) or multinational (operating by agreement across state boundaries), but transnational (acting independently of and sometimes in opposition to the governments of existing nation states).*

It is our hope that we can link rigorous research and the creation of new knowledge with the construction of new social outcomes and practices that can transform the way our cities and our societies function. We are building a collective vision of what cities can be, but not by creating one single utopian vision of one model city that all others are expected to imitate. On the contrary, in our process each city leads from its own particular strengths and its own particular historical and sociocultural base, to find its way forward to a more socially just, ecologically sustainable and vibrantly participatory city of the twenty-first century.

REFERENCES

Chandler, T. (1987). *Four Thousand Years of Urban Growth: An Historical Census.* St. David's University Press.

Perlman, J. (1990). 'A dual strategy for deliberate change in cities' *CITIES, International Journal of Urban Policy Planning*, **7**, 1, February 1990.

Perlman, J. (2004). The metamorphosis of marginality: favelas in Rio de Janeiro 1969–2002. In *Urban Informality*, (A. Roy and Nezar Al Sayyad, eds.), Lexington Books.

Toulmin, S. (1990). *Cosmopolis: The Hidden Agenda of Modernity.* New York: Free Press.

UN Population Division (1999). *World Urbanization Prospects*: The 1999 Revision: Key Findings.

Part Four

THE ECO EDGE

FROM EASTGATE TO CH2: BUILDING ON THE ENERGY WATERSHED

Mick Pearce

one

KINGELEZ'S UTOPIA

Figure 11.1 depicts an installation made of discarded tins by Congolese artist Bodys Isek Kingelez, of Kinshasa. His vision of utopia is a high-energy megacity, unlike the reality of Kinshasa which, according to locals, is a city composed of 'swept up villages'. The expectations people have of the need for *development* is still so very much alive – in Africa, Europe, Asia, the Americas and Europe – despite the energy crisis we face, that I thought, like Kingelez, I would try to make up my own city for the new age, not in tins but in words. But, first I need to remind myself what it means when we say that fossil fuels are fast running out.

To do this I need to describe how two recent buildings that I have been associated with respond to this energy imperative. These are Eastgate in Harare, Zimbabwe, and CH2, which is presently being built in Melbourne. CH2 will be followed by the retrofitting of the existing council house, called CH1. I also need to explore the science of ecology that lies behind the design of these buildings. After a short biographical note which relates to the development of my thinking on architecture and building, I outline the development and predicted fall of the fossil-fuel age. I then consider aspects of the relationship between the city and nature, which leads me to explain and summarize some contemporary scientific theories and laws. I ask in what ways cities are like forests and termitaries, and people are like elks and beavers. I conclude with a brief consideration of the importance of collaborative architecture and of developing fruitful metaphors for the urban architecture we need today.

figure 11.1
THE UTOPIAN AFRICAN CITY
THROUGH THE EYES OF BODYS
ISEK KINGELEZ, ARTIST,
(KINSHASA)

two
THE OIL IS RUNNING OUT

The city today is almost without exception a successful enterprise, in that 80 per cent of the planet's assets are owned by 20 per cent of the people, all of whom live in cities (Carley and Spapens, 1998). Their exuberant lifestyles impose impossible demands on the hinterland through the city's eco-footprint. This lifestyle also imposes unattainable expectations on the remaining 80 per cent of the planet's people. It is a way of life that, we are told, is attained with 'democracy and development' and it carries with it, consciously or unconsciously, a lie – a lie because, in order for all 6 billion people on the planet to achieve this lifestyle, the natural resources of four more planets would be required. Here is the dilemma. There is no question of the rich 20 per cent giving up anything, because it would mean a lowering of their living standards, and there is no question of the 80 per cent giving up the expectations so graphically presented to them every hour from cyberspace.

Yet, the city still functions quite well: possibly it is a bit dysfunctional at the edges but, as the city is where every wants to live, the majority supports the enterprise. The problem is that the lifeblood or energy that is necessary to power cities is not only disastrously harming the environment and social order but it is also running out. The world isn't about to run out of oil, but demand is now at 80 million barrels a day and as this grows, the production of easily extracted oil will peak and then start to decline. The view of when demand will come to a peak varies from 2006 to 2016 for the world outside the Middle East and, for the world including the Middle East, from 2023 to 2040 respectively. There is a growing body of opinion that even these estimates are on the optimistic side (*National Geographic*, 2004).

Such predictions are notoriously bad and depend on the bias of the prophet, but as city designers we have to assume that there will be a shift of the energy base during the life of the developments we are now building. The price of fossil fuels will rise and rise, never to return to previous levels as soon as the peak is reached – and that could be very soon. And where will energy to fuel the city come from then? No city government is preparing for this shift of the energy base. We will remain blissfully unaware of our complete reliance on fossil fuel until the pump runs dry.

three
LIVING BY SUNLIGHT IN 2050

In the year 2050 humans have begun to relearn to live by sunlight just as the rest of the natural world had been doing for the previous 3 billion years. What Fredrick Soddy had predicted in the 1920s has come true. He saw the fossil fuel age as a flamboyant period of history, during which the natural capital stock of entrapped solar energy was used up. He saw the fossil fuel age as a passing phase, after which humanity would return to live by the sun. This vision has now become true, because the limiting factor to growth was the rate of flow of energy supplied each day by the sun. For as long as there had been enough resources to exploit growth, mainstream economics made sense. When oil reserves peaked in 2010, followed by the peak of natural gas reserves in 2020, the price of fossil fuels rose. World poverty and conflict could no longer be solved by development that was driven by economic growth. There were not enough natural resources left to support a high energy-consumptive lifestyle to fulfil the expectations of the 11 billion people on the planet. The price of fossil fuel made burning it in your car like burning diamonds. Three international laws now govern the use of natural resources and, therefore, world economies. These are the laws of scale, allocation and distribution which formed the basis of our taxation system.

The law of scale limits the rate of use of resources. Every 60 minutes the sun delivers enough solar energy to run all human activity on the planet for one year. The problem in the past has been how to harvest it, how store it and, finally, how to use it at a rate, within the capacity of the natural ecosystem, to absorb the resultant entropy. The law of entropy (based on the second law of thermodynamics) has allowed us to explore the great complexities of natural systems. Every living organism has been given a metabolic rating which measured the organism's capacity to transform energy both within its living boundaries (let us call this its skin) and, where applicable, within the inanimate extensions to the organism. Thus, in the case of human individuals, the car, the house and all associated appendages are included as an added extension to their overall metabolic rate, based on their total consumption of energy and matter. In extreme cases this ends up rating a well-equipped human as being equivalent to a 30-tonne mammal.

The law of allocation encourages the efficient use of resources. Ever since this law was passed there has been a burst of innovation unequalled since the early days of the Industrial Revolution. The technologies invented during the machine age continue to be found useful only if they can consume far less energy than they did then. Fossil fuel, which used to be burned, is now used for extremely high-performance materials. Industrial designers and architects use biological forms and the processes of nature for their inspiration. The design teams of the built environment are composed of new disciplines that lean more towards the physiologist than the mechanical engineer, because the human is now seen as the participant in a living system; the building itself. The building is seen now more as an extension of human physiology than the ancient idea that it is a machine for living in.

The law of distribution controls access to resources. This issue used to be the greatest challenge to world peace. International conferences were now focused on two main global crises, security and the survival of the planet. The idea of living by the sun had already begun to drive the energy industries of the post-industrial nations. Most people in the formerly underdeveloped world had not lost the knowledge of living by sunlight and have therefore in many respects led the way out of the survival crisis by their example. They also benefited from this shift in the energy base because there is more sunshine in the south than in the north. However, while this has helped to redress the balance of power between north and south, the expectations of the wealth produced in the city lingered and urban terrorism and its counterpart, the war on terror, persists. On the corner of every street in every city in the old developed world, a camera recorded every movement, and surrounding the earth beyond the ionosphere, satellites monitored all life below.

In the south the cities grew in a totally different way but ended up with the same form. The self-building traditions, which had begun several decades earlier, had improved. They had started originally using recycled materials and as confidence and population pressure had grown, more permanent materials had replaced plastic and corrugated iron. The form of these cities was based on the old traditional rural home but clustered into densely packed villages that were surrounded by intensive agriculture. These villages were networked together with roads for buses and bicycles, and cars for the rich ran on homegrown bio-diesel fuel or biogas. The cities had become vast networks of linked sub-centres. In the developed world the cities had also changed. The central business districts had diminished in size and importance as they became far less viable without access to fossil fuel. The sub-centres had grown in stature and confidence. The roads and all communication and power networks linked the former suburban centres, which have also now grown in importance. The private car is now powered with a fuel cell that uses liquid hydrogen (produced from renewable power) as fuel. The car has become a mini mobile power plant when parked by the house, either feeding the power web or the house directly. The model city is a polycentric, fully networked city, which resembles the ecosystem.

WEB CITY

By 2050 the information age will have moved completely into a new biological age. The fully motorized garden city image will be history. At this time cities will have begun to look more different from each other; reflecting more and more their historical, social, economic and natural context.

In Europe the walled city-state of the pre-industrial era was limited in size to a day's journey by horse. This all changed with the coal-driven machine age. The railways fed the dark, satanic mills and an expanding hinterland of industrialized farming. This all changed with the information age. The dark, satanic mills were replaced with the central business district, where the towers grew higher and higher as the endless network of motorways linked the garden suburbs and vast open fields of the ever-expanding urban footprints. This all changed when the oil and gas began to run out and the eco-footprints overlapped.

So that now by 2050 a new biological age is well under way. Web City is becoming a vast network of small centres linked by webs. An energy web is increasingly fed by the sun, and the information web links the energy web to the cybersphere that now surrounds the planet. The business of growing food without oil has become possible with the introduction of highly intensive solar-powered agriculture, producing food close to the home. The habitat and farming are now becoming culturally linked. The house reflects now much more than ever the business of harvesting solar energy to produce shelter, food, mobility and communication. People meet these days in the centres for social exchange less often than they used to, but with greater celebration.

When I began writing this description I began to think that those who are the losers today could be the winners in the new solar age, or at least, their ability to cope with living by sunshine would place them in a much stronger position. I also began to think of how my life and work can be brought more in line with nature – and the laws of energy and thermodynamics are only one aspect of the marvellous structural integrity and adaptability of natural ecosystems.

four
BORN WHITE IN A BLACK WORLD

Being born white in Zimbabwe was to be privileged from the start. My parents were liberal and I lived a charmed life. I was called *Ishe*, which means 'prince'. I was sent farther and father away from home as I grew up, going to schools and universities in South Africa, Canada and the UK so that I returned to Africa even more privileged than when I had left. In the meanwhile, things at home had changed. Black power was alive. My father died suddenly, leaving my mother vulnerable to white power. She had become increasingly pro-black (against white power). I decided to stay around in neighbouring Zambia, rather than pursue a career as an architect in London, where I had been trained at the Architectural Association. Zambia had achieved black power and had embarked on the fast track to development and I was soon very busy there.

I also became politically involved with the struggle for freedom in Zimbabwe. It was the late 1960s and the world was clearly divided. Because, like my mother, I was pro-black I became increasingly involved in fast-tracking black power at home in Zimbabwe. By the early 1970s my mother had caught the brunt of our efforts and was arrested by white power. She managed eventually to leave and go to the UK. Soon after this my family and I also moved there. We lived in a working-class mining and shipbuilding town called Sunderland in the northeast of England (called by an academic friend the 'armpit of England'). Here, for the next nine years, I helped to start and manage a radical building co-operative called Sunderlandia.

In 1982 we returned to a Zimbabwe freed from colonialism, and became totally absorbed with the development which is tied to western aid and promoted by the west. In 1985 my first seeds of doubt about the idea of development were sown when I heard Bill Mollinson give a lecture in Harare on permaculture. This way of thinking provided a logical connection between ecology and architecture. Fast tracking development in Zimbabwe had caused a foreign currency crisis, due mainly to the demand for imports of plant consuming high levels of energy. I designed and built three major commercial office blocks in Harare during the following six years, each one making a small step in the direction of low energy consumption. By 1991 my low-energy consuming buildings became very attractive to one institutional client I was working for and led to the design

figure 11.2
THE DESIGN OF EASTGATE, HARARE WAS BASED ON A STUDY OF THE ECOLOGY OF THE TERMITARY

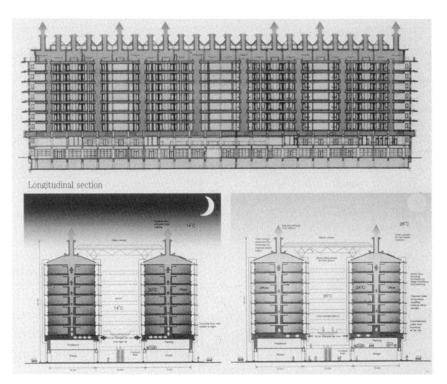

figure 11.3
MAKING USE OF THE DIURNAL SHIFT OF THE CLIMATE IN HARARE TO COOL EASTGATE DURING THE DAY

and construction of the Eastgate building in Harare, a very large mixed-development building in the central business district. Eastgate was also ecologically based. Like a termitary it was 'air-conditioned' naturally. Cool night air was harvested and stored within the concrete structure of the building for dispersal the following day to cool the building passively. A number of smaller buildings followed in which we experimented with using rock stores and wind turbines.

In 1999 Mugabe's fast-tracking ran out of steam. Mugabe was clever enough to hang onto power by replaying the black/white power game. I moved in an opposite direction, to support the opposition to ZANU-PF, his party. As a result I was placed in prison for a short spell. This has led me to leave Africa until things cooled down and I gratefully accepted a job by the City of Melbourne to help build CH2, the new low-energy council offices, in August 2002.

five
CH2 (COUNCIL HOUSE TWO)

CH2 (Council House two) like Eastgate is a mixed use development comprising 1100 m^2 of offices and shops. Also, like Eastgate, it is ecologically based. Like a tree, the building exploits the natural environment of Melbourne and will be seen to do so. The ten-storey Swanston Street façade will appear like a timber box formed of slatted recycled timber shutters which will open and close as the sun moves. At night and each morning when the shutters are open, the building's interior will be revealed.

Five 14 m high transparent tubes will be suspended from the Little Collins Street façade. These will enclose water showers, in which water will rain down onto glass deflectors where the evaporatively cooled water and air will be collected. The water will then transport this harvested cold energy in pipes down to the basement for storing in the phase change materials (PCM) batteries (described below) in the basement. The air is directed into the shops for cooling. These shower towers will express the natural process of evaporative cooling that is achieved by adding water to the dry desert winds that characterize Melbourne's climate.

Six wind-driven turbines top the towers rising up the northern façade. Here, solar energy in the form of wind will be harvested to aid the power-driven fans that are needed to remove exhaust air from the offices.

Unseen from the outside, in the basement two new technologies will operate. One will mine the sewer in Little Collins Street. In this case 100 000 l of water will be harvested each day by filtration processes to produce A grade water, while returning the solids to the sewer. The other will store cold energy in PCMs stored in stainless steel balls suspended in water in four large pressure tanks. PCMs freeze at plus 15°C. In this case the latent energy is exploited to store cold energy when the outside air is cold, usually at night. This is released to cold radiators suspended under the office ceilings to help maintain comfort conditions during working hours.

Both Eastgate and CH2 are forerunners of the city buildings of the near future solar age. The aesthetic expression locates the architecture within its natural, social and economic environment. They do not look like anything that has been copied and pasted from cyberspace. More like a tree, they grow their look from their site in a rain forest.

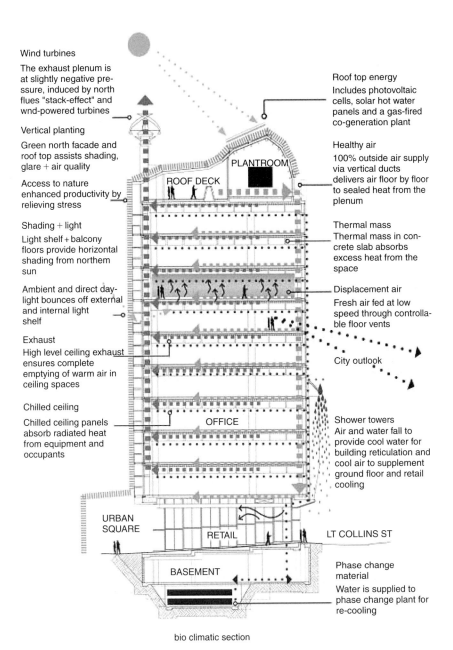

Wind turbines

The exhaust plenum is at slightly negative pressure, induced by north flues "stack-effect" and wnd-powered turbines

Vertical planting

Green north facade and roof top assists shading, glare + air quality

Access to nature enhanced productivity by relieving stress

Shading + light

Light shelf + balcony floors provide horizontal shading from northem sun

Ambient and direct daylight bounces off external and internal light shelf

Exhaust

High level ceiling exhaust ensures complete emptying of warm air in ceiling spaces

Chilled ceiling

Chilled ceiling panels absorb radiated heat from equipment and occupants

Roof top energy

Includes photovoltaic cells, solar hot water panels and a gas-fired co-generation plant

Healthy air

100% outside air supply via vertical ducts delivers air floor by floor to sealed heat from the plenum

Thermal mass

Thermal mass in concrete slab absorbs excess heat from the space

Displacement air

Fresh air fed at low speed through controllable floor vents

City outlook

Shower towers

Air and water fall to provide cool water for building reticulation and cool air to supplement ground floor and retail cooling

PLANTROOM

ROOF DECK

OFFICE

URBAN SQUARE

RETAIL

LT COLLINS ST

BASEMENT

Phase change material

Water is supplied to phase change plant for re-cooling

bio climatic section

figure 11.4
SECTION THROUGH CH2 SHOWING ALL THE SYSTEMS

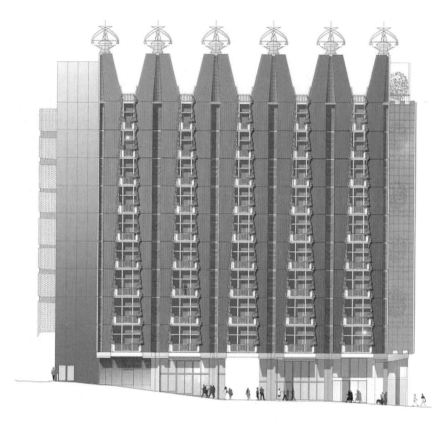

figure 11.5
CH2 NORTH ELEVATION

six

THE CITY AND NATURE

To call architecture 'ecological' implies a new relationship between the city and nature. The idea that the city can be seen in the same way as an ecosystem is at least as new as the word 'ecosystem'. In western culture the city has generally been perceived as something that is separate from nature. As James Hillman (1995) reminds us, ancient Athens kept wild, unruly nature outside the city walls. Nature, to the ancient Greeks, was dangerous and disorderly. It was also the home of Dionysus, the god of wine, intoxication and creative ecstasy, while Apollo, the sun god of male perfection, high art and science, the god of the order created out of disorder, presided inside the walls. The pristine city stood clearly apart from nature.

The idea of creating order from disorder is embodied in the laws of thermodynamics, which state that everything (in nature) tends towards disorder. Energy/matter flows from

figure 11.6
CH2 AS IT WILL BE SEEN
FROM SWANSTON ST
MELBOURNE

order to disorder, while life modifies energy/matter to create order from disorder. Today in the developed world wild, untamed nature is usually regarded with nostalgia, a place where beauty and peace reside. The suburban garden and the park represent nature that is preserved, often fenced in and protected. The car is used (too often) to convey urban dwellers back to these peaceful preserves of wild nature. It is also the urban dweller that campaigns most for nature conservation reservations. On the other hand, it is the urban dweller that demands that the city be kept clean. City pigeons are poisoned, in case they spread disease. This, according to Hillman, is an Apollonian ideal, part of the inherited memory of the west. Thus we still have a city that is pristine but we also have wild nature that is contained either in the park, the suburban garden or the nature conservation area. Therefore, although there are so few scraps of land left on the planet that have not been affected in some way by human intervention and while we want to create order on a vast scale, at the same time we want to fence in and to preserve disorder.

To see the city as an ecosystem is to let Dionysus in. It is not only to see the city as a living system within nature but it is also to apply the sciences of ecology, physiology and psychology into the design of city buildings. I think that there is a need for us to understand the complexities of city in the same way in which scientists are continuously reconstructing nature For instance, the large-scale demolition in a city, such as what happens in China today, may be no different from clear felling in a natural rain forest. And is the regrowth forest any different from the original mature rain forest?

In the case of the forest the difference is palpable, at least to a botanist. The process of regrowth involves the succession of plant species, starting with pioneers and ending, over a period of time, with a diverse, mature forest: a process that can take 200 years. If you take a walk through the large district of a newly built city, it feels very different from a district that is more than a hundred years old. In the latter case there is a presence of historical diversity of style and also the richness of disorder. Biologists call a forest a climax forest when it achieves what they call 'steady state'. When does a city become a climax city? A steady state is a physical state in which checks and balances hold the energy flows through the forest as steady as a spinning top, or as a spinning vortex. This state can be seen as an almost fixed structure, although it is within itself in a state or dynamic movement. This can also be described as state of negative feedback, the way the spinning balls of a governor control a steam engine or a thermostat controls an iron from overheating.

If I am right about the similarity between the city and an ecosystem, are there laws which apply to both? Are there ways of seeing the city which may help us to relate the processes of city building with processes in nature? Is ecological architecture nothing more than the demand for more by-laws that have been invented to protect some human construct of wild nature behind a fence, or is it a new way to see our cities as part of the process of evolution on the planet? In arguing for the latter, I have been influenced by Gaia theory and the laws of thermodynamics.

The Gaia theory is a model of nature, which according to James Lovelock, its originator, sees the evolution of all forms of life as so closely coupled with the evolution of the physical and chemical environment that they constitute a single evolutionary self-regulating process like the steady state described above. As Lovelock (2000, p. 25) says:

... the climate, the composition of the rocks, the air and the oceans, are not just given by geology; they are also the consequences of the presence of life. Through the ceaseless activity of living organisms, conditions on the planet have been kept favourable for life for the past 3.8 billion years. Any species that adversely affects the environment, making it less favourable for its progeny, will ultimately be cast out, just as will those members of a species who will fail to pass the fitness test.

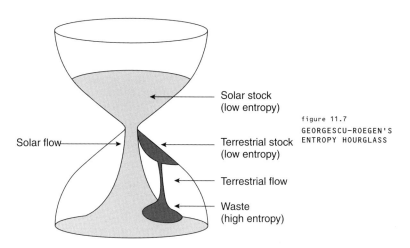

Solar stock
(low entropy)

Solar flow

Terrestrial stock
(low entropy)

Terrestrial flow

Waste
(high entropy)

figure 11.7
GEORGESCU–ROEGEN'S
ENTROPY HOURGLASS

The basis of James Lovelock's contribution to the theory of Gaia is the laws of thermo-dynamics. The laws of thermodynamics are concerned with the relationships between energy, heat and work. The first states that the total amount of energy in the universe is constant. The second states that some fraction of energy is lost to random molecular motion, or entropy (or disorder), whenever energy transformation occurs. Another way of putting the first law is to say that energy/matter cannot be created or destroyed within the closed system of the universe: it can only be transformed from one state to another. Another way to put the second law is to say that in any transformation of energy some amount of energy becomes non-returnable or is no longer able to perform work. Entropy is the measure of this energy.

Figure 11.7 is called Georgescu-Roegen's entropy hourglass. It illustrate these two laws and relates them to the use by humans of time-trapped terrestrial energy/matter, which is usually fossil fuel and is here called terrestrial stock.

The first law: that total energy/matter in the universe is constant; is represented by the sand trapped in the hourglass. The sand in the top chamber, which has the potential to fall and thereby to do work, represents the second law: that entropy increases in a closed system. This top sand is referred to as low entropy matter/energy. The sand in the bottom chamber is high entropy (or used up) matter/energy. But, note that this hourglass cannot be overturned, confirming that the process is irreversible. The narrowing waist of the hourglass causes the rate of flow to be constant, in the same way as for instance, the daily delivery of solar energy to the earth.

Terrestrial, or virtually nonrenewable, low entropy energy (fossil fuels) is stuck to the side of the lower chamber. This time-trapped bio-solar energy called fossil fuel was formed during the last 150 to 250 million years. It was originally derived from the remains of living systems that captured solar energy through the process of photosynthesis and were buried in the form of low entropy energy/matter. This process is continuing all the time. Humans have found ways to transform this energy at whatever rate they chose, unlike solar energy. At present we are burning it up at the rate of one million years' worth in one year – far faster than it is being formed – so that we have to consider it a non-renewable resource. The disastrous consequences of this high-entropy consumption are deal with later.

seven
THE LAWS OF THE ECOSYSTEM

How do these basic laws of physics apply to life? Organisms, which are highly ordered systems, are like eddies of low entropy (being high in embodied energy). They exist only by disordering the universe in which they exist. They are involved in transferring energy from disorder to order. By structurally modifying their environment, organisms manipulate and adaptively modify the ways energy and matter flow through the environment. In so doing, they modify the ways energy and matter flow through them. There are three principle groups of energy transformers in all ecosystems: the photosynthesizers (the plants), the consumers (animals) and the fermenters. The photosynthesizers use the energy of sunlight directly to fix carbon dioxide and water to make sugar and release oxygen to the air:

Sunlight + carbon dioxide + water = organic matter + oxygen

The consumers capture energy by consuming the organic matter and oxygen produced by the photosynthesizers.

Organic matter + oxygen = carbon dioxide + water + body energy

Some of the organic matter escapes oxidation from the above process and sinks into sediments. Here the fermenters digest it and convert it into carbon dioxide and methane.

(Waste) organic matter = carbon dioxide + methane (CH4) + body energy

This is an extreme over-simplification of the process of Gaia. However it gives a picture of a system in balance, in equilibrium, in a steady state.

eight
THE LAW OF METABOLIC RATE

The consumption of energy is the common basis against which to measure both the city and nature. Any living system exists within a dynamic state of flow of energy called the metabolic rate. The metabolism supplies the power that organisms need for growth, maintenance and reproduction. Specifically, the metabolism is the measure of the transformation of energy undertaken by every life form. For example, a large mammal, such as an elk weighing 200 kg, is 10 000 times heavier than a mouse weighing 20 g. However, an elk eats only 1000 times (not 10 000 times) more calories than a mouse. This, for the mathematically minded, means that the metabolic rate per gram of body tissue is proportional to body mass raised to the power of $-\frac{1}{4}$. The metabolic rates of mouse to elk is 0.75 and 7500 respectively. Other biological rates show the same pattern. Lifespans increase with biomass to the power of $-\frac{1}{4}$, meaning that each gram of mouse tissue uses energy at 10 times the rate of a gram of elk tissue and the mouse's heart beats 10 times faster. But the elk lives ten times longer than the mouse and its gestation period is also 10 times longer. The same $-\frac{1}{4}$ power rate applies to plants. The area of leaves relates to the rate of photosynthesis scale as the $-\frac{3}{4}$ power of mass and the lifespan as the $-\frac{1}{4}$ power. Looking beyond the individual, we can see that this provides a method of measuring the geometric structure of an ecosystem and the physical constraints on resource distribution networks within and without organisms. It is a way of measuring the rates of solar-derived energy transformation.

The ultimate niche constructers are humans. As Brown and West of the University of New Mexico say,

> *a woman in one of the most developed nations uses as much energy and has the same reproductive rate as a hypothetical primate weighing 30 tonnes.* (Brown and West, 2004, p. 41)

This finding has important implications for about city construction. Try defining ways in which one might model the sustainable city on the ecosystem and you may find yourself faced with this 'Queen Kong'. Imagine her in a rainforest without the SUV 4 × 4, or any of her first world trappings, and you have a modern Eve with a metabolic rate of 100 watts. Imagine her in a poor country today and her rate would rise to 300 watts; 200 watts more than the modern Eve because the rural peasant has developed agriculture methods and tools in ways which greatly extend her ability to harvest natural resources. Finally, imagine her back as 'Queen Kong' and her rate jumps up to 11 000 watts. Every watt above the original 100 (that is, 10 900 watts) is related to her external physiology which is powered mostly by fossil fuels. Metabolic rate is therefore a method of measuring the consumption of energy/matter by different organisms in a living system. How organisms grow is proportional to their body mass and hence also to their metabolic rate. Thus, the law of metabolic rate is a useful tool to understand the complexity of the ecosystem and the efficiency of the transfer of solar energy from one form to another. We know that it will take decades of further work before we understand just how far the pace of life controls the ecology of life on Earth. However, there are other aspects of this study which link it to the design of the human built environment.

We cannot assume, however, that the forest itself in this scenario is a constant. It, too, has been affected by the increasing CO_2 and temperature levels of the atmosphere, an increase due to human activity, including the introduction of fossil fuel-derived energy leading to global warming.

nine

THE EXTENDED ORGANISM

The story about Queen Kong is a clue to a link between the metabolic law of the ecosystem and Scott Turner's idea of the extended organism.

> *Are animal-built structures properly things external to the animals that built them, or are they properly parts of the animals themselves?... By structurally modifying the environment... organisms manipulate and adaptively modify the ways energy and matter flow through the environment. In so doing, they modify the ways energy and matter flow through them. Thus, an animal's physiological function is comprised really of two physiologies; the 'internal physiology'... [within the skin] and an external physiology, which results from adaptive modification of the environment.* (Turner, 2000, p. 3, pp. 6–7)

In this book Turner argues that animals extend their physiology by modifying their immediate environment in order to increase their capacity.

NICHE CONSTRUCTION

I have recently come across the idea of 'niche construction' developed by Odling-Smee, Laland and Feldman (2003). These authors claim that niche construction, which has been ignored by biologists, is part of the process of evolution. Niche construction is about the extension of an organism (or super-organism). The nest, the burrow or the beaver's dam and, in the human case, the hunter's bow, the farmer's hoe and the megacity are all niches. They are modifications to the surrounding natural environment, which have become embodied into the animal's total physiology. It is as though there are two physiologies, one focused inside the animal's skin and one occupying the space between the animal's skin and the boundaries of the nest. The standard view of evolution is that organisms adapt to a given environment. The new view is that organisms modify their environment for survival. This is a two-way process, in which the environment itself adapts to the niche constructor. By altering the environment to which it is adapting, the organism has a short-term involvement in the evolutionary process. This theory has important implications for the role of human city building.

The termitary is important for me, not only because it helped to inspire the design of the Eastgate development in Harare, but also because it is a clear example from the non-human animal world of niche construction and, as Scott Turner (2000) has shown, is an extension of the organism as architecture. The termite tower can be seen as performing the same function as a lung, and the fungi garden as performing the same function as a stomach. Air is harvested through a mucus-glued earth membrane, probably by using the diffusion of gases by osmosis. A mixing process driven by buoyancy forces and powered by the heat of the metabolism balances the oxygen/carbon dioxide levels. The air and the termites themselves circulate the energy. Water is mined, not only for their own consumption, but also for cooling the air and for their elaborate building process. The queen termite performs the function of the mind and the communication system is the nervous system. In my search for an architecture that goes beyond the age of the machine, this is a perfect model. The building, no longer a machine for living in, has become *the building as a living system*. Unfortunately, not all niche constructions are functionally integrated: some contribute to disorder on a runaway scale. That is, the rate at which they create disorder is faster than the total system can cope with. As we know, this applies to the process of human niche constructions in our cities, our farms and our methods of travel, which are all related to our use of time-unlocked fossil fuel energy.

eleven
ECONOMICS OF LIMITS

Today we are faced with a world population of 6 billion people to be fed, kept warm, transported and entertained in cities whose increase in size is made possible by fossil fuel. The concept of sustainable development must reflect a shift in our perception of how human economic activities relate to the natural world. The ecosystem is finite within its boundaries and it is therefore materially closed. The demands of human activities on the ecosystem for the regeneration of raw material inputs and the absorption of waste outputs must be kept at ecologically sustainable levels. This means we must start to replace the accepted economic norm of growth with that of a qualitative improvement of the ecosystem resulting from creatively managing the way we construct our niches. As Daly (1996) argued in *Beyond Growth*, there are three problems to be recognized in connection with the distribution and use of natural resources – allocation (the efficient use of energy/matter), the just distribution of energy/matter amongst all humanity, and scale (the rate of use in time of energy/matter relative to the capacity of the ecosystem to absorb the resultant waste).

twelve
CONCLUSION

Rome was the last solar city. Before the fossil-fuel age the size of a city was limited to the capacity of the surrounding ecosystem, the transportation systems and the population's capacity to exploit natural resources as well as its power to exploit surrounding communities. The population of ancient Rome peaked at 1 million and declined to 30 000 as the empire collapsed and the ecosystems of North Africa (where most of the wheat came from) also declined.

Or was it Tenochtitlan? The Aztec city of Tenochtitlan, on islands in a now-drained lake upon which Mexico City lies today, may also have reached a population of a million, but this may have been due to the development of an extensive market-gardening system fertilized by human excrement, rather than an empire. Figure 11.8 is a picture of the city seen by Cortés before he razed it to the ground. It was a truly solar city, modelled on an

figure 11.8
THE SOLAR-POWERED AZTEC
CITY OF TENOCHTITLAN

ecosystem. The market garden system, called *chinampas*, produced seven crops a year. The secret (which has only recently been discovered,) of this highly intensive urban agriculture was the existence of a heat-loving microbe similar to those found in hot springs. This bacterium binds nitrogen from human waste, neutralizes dangerous pathogens in sewage and speeds up the decomposition of organic waste. The gardens were made on narrow promontories built out into the lake and they were watered and fertilized by skin buckets, which scooped up water and sludge from the canals between promontories. This sludge was rich in human waste. If this is a true description of what happened, this is a model of sustainability.

REFERENCES

Brown, J. and West, G. (2004). One rate to rule them all. *New Scientist*, **182**, 2445, 38–41.

Carley, M. and Spapens, P. (1998). *Sharing the World: Sustainable Living and Global Equity in the 21st Century*. Earthscan.

Daly, H. E. (1996). *Beyond Growth*. Beacon Press.

Hillman, J. (1995). *Beauty Without Nature*. Audio Cassette: Sound Horizons Audio-Video.

Lovelock, J. (2000). *Gaia, the Practical Science of Planetary Medicine*. Gaia Books.

National Geographic (2004), **90**.

Odling-Smee, F. John, Laland, K. N. and Feldman, M. W. (2003). *Niche Construction*. Princeton University Press.

Scott Turner, J. (2000). *The Extended Organism: The Physiology of Animal-Built Structures*. Harvard University Press.

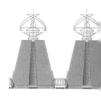

CURITIBA AND SUSTAINABILITY

Cassio Taniguchi

Brazil underwent massive urbanization – or perhaps what is best described as de-ruralization – at such a scale and rate from the 1960s onwards that the country's municipal administrators have had to face immense new challenges in a very short period of time. New regulatory frameworks coupled with political will and public support were needed for sustainability to become a reality in the lives of a city's inhabitants. As Mayor of Curitiba, Brazil, for two terms in a row (1997–2000 and 2001–2004), and as a member of the city's planning team for three other terms, I am proud that urban planners and environmentalists around the globe now point to Curitiba as a world model for sustainable cities.

Curitiba faces the same problems as other cities around the world, including overcrowding, traffic, poverty, pollution and limited public finance. However, in Curitiba we have developed creative and cost-effective strategies for solving these universal problems of cities. These strategies include a city-wide bus system that is 90 per cent cheaper to operate than a subway. In 1989, we were the first Brazilian city to implement garbage recycling and linked local employment schemes and a 'green exchange programme' as a way of addressing poverty. We have also worked hard and successfully to attract new industries while expanding green spaces, at the same time as preserving historical areas to transform neighbourhoods and encourage tourism. Through such strategies, Curitiba provides practical evidence of the long-known fact that integrated transport, the preservation of the environment, and encouraging job creation and urban and social integration are the keys to good urban design.

Curitiba is the capital of Paraná, one of Brazil's the southernmost states, and is located 400 km south of Sao Paulo. Settled in 1693 by Portuguese explorers, Curitiba quickly became a supply centre for gold prospectors who were followed by the cattle ranchers who chose the name 'Curitiba'. These early settlers were our first conservationists as they passed regulations that limited the number of trees that could be cut and required houses to have tiled, not wooden, roofs. By the end of the nineteenth century, when a tide of immigrants from as far away as Japan, Syria and Lebanon arrived, Curitiba's population reached 50 000. This rapid growth continued and reached 430 000 in 1960. Today, we have over 2 million citizens. With a growing population, Curitiba has long faced increasing demands for water and sanitation services, housing and transportation. A town plan in 1940 sought to address these needs but did not anticipate future waves of newcomers. As a result, Curitibanos began to fear that the loss of green spaces, sprawl and increasing poverty would follow the increasing numbers of people.

In 1964, a call from Mayor Ivo Arzua for ideas to address these problems was answered by a team of idealistic architects and planners from the Federal University of Paraná, led by

Jamie Lerner. Their proposals, which eventually came to be known as the Curitiba master plan, sought to control urban sprawl, reduce downtown traffic, preserve Curitiba's historic district and provide accessible and affordable public transport. An Institute of Urban Planning and Research was established under Lerner. With environmental, economic and social balance as the key priority, the Institute and the city leaders focused on two key questions: how will the city grow and how will its inhabitants live? Some forty years later, the Curitiba master plan has become Brazil's showpiece of urban planning and an international blueprint for sustainable urban design.

one
IMPLEMENTING CURITIBA'S MASTER PLAN

The basic goal of the master plan was to meet the daily needs of citizens, such as mobility, shopping, work, recreation and entertainment, through the provision of urban services. The street network was allied to zoning rules, with public transport being established as the main instrument of the city's growth. The implementation of this master plan from 1971 on brought about and backed up three basic transformations in the city: physical, economic and sociocultural. It would be simplistic to describe any single one of these transformations as contributing to environmental, economic and social sustainability, respectively, because of the interdependence of these policies. Thus, elements of all three aspects of sustainability can be seen in each of the three types of urban transformation.

PHYSICAL TRANSFORMATION

Addressing transportation problems was the early key to reform. Our planners designed an economical, accessible and efficient public transport based upon existing roadways. The master plan provided for the future expansion of Curitiba to be directed along public transport-based axes radiating from the city's centre. An extensive bus system was developed along five radial corridors and several circumferential corridors to serve suburb-to-suburb travel. The radial corridors include exclusive bus lanes to serve high-capacity buses, providing a rapid transit means of travel. That is, each axis has three lanes – one flowing in each direction, and a central lane used solely by buses (see Figures 12.1 and 12.2). The full system of express buses, rapid transit buses, the inter-suburban bus service, inter-hospital buses and local feeder services quickly and cheaply moves over 70 per cent of the population every day. Flat fares, independent of journey distance, and the distribution of bus tickets by the city in place of social welfare help to ensure that the poorest can afford the system while reliability and comfort ensure that the more well-to-do use it also. At peak times, buses arrive every 60 seconds with the throughput of commuters increased by having enclosed bus stops where customers pay their fare. When the bus arrives, they simply climb aboard, thereby increasing loading speed by 300 per cent. As a result, Curitiba's road design and its efficient public transport system effectively created a demand for bus use in the same way that the infrastructure of traditional cities creates a demand for car travel. Thus, while Curitiba's population has increased by more than 500 per cent to 2 million since 1964, car travel has decreased by 30 per cent.

figure 12.1
THE THREE LANES IN TRANSPORT PLANNING IN CURITIBA

As economic growth is tied closely to the public transportation system, the city's mixed-use zoning has encouraged local self-sufficiency through locating development near transit stations so that bus stops have become nodes of civic activity where shopping, recreation, police stations and businesses concentrate (Figure 12.3). Congestion is contained within the civic areas, allowing room to develop parks areas and extensive pedestrian and bicycle networks. Curitiba's integrated land use and transit development policies have resulted in one of Brazil's lowest air pollution levels, with little traffic congestion and an optimal environment for its residents.

figure 12.2
MIXED-USE ZONING ALONG TRANSPORT CORRIDORS

The expansion of parks and preservation of open space also contribute to the maintenance of environmental quality. Curitiba has a higher rate of green space than any other Brazilian city. Our twenty-eight parks and undeveloped open space cover about 20 million m² and provide more open space per capita than any city in the world. Many of Curitiba's parks were reclaimed and converted from industrial or commercial use. For example, a quarry was rehabilitated for the garden campus of the Free University for the Environment, Curitiba's environmental learning centre. On a larger scale, Saõ Lourenço Park was once a *favela* along a river that flooded every year. In the early 1970s, the city built low-income housing for these people away from the floodplain and converted the land into a park. The Curitiba Zoo also doubles as a free public park while community gardens contribute to nutrition, health (via medicinal plants) and community spirit. Since the 1970s, volunteer citizens have planted over 1.5 million trees along streets and avenues (Figure 12.3). Privately held trees and habitat are also protected under a 'two-for-one' rule which requires a landowner or developer to replace any tree they want to remove with two semi-mature ones.

ECONOMIC TRANSFORMATIONS

The second goal of Curitiba's master plan was the economic transformation of the city, with the establishment of an industrial city in 1973. The Institute of Urban Planning and Research developed an aggressive incentive scheme to provide mechanisms that would preserve the environment and consolidate the city's quality of life as well as transform the landscape. In the beginning, it was necessary to provide financial incentives to foreign industries to set up here, since local firms had refused to take the risk. This attracted some old industries that were still polluting the city centre. These have now sold their old premises and rebuilt their operations, modernizing them to be non-polluting, in new areas especially designed for them. These areas are not solely reserved for industry, but contain a mixture of accommodation, enclosures, services and recreational areas, and are equipped with a good system of internal and external transport. Time for travelling to work is reduced, either because people live nearby or because they have a special line connecting them to the main working areas.

Zoning rules encourage economic activity close to the structural sectors along the axes. The ground floor and the first floor of buildings have been set aside for commerce and services. Along the avenues used by the mass-transport vehicles in residential zones, clusters of commercial and medium-sized service activities are allowed. Termed 'collectors', these lanes concentrate the traffic of residents, commerce and public transport.

Waste recycling has also been a major part of the economic transformation of Curitiba. With sites for landfill scarce and incinerators too polluting and expensive, Lerner, who had become Mayor and was to serve for three terms, commenced a television campaign with the slogan: 'Waste which is not waste'. In a short period of time, most people were

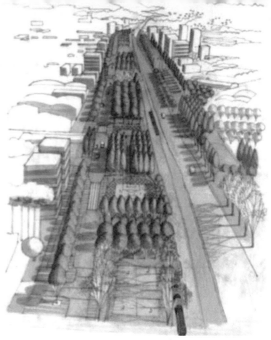

AERIAL VIEW OF ROUTE BR116
LOOKING SOUTH

AERIAL PERSPECTIVE OF THE
PROPOSED AVENUE FOR THE SOUTH
SECTOR OF CURITIBA

figure 12.3
TRANSPORT CORRIDORS AS OPEN SPACE

sorting their waste for collection, over 40 per cent of which is recycled. The waste is carried to a factory outside the town and is sorted for sale. The people working the sorting conveyors or bringing in waste are often very poor, alcoholics or homeless who are paid for their rubbish. They sort the rubbish from the town and are paid with vegetables, fruit, bus tickets and so on ('green exchange').

SOCIOCULTURAL TRANSFORMATIONS

The memory of three decades of efforts to build a sustainable city is today ingrained in the community identity of the people of Curitiba and continues across the generations. We have the feeling of sharing in an innovative experiment that has made us world famous and encourages a culture of continued concern. The cultural transformation of Curitiba began when a section of November XV Street in the heart of the city was made into an exclusively pedestrian mall for citizens to discuss ideas for planning the city. This has helped develop a culture of collaboration between citizens and the city council and improve the credibility of local politicians and planners and has also helped people to identify with, and feel part of, their city. Curitiba now has several 'citizenship streets' of government branch offices located throughout the city. All are located at major bus terminals throughout the city and help reduce 'City Hall' to the local scale. Each citizenship street houses a regional branch of the various city offices as well as libraries, markets, sports facilities and community meeting rooms. Nearby residents and commuters can access municipal departments, banking offices, state and federal agencies and special courts all in one location.

This focus on city identity and localized civic services means that, in Curitiba, culture is seen as related to the quality of life of the inhabitants and a system of neighbourhood relations, on the scale of a village rather than a large city. This attachment to a locality provides Curitiba with an identity and multiplies the effects of one action on another.

Two other aspects of the socio-cultural transformation of Curitiba into a sustainable city are our focus on heritage and social well-being.

The aim of the Curitiba master plan was to accommodate growth without the loss of its history. Thus, it provided for more parks, museums and cultural centres around old Curitiba landmarks and a historic zone that preserved old buildings by permitting the transfer of building rights from historic plots to vacant ones. This allowed owners of heritage buildings who lacked the resources to restore them to exchange them with vacant city land. As a result, several stretches of historic blocks with 100-year-old buildings are now restored and preserved. This has aided both a growing sense of pride in Curitiba's heritage as well as the development of a tourism industry focused on these historic precincts.

Despite our many improvements, Curitiba remains a city with many poor people in a rapidly growing developing country. Our population continues to swell daily with new migrants from the countryside and it is difficult to keep up the supply of accommodation. Nearly 5000 new homes are being built each year but there is still a shortage of 80 000 homes and 7.5 per cent of inhabitants are in temporary accommodation. Any process of urban development that prioritizes human needs requires a detailed understanding of the territory and the conditions of life of the inhabitants who live in each and every district of the city. The collection of detailed information has opened the way to making investments in infrastructure and defining the managerial priorities to find a harmonious balance between development and the residents' quality of life.

In 1997, when I began my first term of office as Mayor, this information told us that there was an imbalance of incomes between our newcomer citizens and those who were resident in the already consolidated areas of the city. This had led to an economic and social division along a north–south axis, in which the southern residents were the most needy portion of the population. Investments in urban infrastructure, allied to the new public transport corridor and environmental preservation, began the process of integrating the two needy regions of the city, with a foundation in providing jobs for the newcomers. Using a vacant area along the corridor of electric towers that supply the city, which at the time represented a place in which slums could thrive, we created a special 'Job Line' sector, named after the high-tension electricity lines in the area (Figure 12.4). With the agreement of the energy company that transferred the use of the area to the Curitiba municipality, a large, 34 km avenue crossing through eighteen districts between the city's north-eastern and south-western areas was developed (Figure 12.5 and Figure 12.6).

Once City Hall stimulated the creation of productive activities along its route, the Line has provided thousands of job and income opportunities, becoming the most comprehensive job and income-generation programme in Curitiba since the development of Industrial City in the 1970s. The city has invested in professional training for new

figure 12.4
THE SITE OF THE JOB LINE

figure 12.5
VIEW OF A SECTION OF THE JOB LINE
TODAY

Terminal Atuba

Estação Fagundes Varela
Estação Vila Olímpica
Estação Tarumã
Estação Central

Estação Jd. Botânico
Estação UFPR
Estação Av das Torres
Estação PUC
Estação Mal Floriano
Estação Vila Fanny
Estação Santa Bernadete
Estação Xaxim
Estação São Pedro

Terminal Pinheirinho

figure 12.6
THE SCALE OF THE JOB LINE LINKING THE CITY'S NORTH-EASTERN AND
SOUTH-WESTERN AREAS

entrepreneurs and established ten business incubators to help them put their skills into practice and begin to manufacture at industrial scales. These entrepreneurs have the right to use the incubator for up to two years rent-free, in order to accumulate capital and experience, gain customers, enhance production and consequently generate jobs in a region that had previously divided the city in economic terms. The successes of the programme include the regional development of the districts crossed by the Job Line and hundreds of new enterprises, which have created 15 000 new jobs.

However, for this and other job creation schemes to work, they need to be grounded in an effective social inclusion policy that promotes the well-being and emancipation of the needy citizen. This was the focus of my second term as Mayor. It is my personal belief that no-one can suppose we live in an equal world that offers opportunities for everyone. With this in mind, we implemented a policy of encouraging individual self-esteem through participation in collective causes. Curitiba's social assistance network was established to address these needs through the participation of communities in inclusion projects. Emergency assistance focusing on the rescue of those who are at risk was our first step. The second step was to assist citizens at risk towards emancipation by providing opportunities and assistance towards self-sufficiency, by identifying their skills and vocations and providing them with incentives to undertake professional training as well as support. The training offered was aimed at inserting the citizens in the job market and strengthening their self-confidence. Training was provided by means of partnerships with the private sector, which offered instructors for skills improvement, thus generating an income to the citizens involved in the process.

Curitiba has a strong tradition of providing extensive social services and aid to its poor, who make up about 7.5 per cent of the population. Thus, besides aiding needy citizens, our inclusion programme has addressed basic needs such as health and education. Curitiba has reduced to zero, for instance, the transmission of HIV from pregnant mothers to their babies. This was achieved through the Curitiban mother programme which, assisted by the public health system, provides assistance to 97 per cent of pregnant women. This programme also guarantees mothers the right to free prenatal examinations and has been a key factor in a drop in infant mortality rates from 16.6 deaths per 1000 live births in 1998 to 12.4 in 2003 and a decline in maternal mortality rates from twenty-one deaths per 1000 mothers in 1999 to seven in 2003.

Children are often major victims of Brazil's urban explosion. Grinding poverty also forces many to be abandoned without protection or shelter. Many of the homeless have formed dangerous gangs for survival. To assist them, a *pia* ('street-kids') programme collects those who are in a critical situation and provides shelter, work, food and education. We will soon have 11 000 young people and children in forty such establishments. Many businesses have also been encouraged to adopt small groups of ten to fifteen children, feeding them and giving them work and, where possible, teaching them a trade.

Many of Curitiba's more established social programmes are mobile services. Old converted buses, some even equipped with classrooms, travel to the neediest areas of the city, bringing basic services such as food, education and health care. The five buses in the *Linha da Economica* programme serve as mobile markets at more than ninety sites in the city's poorest areas. Stripped of seats and modified to have narrow shopping aisles, the *Economica* buses provide government-subsidized goods at a third of regular market prices. This programme also supports Curitiba's farmers by selling their blemished or surplus produce, which might otherwise have been destroyed. The *cárie zero* ('zero cavity') bus travels to schools and parks to teach oral hygiene and, in recent years, many industries have booked visits from *cárie zero* in order to teach dental care to their employees. The *linha do lazer* ('leisure bus') is staffed with instructors who offer games and activities to children in schools that do not have a physical education curriculum. These buses also visit centres for senior citizens and children's hospitals. The *olhos da agua* ('eyes of water') travels to low-income areas along river banks to teach environment studies and develop skills for water-quality monitoring through which citizens, youth and scientists can work together to help safeguard Curitiba's water quality.

Preparing a city to be service based, which is a feature of all successful metropolitan capitals, demands investments in technology. Bearing this in mind, I stimulated the use of technology as a planning tool in Curitiba and promoted the use of information technologies by strengthening the Curitiba Information Technology Institute (ICI). As a non-profit-making organization, ICI invests its financial surplus in science and technology to develop new products and services in the fields of IT and telematics. Part of this surplus is also invested in social responsibility programmes, such as our current project to provide the first free public network for Internet access in Brazil. Our efforts towards information democratization may be seen on several fronts: e-inclusion, e-education, e-government, e-health and e-transport.

The further to promote social inclusion, Curitiba has also been a pioneer in Internet access centres for people with special needs. Two facilities were inaugurated in 2004. The first is located at the 24-Hour Street, and the second at Fazendinha's Citizenship Street. Both provide computers suitable for people with physical, motor, mental and visual disabilities. In November 2003, we launched the InterClick programme, consisting of a bus that takes free Internet access to the districts and to tourist attractions in the city. The result of a partnership between ICI and the private sector, the InterClick bus parks at strategic points in the eight regional administrations and central plazas on weekdays and, on weekends, may be found in parks and events taking place around the city. The InterClick bus has eight computers equipped with a printer, scanner and a CD-ROM recorder. In order to use the service, it is necessary to be registered with 'Keying the Future' web-mail. As the first Brazilian public network to offer free Internet access, Keying the Future provides fast and integrated assistance to citizens, granting them closer contact with information technologies and the Internet, facilitating their access to information and education and thus enhancing their opportunities and improving the quality of life of all Curitibanos. In addition, a Web application was developed in order to allow the user to book public space by means of a Smart Card, which is also used in schools, health-care centres and for public transport. In addition, this card is used for borrowing municipal library books. Technology in Curitiba is thus not an isolated solution to an isolated problem, but the key to a highly integrated set of projects.

In 2004, at the end of my term as Mayor, Curitiba was at the top of the Brazilian quality of life index and showed the second highest human development index in the country. In the last decade, the proportion of people in poverty in Curitiba dropped from 13.48 per cent to 7.52 per cent of the population. Average income increased from R$6686 in 1995 to R$10 275 in 2000. The number of children attending school in Curitiba has reached 100 per cent and illiteracy has fallen to 3.38 per cent in 2004. Gender equality in education has also been promoted, with girls and women taking up 47.8 per cent of the openings in basic education and 52.7 per cent in high school.

two
CONCLUSION

As more and more people worldwide see the city as their hope for a better life, the challenges for urban planners and leaders also grow. We are proud that many are looking to our city for real solutions. Many cities have adopted our planning approaches to individual urban problems and adapted them to local needs, but very few have been able to emulate Curitiba's comprehensive, integrated approach to urban planning and design. This chapter has concentrated on the strategies that we have used to bring about physical, economic and sociocultural transformations of Curitiba as a sustainable city. What it has not done is explain why Curitiba was an 'early adopter' of sustainability and how it has been able to maintain its vision for such a long period of time. Curitiba did not become a success overnight. Our innovations came through research and experimentation and evolved over a generation with strong direction from an independent and progressive planning office. We have also had the advantage of mayors who were experienced architects and planners. These factors help to explain 'why Curitiba', while the partnership model developed between City Hall and citizens, together with the obvious benefits that citizens have experienced in expanded income and employment opportunities, a greener environment and reduced commuting times, go a long way to explain why we have been able to maintain our momentum. In a nutshell, Curitiba is well on track in anticipating solutions, firmly grounded in the already anticipated need to alter the city's zoning rules and land-use laws.

In a little more than 7000 years of known and recorded history, we have observed the development of the gregarious spirit of humanity. Alone, we are nothing. First we gathered into groups, then in families, tribes, villages and finally cities. In our time, cities have probably become the most important basic social unit. People build their lives in cities. Cities are the depository of our dreams and our children's dreams. Obviously, as a result of being so remote from our natural origins, cities cannot be considered the best places in the world, as, Voltaire's optimistic Dr Pangloss believed. Nonetheless, the story of Curitiba shows how the city can be transformed so that people can feel at home and develop their civic pride, artistic spirit and livelihood naturally within its boundaries.

Note: The original text of this chapter by Cassio Taniguchi was revised for this book by John Fien.

#13

SUSTAINABILITY AND METROPOLITAN PLANNING
MELBOURNE 2030 – A CASE STUDY IN GOVERNANCE AND THE MECHANICS OF CHANGE

Stuart Niven and Cathy Wilkinson

one

SETTING THE SCENE FOR SUSTAINABLE DEVELOPMENT

In 2000 the newly elected State Labor Government in Victoria, Australia, decided to redirect and restructure the way growth planning and economic development was conducted. It aimed to create a long-term urban development strategy that would be both sustainable – reversing unsustainable trends that were becoming evident – and achievable. Practical implementation – the process for achieving the targets set – was of paramount importance, as recent international research shows that around 90 per cent of such strategies are never implemented (Harvard Business School, 2003). Within the state as a whole, the focus of the project was metropolitan Melbourne, Victoria's sprawling capital city and its hinterland of small regional cities and towns. Melbourne's current population is more than 3.5 million, with the overall population in the state touching the 5 million mark. By 2030 Melbourne itself is projected to grow by a further 1 million people. This means some 620 000 additional households must be provided for within the metropolitan area, with growing demand for one- or two-person households.

Putting this in a global context, according to the United Nations population division more than half the world's population will live in urban areas by 2007 and all population growth up to 2030 will occur in cities. Growing urbanization makes the planning function increasingly important. Cities are engines of growth, but with this growth come complex problems that threaten liveability and prosperity and are in conflict with the principles of sustainability. Cities are becoming congested and their civic infrastructure overburdened. They are impacting heavily on the natural environment. Those in charge of governing them need to identify and put into action more sustainable courses of action.

What do we understand by sustainability? Portney's *Taking Sustainable Cities Seriously* (2003) examines approaches to sustainability in a number of North American cities and develops the premise of 'carrying capacity'. In these terms it is about maintaining and improving the carrying capacity of the earth – its land, water and air – in the face of human activity, which '…depletes rather than replenishes or sustains the earth's resources that contain the capacity to carry life …' (Portney, 2003). The Brundtland Commission's report, *Our Common Future*, defines sustainable development as development activity that '… meets the needs of the present without compromising the ability of future generations to meet their own needs ...' (Brundtland Commission, 1987). While the underlying principle of carrying capacity is evident in *Melbourne 2030*'s programme and objectives, it is the more familiar Brundtland definition of sustainability that *Melbourne 2030* adopts as its specific long-term objective. This involves

- Formal recognition of the interdependence of environmental, economic and social issues;
- Respect for all forms of capital (natural, human, social and financial) and for living as far as possible on the 'interest' generated by that capital;
- Joint consideration of economic, environmental and social costs and the benefits of planned actions and activities;
- Assessment of the impact of activities on all people, across all places and over time.

Melbourne 2030 has been designed to address the question of how best to manage development in the context of evolving community and economic concern about sustainability. It also acknowledges the state government's position that doing nothing in the face of Melbourne's expanding city growth is not an option.

Five key concerns have fuelled this perspective:

- The quantity and the future household make-up that is likely to characterize Melbourne's projected population growth;
- The sprawl effects of unchecked residential growth at the city fringe that leaves new residential areas with poor access to shops, services and job opportunities – the issue here being equity of access as one of the major, underlying causes of social inequality;
- Infrastructural backlogs in the city's outer suburbs, coupled with a growing demand for transport and social infrastructure to serve new developing areas – at a significant cost to the state and local government;
- Strong interest group and local community pressure to provide better protection to areas of environmental value that are coming under pressure from urban expansion;
- A need for a clear government policy and commitment within which industry, local government, communities and investors can act with certainty over time.

two
A GLOBAL CONTEXT – INPUT FROM THE OECD

Early in *Melbourne 2030*'s formulation, the state government sought to put its efforts to plan for sustainable development and growth into a much wider context. It commissioned the international body, the Organization of Economic Co-operation and Development (OECD), to examine the direction, objectives and content of *Melbourne 2030*, its terms of reference being drawn in part from the OECD's earlier report, *Cities for Citizens – Improving Metropolitan Governance*. This report includes a set of governance principles to '... help Member countries reap the benefits which good governance and "smart growth" offer and to achieve more sustainable forms of urban development ...' (OECD, 2001).

Based on knowledge of current urban development experience and practice within OECD member countries, the report notes that

> ... because cities are the engines of growth, member countries have every interest to examine how policies to improve governance at the metropolitan level can develop competitiveness, promote more sustainable development, and enhance social cohesion'. (OECD, 2001, p. 324)

As a partial reflection of these principles *Melbourne 2030* addresses five strategic questions. These are:

- How best to provide for a growing population and ensure that this growth maintains our ability to live within the available resources of water, land and energy?
- Where should development be discouraged or prevented to retain the quality of the natural environment across the city's catchment areas and beyond?
- How should development be focused, and what pattern of land use and transport should be invested in for a better future?
- What changes should be made to lifestyles, technologies used and the organization of the city to reduce the use of resources and its impact on the city's living environment?
- What additional social infrastructure will be needed to support a growing city and best ensure that this is available for all when needed?

It is significant that the OECD's commissioned report on *Melbourne 2030* concluded with this comment:

> the Victorian State Government, through its policies and the Melbourne Metropolitan Strategy, is in the vanguard of metropolitan areas in OECD in terms of governance and is in line with the OECD Principles of Metropolitan Governance. The reform and modernisation of State planning currently under way ... all combine to create a framework for a very high level of economic, social and environmentally sustainable development which should underpin a prosperous future for Metropolitan Melbourne and the State of Victoria.' (OECD, 2003, p. 327)

While the OECD also indicated there was room for improvement, this is an extremely positive assessment of the Victorian Government's response to the challenges and opportunities facing Melbourne.

three
MELBOURNE 2030 – DIRECTIONS AND INITIATIVES FOR SUSTAINABILITY

Melbourne 2030's plan for Melbourne's future growth is a framework structured around nine strategic directions, spelled out in fifty policies and 226 specific initiatives. In essence, it involves the targeted redirection of the city's anticipated growth over a thirty-year period. This redirection embodies a comprehensive programme of sustainable development that is intended to:

- Curtail sprawl and internally redirect the city's future urban growth;
- Reorient and strengthen the city's transport and general movement patterns so as to emphasize and significantly extend the use of public transport in the city;
- Guide, direct and structure Melbourne's future patterns of urban growth to new targeted locations that have a strong relationship to an improved and extended public transport system;
- Provide for a future range of diverse and changing housing needs within mixed use (rather than functionally isolated) areas and with a closer physical relationship to a spread of employment opportunities;
- Ensure that the city's future development patterns encompass and incorporate all that has been learnt (and will be learnt) about the sustainable use of resources – reflected in new, or revised, strategies for water and energy use and for waste disposal coupled with practises of resource retention and reuse.

To *curtail sprawl, Melbourne 2030* introduces an urban growth boundary at its fringe. This will contain development into major identified transport and infrastructure corridors and stop urban growth from spreading onto land that is valued for its agricultural and tourism functions and its environmental content. Five growth areas are identified on the city's fringe, in locations associated with transport and infrastructure corridors, where 'green field' development can still occur. Defined non-urban areas at the city's periphery and outside the urban growth boundary, referred to as Melbourne's 'green wedges', accommodate agricultural, recreational and urban support uses (such as airports). Legislation has been enacted to support the urban growth boundary and the green wedges.

To *reorient and strengthen transport and movement patterns, Melbourne 2030* involves the expansion of the City's principal public transport network, applying a mosaic of cross-town routes to its traditional radial pattern. This improved public transport network will emphasize and strengthen links between the city's dispersed major activity centres and will help achieve the Government's key target 20/2020 target – that by the year 2020, the proportion of motorized transport trips taken on public transport will more than double, from the present figure of 9 per cent to 20 per cent. The review of the city's transport network extends beyond metropolitan Melbourne to include improved and more efficient road and rail access between Melbourne and key regional cities. This will help control growth at the city fringe and will spread employment and residential patterns and opportunities. *Melbourne 2030* also places significant weight on the strategic protection and development of the city's international trading gateways – its airports and ports – on which Victoria's economy depends so heavily.

To *direct future patterns of urban growth, Melbourne 2030* identifies more than one hundred activity centres (categorized as principal, major, specialized and neighbourhood centres) across metropolitan Melbourne where new development will be encouraged. This sets a

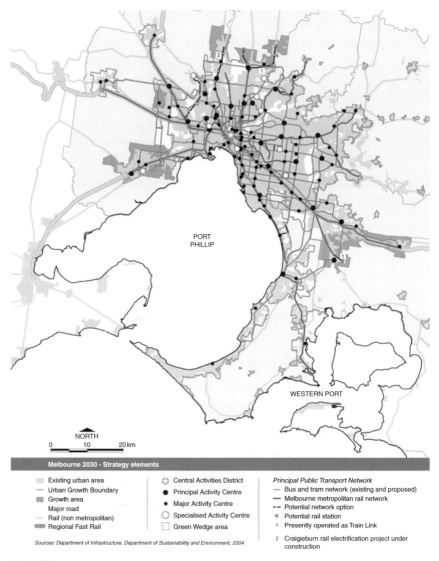

Melbourne 2030 - Strategy elements

▨ Existing urban area	⊙ Central Activities District	*Principal Public Transport Network*
— Urban Growth Boundary	● Principal Activity Centre	— Bus and tram network (existing and proposed)
▨ Growth area	• Major Activity Centre	— Melbourne metropolitan rail network
Major road	○ Specialised Activity Centre	-- Potential network option
-- Rail (non metropolitan)	□ Green Wedge area	⊟ Potential rail station
▬ Regional Fast Rail		1 Presently operated as Train Link
		2 Craigieburn rail electrification project under
Sources: Department of Infrastructure, Department of Sustainability and Environment, 2004		construction

figure 13.1
MELBOURNE 2030 IN SUMMARY

new, more intensive development agenda for these existing centres as well as reinforcing the evolutionary process of the city's existing pattern of established and emerging centres. Within these activity centres, nine principal metropolitan mixed-use centres have been iden- tified for the Government's Transit Cities programme, where the state and local government are working together with private investors to focus higher density mixed-use development around activity centres. Each Transit City involves a major public transport hub (tram, train and bus) and interchange. The increased efficiency and public comfort of these interchanges is closely tied to their related town centres – which in turn are supported by a range of uses, public spaces and a well-structured walking environment. The government has also committed to the introduction of 'priority development zones' to help facilitate activity centre policy and decision-making on major urban renewal and regeneration projects.

To *provide for future housing needs, Melbourne 2030* encourages higher density housing around designated activity centres, where employment and services are located, and will promote an increased supply of well-located, affordable housing. In new development areas it will ensure that the installation of infrastructure and services is co-ordinated to keep pace with housing development. To support new or expanded residential development, it proposes the creation of a network of new public parks. Particular emphasis is placed on the western suburbs, to help rectify shortages of public open space and outdoor recreational opportunities there.

To *ensure the sustainable use of resources, Melbourne 2030* addresses environmental sustainability through a range of new state initiatives that include the management of water, waste and energy, stormwater management, air quality and biodiversity. Examples include specific water targets – such as reduced consumption, investigating the reuse of grey water and other significant reform initiatives, which are set out in the government's White Paper, *Securing Our Water Future Together* (Department of Sustainability and the Environment, 2004). Energy-efficient design is promoted through the requirement that all new homes must achieve a five-star energy rating.

GOVERNANCE AND THE TASK OF IMPLEMENTATION

If this is the substance of *Melbourne 2030*, how does it move from being a sophisticated, comprehensive statement of policy and intent into the far more turbulent waters of implementation? What makes it not just a very good plan, but a concerted programme of action? The answer is the right management, or governance. From the outset those responsible for *Melbourne 2030* have paid particular attention to the governance arrangements and decision-making structures that would be needed to implement it. They have done so in light of the OECD emphasis on governance arrangements:

> *... the governance structures of large cities need to be reformed in order to ... meet the challenges of today – sustainable urban development, increasing competitiveness in a global economy, strengthening social cohesion and nurturing local democracy.* (OECD, 2001)

In Victoria, this understanding is central to the implementation of *Melbourne 2030*. It underlines the key role of the state government as both the source of *Melbourne 2030* and its key driver.

AUSTRALIA'S GOVERNANCE TRADITIONS

Victoria is one of six states and two territories within Australia. The country's constitutional structure involves a fusion of British parliamentary democracy and the federal system of the United States, where the states are self-governing and significantly independent, and the federal government takes prime responsibility for the country's economy, defence and international relations. Across Australia, and within each state, governments at any one time are elected for a set term by popular vote across independent geographical arrangements of state and federal electorates. Under each state government extends a patchwork of local governments (referred to here as local councils) whose governance responsibilities combine the delivery and administration of state government policy with the articulation and representation of community interests. The balance is delicate and often leaves local councils with the task of mediating between state government policy and local concerns.

It is in this context that the state government implementation of any large-scale regional plan for change and future sustainable development, needs to be understood. *Melbourne 2030* has been introduced by a Labor Government which has sought to distinguish itself from its predecessor by making a strong political commitment to the independence and autonomy of Victoria's local governments. In practical terms, this means that significant responsibility for the delivery of *Melbourne 2030* has devolved on local government in a partnership role with the state government.

THE SPECIAL ROLE OF THE STATE GOVERNMENT

State governments have considerable power and influence within the Australian constitutional system. In the pursuit of a defined policy objective or strategy, they can marshal significant resources and activity across the full range of relevant state government departments and agencies. They also have considerable ability – through direct action (such as regulation), or indirect action (such as leverage) – to influence the behaviour of many players crucial to the success of government policy. In formulating *Melbourne 2030*, it was acknowledged that implementation of such a complex development plan would involve many players within and beyond the state government, its institutions and agencies, and many activities beyond the state's formal planning system of legislation and regulation. This is why the state government put *Melbourne 2030* through extensive consultation within and beyond government and then made sure its approval was undertaken by the whole government. *Melbourne 2030* has been adopted by Cabinet as government policy, binding on all state government ministers, departments and agencies that have a responsibility to pursue its policies. This has been done deliberately to instil a strong awareness that any such plan or strategy has significance within the overarching frameworks of governance for the city, irrespective of the means by which it is implemented.

While a state government can single-mindedly drive the delivery of a key state strategy, the real picture of whole-of-government co-ordination is often less clear. Such co-ordination will often involve lengthy processes of trial and error to identify and negotiate changes in institutional behaviour. It will require careful strategies for how best to keep moving forward in the face of external resistance. In implementation terms it means striking and maintaining a fine political balance between direction and persuasion. At any one time there are real limits to the mix and emphasis given to these two implementation processes, since *Melbourne 2030*'s sustainability objectives mean it is essentially about engineering large-scale, regional change in attitudes and behaviour. That is why much time and effort has gone into establishing the structure and details of the crucial working relationship between the state government and local councils – a relationship that will need to be extended by drawing key private-sector players into the implementation process.

GOVERNANCE TOOLS FOR URBAN MANAGEMENT

Governments – federal, state, local – have specialized tools, or management techniques, at their disposal to use in urban management (Neilson, 2002). Eight of these are listed below.

Policy – the basic, overarching philosophies that guide actions and behaviour.

Legislation/regulation – the laws that prevent certain behaviour, which are the source of most conventional town-planning activities.

Fiscal – raising money through taxes and charging for services.

Financial – how they spend the money they raise, usually on other services like health or on major infrastructure like roads.

Institutional – the agencies, bodies and authorities that are empowered to govern.

Asset management – looking after the vast range of public assets, including overall responsibility for urban spaces.

Knowledge management – investment in research and dissemination of the results to improve understanding and decision-making.

Advocacy – demonstrating leadership by taking a stance and encouraging others to do the same.

All these techniques are vital in implementing *Melbourne 2030*.

four
'START UP' IMPLEMENTATION – THE *MELBOURNE 2030* PROCESS

Portney asks how seriously cities are taking the pursuit of sustainability. Most of the North American cities he identifies for study are in the earliest stages of applying such policies. Consequently, while he points to a range of objective indicators of performance as a way of eventually unravelling an answer, he is forced to rely on a more subjective gauge of serious commitment. More often than not, this involves scrutiny of the 'style' of implementation, the processes and structures initially selected and what these indicate about an understanding of the complexity of implementation and the scope of change it needs to address.

How seriously is *Melbourne 2030* being taken? Just two years into a 30-year programme, this can be gauged only by looking at the efforts made to meet implementation targets and integrate this with the more complex issue of tackling attitudinal and behavioural change. Tackling behavioural change on this scale involves introducing changes to the usual practices of state and local government decision-making and implies involvement beyond the bounds of purely government activity. Some mechanisms and processes of this sort are already under way, leading to changes in terms of both attitudes and action.

NEW INSTITUTIONAL STRUCTURES

In late 2002 a new government department was created. The Department of Sustainability and Environment (DSE) integrates the state's strategic planning functions and its water, parks, environmental and land management agencies. DSE has become the home and the implementation base for *Melbourne 2030*.

While the state's Minister for Planning has the principal political responsibility for *Melbourne 2030*, DSE initiates its delivery and drives it from day to day, assisted by refinements in its internal structure and the arrangement of functional areas and task groups. For example, the Metropolitan Development Group within DSE is divided into four specialist areas to manage implementation, specialist consultants, the development of guidelines, the establishment of key working groups and the negotiation of particular development proposals.

BUILDING LONG-TERM PARTNERSHIPS

The implementation reference group is a high-level advisory and review group set up by government. It reports to the Minister and the government on any matter relating to *Melbourne 2030*'s implementation. Its broad agenda and scope of action includes championing policies, advising on opportunities, reviewing process, identifying emerging opportunities, giving feedback and helping promote understanding between business, government and the community. Its members are influential people from a range of peak bodies representing all parts of the community and it can set up specialist working groups as required – already this has proved a highly effective implementation device. Independently chaired smart growth committees have also been set up to advise the government on structure planning options and the final configuration of the urban growth boundaries for each of *Melbourne 2030*'s five growth corridors.

TRANSIT CITY INITIATIVES

Another approach to building partnerships can be found within the Transit Cities programme, which is one of the most intensive and innovative of the *Melbourne 2030* implementation projects. The Dandenong Transit City is located in Melbourne's east, where Dandenong is the fastest growing urban centre outside the central business district. While the Greater Dandenong Council is generally well resourced and has a sound skills base, like many local councils it finds it difficult to marshal independently the necessary leverage, development and intervention powers necessary to successfully drive the ambitious Transit City concept. Thus the Dandenong Development Board has been created as a joint state/local government initiative. The aim is to focus at a high strategic level on the Transit City's development objectives while bringing to bear the full, co-ordinated weight of state and local government resources in partnership with key private development players and local business representatives. The Board is made up of senior public and private decision-makers and is focused on achieving exemplary public transport and interchange facilities at the heart of a recast, mixed-use town centre of markedly increased residential density, in a public space setting of exemplary physical quality – in short, the Transit City. The Board does not need to address the full gamut of local government responsibilities. While primarily advisory in its make-up and terms of reference, it can broker decisions and attract infrastructure support – always supporting the local council's responsibility of carrying the community of Dandenong with it as it engineers change.

five
DESIGN-BASED INITIATIVES

Beyond the landscape of independent strategic advice and review, other implementation devices are being put to trial. These must acknowledge the balance that *Melbourne 2030* seeks between future physical change and the attitudinal change necessary to support and secure this change. If that physical change is not well designed and attractive to look at, no matter how functional, it is unlikely to achieve popular success. So at this level of implementation activity, design assumes increased prominence in the form of urban design initiatives, advice and skill. Design-based implementation initiatives are grounded in a precisely imagined future and are invaluable in helping people visualize the eventual result of policy. Skilled design input is vital in obtaining and putting in place the rich public environment qualities that are sought for the new metropolitan communities of *Melbourne 2030*. Three kinds of design-based initiatives are utilized in implementing *Melbourne 2030*. All have a track record for effectiveness, not just in obtaining the desired result, but also in their ability to influence attitudes to change – now and in the future.

DESIGN GUIDES

This involves establishing standards for a visual environment of high standard in the design of public space and its surroundings. Three major design guides have been produced to address different aspects of development that will be generated by *Melbourne 2030:*

- a design guide for higher density housing for new residential development within activity centres.
- an activity centre design guide, with an emphasis on the quality of public space in these centres.

- a safer design guide – broader in scope, seeking to influence everything from the structure of the city and new subdivision patterns down to the design of small local parks and the way that buildings edge streets.

As with all urban design there is an element of negotiation in these guides, but what is not negotiable is delivery of the design principles they embody for any new public or private development. This is spelt out in *Melbourne 2030*. Successful application will involve informed discussions between a developer, the developer's design advisor and the approval authority (typically, a local council planning officer). The key public component to this negotiation is the presence of somebody capable of exercising a design-trained assessment of the best a particular negotiation might achieve. This person may also have to make a judgment on the standard of design ability being used by the developer. Accessing the skill base for these negotiations (where the true effect of design guides will be revealed) will be a major challenge for implementation of *Melbourne 2030*.

THE DESIGN CHARETTE AND THE VISUALIZING PROJECT

Both the 'design charette' and the visualizing project are techniques used to develop and project images of what a *2030*-influenced city might look like. They have slightly different, if complementary, aims. The design charette has been applied in the Transit City of Frankston, south of Melbourne, along the urban edge of Port Phillip Bay. Frankston is the site of major regional retail development, but far less attention has been paid to the quality of its public spaces and downtown commercial buildings. The public environment is harsh and car-dominated and pedestrian facilities are largely inadequate.

Five award-winning architectural/urban design firms were invited to focus on two different precincts – a tidal creek parallel to the beach on the western edge of the town centre and the train and bus interchange on the eastern edge of the town centre. Each design group was briefed about the specific development circumstances of Frankston and community concerns and aspirations for each precinct. Each devoted a day's design workshop to developing a strong conceptual approach for each precinct, which at the end of the day was presented to the workshop group and the local council in an open public forum. Two more weeks of work produced enough material to mount a local exhibition of the results and publish a promotional booklet setting out the design proposals. The exhibition and the workshop booklets have had a telling effect on local pride with a noticeable change in local expectations in a town that is often talked about disparagingly. The visual material is being used to excite interest in the development possibilities for the water edge zone of the town. At the same time the workshop process and its results have further shaped the local council's understanding of conceptual preferences and the general principles of layout, building alignment and walking links that might apply to each precinct as a whole.

The *visualizing project* involves developing images of what a *Melbourne 2030* future might look like. The focus is on change and how a place might look at different intervals over a thirty-year process of physical change. Three high streets at the centre of three different

figure 13.2
DESIGN PROPOSALS FOR FRANKSTON KANANOOK CREEK RESULTING FROM THE URBAN DESIGN
WORKSHOP

figure 13.3
DESIGN PROPOSALS FOR FRANKSTON KANANOOK CREEK RESULTING FROM THE URBAN DESIGN
WORKSHOP

figure 13.4
DESIGNERS AT WORK DURING
FRANKSTON KANANOOK CREEK URBAN
WORKSHOP

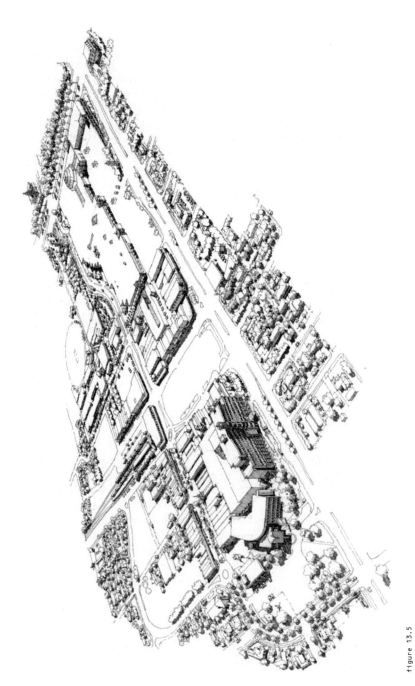

figure 13.5
PELIMINARY SKETCH – ACTIVITY CENTRE VISUALIZATION PROJECT

kinds of activity centre (the historic inner city, the outer urban fringe and the middle suburb) were selected for treatment. Using the activity centre design guide as a basic imaging script for possible future change, sketches were prepared to show each street and its surroundings three times over a thirty-year period, each time expressing the cumulative impacts of change. The sketch sequences in a number of different presentation formats will be used as an explanatory and discussion tool as part of the communication strategy of *Melbourne 2030*. They may also help people understand the rate of change over time, the fact that change is not always for the worse and the balance that should be sought between change and the valued local qualities of particular places.

DESIGN NEGOTIATION

The strategic use of specialist design review panels as a support to local government in its role as a planning and development approval authority is a relatively new procedure in Australia. With the process having been given a successful trial in New South Wales and briefly in Victoria, the Frankston design review panel is the first formally constituted design review panel to be appointed in Victoria. It is hoped to be the first of many, as part of the *Melbourne 2030* implementation process. The panel's role is to assist the local council in significantly improving the general standard of development design in the town and to provide the council with a consistent, specialized source of strategic urban design advice for the development of its Transit City precinct plans and implementation. While the panel is yet to assess its first development application, it has already discussed with the council its role in negotiating a design result on the council's behalf, rather than simply advising it on the shortcomings or advantages of a particular design proposal.

A further initiative focuses on the one-off problem and hence is more tactical than strategic. As part of its *Melbourne 2030* implementation team within the DSE, the state government can provide development facilitation and urban design skills to address major development proposals where issues of design and development intensity may mean the difference between development approval or refusal. This has given weight to the early stages of *Melbourne 2030* implementation, where the local council's activity centre structure plans – their strategic account of acceptable development potential within activity centres – are still in progress. Design negotiation is a lengthy hands-on process, but a useful one where standards are set for use and reuse. Within the *Melbourne 2030* framework, the negotiation pair of the development facilitator and the skilled urban designer can be a particularly persuasive partnership.

six
CONCLUSION

Implementing a plan of *Melbourne 2030*'s dimensions and aspirations involves sustained hard work and commitment from all parties as well as understanding and accepting its long-term aims, and being willing to be flexible when required. This is doubly important when sustainability is an object of the plan, as sustainability will not be achieved without planning for change. The OECD observed as much in its territorial review of Melbourne, commenting:

> *What was utopian 10 years ago is now a matter of practical policy implementation. Remaining with the status quo is not an option: doing nothing different translates into lost opportunities, higher transaction costs, and higher costs to cope with social distress and environmental problems.* (OECD, 2003)

Indeed the need to challenge the *status quo* was part of the reason why the Victorian Government decided to prepare a new metropolitan strategy. Since the launch of *Melbourne 2030* in 2003, much work has taken place at many levels even beyond that indicated in this paper. The implementation reference group has identified a number of priorities for government in implementing *Melbourne 2030*, notably investment in improved and extended public transport facilities and better communications. The Premier has also established a new *Melbourne 2030* Cabinet committee, which demonstrates a whole-of-government commitment to making the difficult policy and budget decisions that will ensure successful implementation.

It is clear from public comment that even more work needs to be done with the community to ensure that, as structure plans for activity centres are completed, local communities have a genuine opportunity to participate in determining the future form and character of their local centres. This won't happen overnight, of course. An implementation agenda of this extent, applied to a city of Melbourne's size, takes time to introduce, develop and bed down. After all, many years of effort went into the urban renewal of Southbank and into improving water quality and creating a public open space network along the Yarra River. And many years of effort are still needed to realize the vision of Docklands. But the government should be applauded for its open approach to implementation and its willingness not only to invite peer review from such a wide range of peak bodies, but to respond to criticism as it endeavours to keep the large picture in view.

Portney notes in *Taking Sustainable Cities Seriously* that:

> *…The concept of sustainable development, to a large extent, shifts the emphasis away from mere concern about the environment to include explicit concern about economic development. The argument often put forth is that the wrong kind of economic development will not only deplete the earth's resources and damage the earth's ecological carrying capacity, in the long run it will also undermine achievement of economic growth itself. Unsustainable economic development is just as much about being unable to sustain economic growth as it is about exceeding the earth's ecological carrying capacity…* (Portney, 2003)

In many ways this captures the essence of the government's vision for Melbourne. Its take on sustainability is as much about securing the city's economic future (its competitive edge) as it is about addressing the city's impact on the carrying capacity of its ecological setting. What this means in practice is making endeavours on a broad scale. While there will be many opportunities to falter, the intent and spirit of implementation, as it is currently being crafted in Victoria, provides a practical and optimistic application of the OECD's four aspirational principles of flexibility, sustainability, liveability and an interconnected holistic focus. As long as we guard against becoming complacent and recognize that there is room for improvement – as indicated by the OECD – then the aims of *Melbourne 2030* should ultimately be fulfilled.

REFERENCES

Brundtland Commission (1987). *Our Common Future*. World Commission on Environment and Development.

Department of Sustainability and the Environment (2002). *Melbourne 2003*. Available online at http://www.dse.vic.gov.au/ Government of Victoria.

Department of Sustainability and the Environment, (2004). *Securing Our Water Future Together*. White Paper Available online at http://www.dse.vic.gov.au/ Government of Victoria.

Harvard Business School (2003). *HBS Scorecard Report: Managing Innovation*. January–February.

Neilson, L. (2002). *Instruments of Governance in Urban Management*, Joint Royal Australian Planning Institute and New Zealand Planning Institute Conference, *Australian Planner*, **39**, 2.

OECD (2001). *Cities for Citizens – Improving Metropolitan Governance*. OECD.

OECD (2003). *Meropolitan Region of Melbourne, Australia*, OECD Territorial Reviews.

Portney, K. (2003). *Taking Sustainable Cities Seriously*. MIT Press.

14

FROM NEW YORK TO DARWINISM: FORMULARY FOR A SUSTAINABLE URBANISM

Michael Sorkin

Although this may be hard to believe, New York State is second in the US (after balmy Hawaii) in its efficient use of energy. This remarkable situation is due to a single circumstance: the very high rates of public transportation use in New York City, greater by far than anywhere else in the country. That such a single factor should – in a place of demanding climate and profligate levels of consumption – be so influential is hugely suggestive. Urban sustainability requires thinking at appropriate scales.

This doesn't come easily. The mood of voluntarism is endemic, a result of national policies that are little concerned with the fate of the planet as well as the origins of the environmental movement as part of the counter-cultural coalescence of the 1960s. The movement for a green architecture has, true to its origins, been largely preoccupied with the power of individuals, with thinking small. As a result, the literature – and to a lesser degree, the environment – abounds with examples of buildings that seek to conserve energy and to achieve higher levels of environmental autonomy. Vital though such disciplines are, such local practices – bromides notwithstanding – can hope to be only part of the story.

However, the way in which such efforts are judged is crucial, even foundational for urban environmentalism. The core idea that self-sufficiency – life 'off the grid' – represents a meaningful test of accomplishment, is something that can be logically scaled. The sustainable city is also one that fends for itself. While it would be foolish to argue that every city should or can be wholly autonomous, self-sufficiency provides the logical means of measurement for the calculation of urban success. Furthermore, it has particular relevance politically, as cities emerge as bulwarks of participation and resistance in a world culture increasingly characterized by dysfunctional national governments and the growing hegemony of transnational corporations. Indeed, the vitality of the city is crucial to the success of democracy itself.

one
FOOT-PRINTING THE CITY

One of the most succinct measures of the place of cities in the global environment and of their self-reliance is the so-called 'ecological footprint'. This is no more than a convention for calculating the area of a city (or building or person) in terms of the totality of the resources it consumes, but it has the power to change dramatically normative conceptualizations of the urban. Unlike a political boundary or even a standard metropolitan statistical area, an ecological footprint does not simply measure the extent of a contiguous conurbation or an area under a particular administrative control. Rather, it seeks to quantify just how much of the earth a city requires to sustain itself. This includes inventories such things as food, oxygen, water, CO_2 uptake, raw materials and so on. A variety of more or less credible algorithms are available to convert these quantities into areas, and the results can be striking. For example, by one set of calculations, the ecological footprint of Los Angeles is equivalent to the total area of Peru.

This has a number of deep implications for urbanism. First, foot-printing suggests that we must conceive of cities in a way that exceeds their immediate territories, however these may be defined. The footprint vividly reveals the way in which cities function globally, given the long distances its resources are obliged to travel and the distant victims of urban effluent. It also exposes – with depressing clarity – the utter disproportion of the rates of consumption and the skewed directionality of resource flows. Clearly, if all cities consumed at the Los Angeles (or New York) rate, the surface of the planet today would be insufficient to supply them all with the means of life. According to a 1997 calculation by Matthias Wackernagl – one of the pioneers of such calculations – the United States as a whole has a capacity of around 18 million square miles but a total footprint of nearly 28 million. This is the very definition of the unsustainable.

This disproportion is rendered even more grotesque by the fact that huge numbers of the world's population (of which half now live in cities) do not have even the minimum necessities of life. Close to one and a half billion people live on under $1 a day. More than a billion people lack safe drinking water and three billion do not have access to adequate sanitation. Life expectancy rates – and the other components of human development – vary appallingly between the rich and the poor. Capitalism – now the planetary economic system – argues that only the neoliberal engine of 'free' trade and fiscal bondage to the global banking regime – will, in its rising tide, lift all boats. In practice, this has been abundantly proved not to be the case, as agribusiness has wiped out 'inefficient' local farming and onerous debt servicing has crippled the ability of governments to provide basic services to their people. Indeed, economic and cultural globalization – with its skein of distorted interdependencies – has helped thwart the possibility for local autonomy and, by extension, self-sufficiency.

What this suggests – like the model of green architecture – is that only a radical reduction in either the size of the population or rates of consumption can save us. This requires – to put it mildly – a certain level of strategic thinking, which can resonate in a wide variety of ways. For instance, if the world were to go vegetarian, the footprints would be dramatically reduced. Beef – the gold standard – is, from a planetary perspective, perhaps the most inefficient protein delivery system imaginable. This first world piggishness is also reflected in the consequences of our styles of mobility. We Americans are wedded to our motorcars, which generate a tremendous range of problems. The projected carbon emissions of the 114 million people by which the US population is likely to grow in the next 50 years is roughly equal to the projected emissions of the expected 1.2 billion increase in the population of Africa. Unfortunately, too many still see the US experience as a model. One of the most depressing news stories of recent months announced the decision of the Chinese authorities to restrict bicycle traffic on major thoroughfares in Beijing and Shanghai. This is an instance in which keeping up with the Joneses is a formula for suicide. Ironically, this is a reversion to the old Marxian theory of the stages of development, as the party leadership mindlessly goes back to pick up a lost step.

two

THE ECONOMIC MODEL

The economic model that most closely describes the mechanism of urban self-sufficiency is that of import substitution, or import replacement, as Jane Jacobs calls it. In her classic *The Economy of Cities* (1970), Jacobs argues that this process has been through history the driver of rapid urban growth and differentiation from the earliest days of cities. Although it is generally used to describe a strictly economic dynamic, the idea also contains a possible teleological component. Likewise, it raises the question of why cities grow and, implicitly, contains a notion about the limits of growth. If there is an urban phenomenon today that marks out the contemporary stage of urbanism from previous ones, it is the rise of the so-called megacities, cities with populations in excess of 10 million. Although cities of a million have been know for millennia, the predominance of these places is of much more recent origin. At present there are approximately 500 such cities and, among them, 20 cities of 10 million or more, the majority of them in the developing world.

The difficulty of such places is both their unsustainability in environmental terms and their political and social *apraxia*. Like systems and organisms of many other types, cities too can reach a scale at which they are simply unable to perform co-ordinated movements. Beyond a certain scale, cities become inaccessible and beyond management. Services are undeliverable and politics – which, in cities needs a local predicate – cease to be a meaningful element in everyday life. Moreover, since these cities are increasingly the product of the in-migration of the poor, they become factories of despair, forcing their inhabitants into ever more desperate margins in which any hope of individual autonomy becomes an impossible dream. And yet, as Jane Jacobs has so eloquently pointed out, large cities are also – in their multiplication of useful margins – the indispensable setting for freedom and choice.

This balance between political autonomy and environmental self-sufficiency has a clear component of scale. Thinking about the future of the city, it is evident that the only reasonable formula is to create new cities, and lots of them. Of course, this process is taking place all the time but the degree to which urban creation proceeds without anything that might properly be called environmental planning is astonishing. The vast majority of our cities are simply accidents, the undisciplined growth of existing towns or – most characteristically – the global spread of the interstitial ooze commonly called the 'edge city' or simply, sprawl. Indeed, American leads the way: our economy directs the major portion of our urban investment and development, not to traditional urban areas, but to the endless periphery of the multinational globopolis.

three
THE TECHNOLOGICAL MODEL

One of the cultural resistances that must be overcome by a sustainable urbanism is our own inclination to think in terms of technical solutions to environmental problems. This is not to slight the importance of technology – one need only think about the revolution that might ensue from the invention of cheap photovoltaics or desalination – but instead to point out the conflict between the idea of technology as the medium for overcoming difference and the predication of the sustainable in the idea of locality. Our building and environmental technologies have long striven to offer homogeneous possibilities in the construction of buildings and cities. Air-conditioning secures a constant indoor tempera-ture everywhere. Fertilizers and genetic engineering bring local diets into conformity with multinational nutritional norms. Automobile ownership assures territorial smoothness. Electronic technology throws body-based styles of adjacency into radical doubt. The advertising industry – which misses no cranny on earth – persuades us that this is what we want and need.

The corrective is to think of technology not as an autonomous force that seeks solutions measured only by internal standards of 'efficiency' and uniformity, but as an instrument that can secure the benefits of the local – an adjunct to difference. This means that par-ticularity must be valued for itself and that the paradigm of uniformity must be resisted at all levels, from the technical to the cultural. The fight for diversity is not simply senti-mental: a result of nostalgia for vanishing habits of a life that technology has rendered obsolete. Rather, as we know from biology, diversity is crucial to renewal and health. This is equally true in the political and social registers. Freedom is the byproduct of authentic choices and a uniform environment, directed by the needs of the global circuit of capital, is the enemy of both our rights and our opportunities.

Devising urban practices and morphologies to produce this dialectic of difference is the task for green urbanism. To state such principles is to beg their inflection – the argument for a consistent agenda is very different from arguing for a uniform collection of forms. This said, what are the elements of a sustainable urbanism that have widespread applica-tion, including practices that are both protective and stimulating? If the goal is to promote urbanism that is just, beautiful and sustainable, what follows below might be a preliminary list:

four
DELIMITATION

The debate over compact cities has been especially fervid in Europe, less so in the United States. Nevertheless, one of the primary agendas for urban growth is the retention of the difference between what is urban and what is not, a proposition about both character and edges. While we may prefer to think of nature as an artifact, an artificial construction, a remnant of eighteenth century territorial ideology, we all know that, as a practical matter, the continued existence of the 'natural' environment is crucial for both our psychical self-construction and for our physical survival. The only cure for sprawl is to call a halt to it, to build cities with clear boundaries which are able to inventory continuously the means of their own survival, differentiation, hospitality and assets. This will produce a double cycle of growth. The first phase – that of enlargement – will delineate the expanded territorial requirements of the city. The second – characteristic of 'historic' cities – will be an ongoing differentiation in place. As cities mature and become successful, the differentiation will devolve on a set of shrinking physical sites and will result in the continuous growth of complexity, rather than extent. In a democratic city, this will lead to an accumulation of consent that will serve to limit the ease of radical transformation, favouring the most widespread styles of agreement, rather than the autocracy of the top-down.

five

BODY–BASED

Green urbanism is the recognition that cities are *habitats*. This implies a radical redescription of what it means to measure urban success and what exactly it means to live in the city. The city, treated as an ecology, must lead to both the mental and physical health of its inhabitants and structure itself – in the first instance – to the capacities and needs of the human body. The wave of tele and cyborg technologies – well reflected in our chosen contemporary forms of paranoia – tend toward a disembodied subjectivity. Freedom of movement is the root expression of democracy in space and the sustainable city will privilege a particular means of motion – human locomotion. This will have a number of consequences for the ways in which we both measure and use the city. Indeed, the requirements of the body are the single most crucial measure for urban design. This will reproduce itself in various registers:

Mobility. If walking is the alpha means of urban circulation, then the basic construct of urban organization – the neighborhood – will be both sized and differenced to accommodate people on foot. This suggests that neighborhoods be highly mixed in use, supporting the range of daily necessities – employment, education, commerce, conviviality – that are crucial to a full and active life. The walking city also ramifies in its architecture. If the test of regular accessibility by foot is applied to urban building, it will tend to generate an architecture that is low. Although there is an ample range of variations, this architecture will be five or six storeys high, the natural limit for stair-climbing on a regular basis. Local mobility – in both horizontal and vertical axes – is also crucial to the health of the organism. As the Centers for Disease Control in the US have reported, our current epidemic of diabetes and obesity are directly related to our settlement pattern and its sedentary styles of circulation. What we beleaguer as an inconvenience is actually central to our well-being. Messages that urge us to live this way, patterns that offer no alternative, and the fantasy of the infinite reparability of our bodies – whether through drugs, surgery, or other centrally administered forms of 'self-help' – all contribute to the marginalization of the body as a driver of form.

Propinquity. Throughout the world the green agenda has begun to displace the red as the focus of political activity. This is not simply a distraction from what might seem more pressing principles, but a reformulation of the terms of the struggle for a world arriving at the 'end of history,' a re-articulation of the terms of political argument for a globalizing culture. To the degree that the ownership of the environment – and America is pressing for the rapid devolution of the global commons into private hands – is the register of the world distribution of wealth, its stewardship becomes the marker of what once was called class struggle. However, equally crucial to the character of the green city – which I understand as fully interchangeable, conceptually, with the idea of the just city – is the way in which it fulfills the primal role of democratic space, providing the setting for both the deliberate and the accidental meeting of bodies. To facilitate this interaction is our most important task and the measure of such interactions is our most useful index of urban success. We have increasing difficulty in speaking of public space, both because of the surge of privatization and because of a suspicion of its traditional physical forms, the streets, and squares, the parks and cafes of traditional urbanism. Such places, however, are bulwarks for the expression of our rights and are still strong symbols of the meaning of collectivity. The bodily right to the city is utterly fundamental.

Respiration. Le Corbusier's famed formulation of a trinity of architectural desires – sun, space, and greenery – is a good enough mantra for the tectonics of body-based architecture. Although this seems basic, its implications are ever more deeply ignored. Faith will not assure breathable air, cross-ventilation, comfortable insulation, thermal management (the urban heat island), or room for the necessary pleasures of physical culture. Green urbanism, at its roots, is a strategy for survival.

Self-sufficiency. The idea of the self-sufficient city is not meant to gainsay the value of co-operation. Indeed, such co-operation is the precondition of self-sufficiency. Nor should the idea of self-sufficiency suggest the elimination of exchange, whether economic, social, cultural, or biological. Rather, the goal of self-sufficiency will provide a primary measure of a city's responsiveness to the biosphere and an inventory of global economic and environmental justice. Moreover, a city striving to support itself will – via this predicate of economy – find – as suggested above – a more meaningful and defensible place in a world community increasingly characterized by weak states and powerful corporations. Equally crucial, the self-sufficient metropolis will limit its growth by harmonizing its production with the bearing capacity of its site and the desires of its population. Economies of scale are not based on an ever-increasing gyre of size. True economy is a proportioning system, a means of balancing needs, wants and resources. The self-sufficient city will find the medium of its own singularity by evolving an economy that does not simply reproduce a universal pattern of supply and demand based on the corporate invention of want, but which engenders forms that incorporate historic habits, desires and uses, specializing for both competitive advantage and self-identity and – because of the depth of its internal economy – promoting welfare and exchange among its citizens.

The local. Given the rapid evisceration of the idea of locality by the onslaught of multinational culture, new strategies must emerge for authenticating the individuality of place. A green and self-sufficient city will be closely attuned to the particulars of its bio-climate, culture and resource base. By understanding itself as habitat, the city will aim for a style of homeostasis that encloses a description of the particulars of place. Rejecting the paradigm of the continuous sealed environment of the multinational corridor and of the endless city of sprawl, this city will engage both the politics and the forms of its own particularity. There are three potential sources for such differentiations of form.

Firstly, the weight of culture and history – the fabric of memory and of consent – must be served. This does not mean the limp conservation of forms that have been totally wrested from their originating contexts of meaning. Rather it means that forms and habits that remain vital are reproduced and that vital textures are reused. The expectation that when a form is decontextualized it will still somehow retain its primal vibe must be dismissed. Secondly, appropriate technologies of sustainability – however simple – will be foundational in the disposition of the elements of the city and in their particular configurations. The repertoire of shading and insulating, the management of wind, the use of indigenous materials, the careful consideration of lifecycles from cradle to cradle, the reduction of embodied energy, the use of a specific means of creating electrical energy, will all contribute to the formulation of an architecture of particularity and suitability within the larger context of local wishes and memories. Finally, the true signature of cultural locality lies in both functional and expressive singularity. Such singularities – whether those of Venice or Fez, Paris or New York – are neither automatic nor natural. Particularly today, in a situation in which visual culture is ever more dominated by global taste-makers and in which any object is visually accessible to anyone with a computer, the idea of cultural inevitability becomes increasingly suspect. In lieu of an illusory theory of the emergence of particularity from the crucible of culture, we must – to preserve and legitimate difference – increasingly rely on artistic invention to set the terms of urban singularity. We have arrived at a moment in which the design of cities can be dramatically re-engaged as a discourse of the harmonization of the received and the imagined. It is possible to speculate about forms that are both logical and have never before been seen.

The green. Our urbanism is still greatly in the thrall of the idea of the garden city. This makes sense: the garden city and its heirs were responding to the nineteenth century predecessors of the dysfunctional urbanism of today. The dark and satanic cities of the Industrial Revolution were early detected as an affront to health and civility as well as a medium for producing and reproducing the oppression of the working class, the ideal theoretical subject of progressives of the time. Indeed, the garden city – in a number of its classic formulations – articulated a number of the principles advanced above, although its hostility to industrial production – motivated by the alienating circumstances of its human character – remains problematic as a broader urban strategy. Garden cities sought self-sufficiency, compact dimensions, human scale and a kind of proto-environmentalism that reflected the rapid rise of the natural sciences and the first stirrings of the concept of a global ecology.

However, a salient characteristic of the garden city – almost too much of a truism even to state – was that is was green. Garden cities represented an early effort to redress what was perceived as a dramatic imbalance in human relations with the natural world. Just as contemporary Darwinism resituated the species within the family of worldly creatures and dealt a mortal blow to received ideas of the uniqueness of humans, so the garden city movement – and the ideas of Ebenezer Howard's successors, like Patrick Geddes – redescribed urbanism as a sheltering activity with a prominently biological basis. This opening up of the city to an idea of necessary cohabitation with the plant and animal kingdoms produced a new morphology of inclusion, derived from a fantasy of the balance represented by the village life of a previous age. This restoration of the putatively superior social principles of small town and village life was abetted, not simply by a turning back to history, but by new technologies of movement and communication that allowed the garden city not simply to be scaled up but networked with a hoped for galaxy of new towns of similar character.

six
CONCLUSION

We still have much to learn, not simply from the example of these propositions but also from the way in which the ideas of the garden city have been twisted and degenerated as they have morphed into a vapid suburbanism and one-dimensional visions of new towns, too simple, too monochrome. The lesson of these places and this movement, however, must be redirected. The creation of new towns is not an antidote to the idea of the big city in general. Big cities remain central to the human project and are unique in their ability to deliver lives of richness and diversity. Rather, the idea of the garden city must be applied to its own bastard, suburban sprawl; the real nemesis of urban and planetary sustainability.

Our new and newly green cities will owe a great deal to the earlier garden city project, and not only in the terms suggested above. If one can make a blanket statement about the character of these cities, it is that they will be literally green. This proposition might seem both too obvious and too simple. But an abundance of greenery in cities will be the mark of their efficiency and progress in the future. For virtually every issue that cities confront, nature has an answer. Our new urban gardens – ubiquitous on every horizontal plane – will supply us with oxygen, sequester carbon dioxide, control our temperatures, provide a habitat for our fellow creatures, offer us food, grow construction materials, calm our gaze and instrumentalize our autonomy. This condition must become the default. Our lives depend on it, on the incorporation of a universal we have always had.

REFERENCE

Jacobs, J. (1970). *The Economy of Cities*. Vintage Books.

#15

BEYOND THE CITY EDGE

John Fien

Humanity's future lies in cities. If we take action now, cities of despair can become cities of hope and joy. (Toepfer, 1999)

This chapter provides the beginning of a synthesis of the lessons to be learnt from the case studies in this book. As Esther Charlesworth told us in Chapter 1, a major revolution in human affairs has taken place: for the first time in human history, more than half of the world's population now lives in cities rather than the countryside. This urban revolution will escalate over the next three decades when urban populations will grow to twice the size of rural ones. Most of these new city dwellers will be in Africa and Asia, joining the vast pool of urban citizens in Europe, North America, Latin America and Australasia, where three-quarters of the population is already urbanized. Africa, currently the least urbanized continent, will have two-thirds of its population living in cities by 2020. And the biggest, most densely populated megacities, with populations of over 10 million, will be located in countries of the south, not the north.

Cities are – and will remain – the focal points of national and global culture, politics, finance, industry and communications. While immensely productive, creative and inno-vative, cities have also become centres of great poverty, violence, pollution and conges-tion. Unsustainable patterns of consumption, transport and waste have also extended the ecological footprints of cities to such an extent that, for example, London's footprint is an area of land equivalent to nearly 90 per cent of the total area of the British Isles, while Tokyo's impact is 1.66 times the size of Japan and the footprints of 29 major cities around the Baltic Sea range from a minimum of 500 to over 1100 times that of the cities them-selves (Folkes et al., 1997; Rees, 2003). The major environmental problems of the future will be urban ones.

However, as we saw in the chapters in the eco edge section of this book, environmental problems are interdependently entwined with social and economic ones. More than 600 million people living in cities in the south – one-tenth of the world's population – have homes of such poor quality and such poor water, sanitation and drainage services, that their health, indeed their very lives, are under continuous threat. At the same time, visitors to the USA and Europe are often shocked by the vast areas of deprivation that cast a shadow over so many great cities. These ghettoes, these 'edge cities', seem strangely out of place in such prosperous lands – a sad reminder of the racial, ethnic and class divisions that undermine the urban dream. As Klaus Toepfer, the Director General of the

United Nations Environment Programme laments,

For many millions of people around the world, urban living has become a nightmare, far removed from the dream of safety and prosperity held out by city visionaries. (Toepfer, 1999)

Despite these problems and challenges, cities continue to grow and flourish – a testament to the power of the urban dream and the dedication and plans of so many city visionaries. The ongoing decline of rural areas is also a powerful push factor, and a clear sign that the world needs rural transformation visionaries to match the urban design politicians, architects and planners whose experiences have been shared in the case studies in this book. However, just as in rural areas, poor governance and inadequate policies have led to the deteriorating living conditions and environmental degradation found in so many cities. Many metropolitan governments have been too underprepared, underskilled and under-resourced to respond, let alone anticipate and prepare for, the problems they now face.

What are the lessons that can be learnt from the urban design case studies in this book? No doubt there are many and the set that follows is not comprehensive. It also reflects the views of a student of sustainability with a passion for just, liveable cities rather than those of an urban specialist with an interest in sustainability. Perhaps this set of lessons might best serve as a mirror into which others might look to see points of agreement and disagreement, and find for themselves the lessons that can help make each of our cities 'cities of hope and joy'. The four themes in this book have organized the analysis of urban design and (re-)development into a consideration of the balance of public versus private investment and control, the relative importance of the central cities and their peripheries, cities on the edge of direct and structural violence and the hope of the urban sustainability movement. The four lessons I have distilled from the case studies relate to these four themes.

one

PRIVATE DEVELOPMENT VERSUS PUBLIC REALM

The contrast between the privatized management of the *centre ville* of Beirut by the Solidere corporation (Chapter 1 by Angus Gavin) and the public control of Barcelona's urban renaissance (Chapter 2 by Joan Busquets) could not be more marked. Yet many approaches to urban design are shared by both cities. Port redevelopment is a feature of both cities, sharing, as they do, the Mediterranean coast. Both have sought to provide much needed residential accommodation and both have emphasized the central importance of public space through the renewal of the Ramblas in Barcelona and the Martyr Square in Beirut. Both have emphasized the importance of attracting tourists to fuel economic recovery and the consequent development of recreation, retail, eating and entertainment precincts. The lesson for us here is that the approach to urban design needs to be culturally appropriate and responsive to local contexts. The Barcelona approach is a reflection of a liberal, western, semi-socialist tradition of European planning and the Catalonian response to so many years of control by Franco from Madrid. Beirut, once the 'Paris of the Levant', is a city being rebuilt after nearly twenty years of fierce and destructive civil war. Whole parts of the city along the Green Line were destroyed to make a clear-fire range between the warring factions who were responsible for over 300 000 people wounded and 170 000 deaths. In a country of only 3 million inhabitants, another 500 000 were displaced and at least 1 million people emigrated permanently, taking with them their valuable abilities, energies and capital. One-third of Lebanon's population left the country. The cost of destruction in Beirut was estimated to be at least $US1 billion (Dagher, 2000). How was a government to pay for this level of reconstruction and undertake it is as short a time as possible in order once again for Beirut to drive the Lebanese economy? Perhaps the creation of a private development company, in which major political figures invested, but which was also capable of borrowing funds and raising more on the stock exchange, was the best and only solution.

Yet, while the 'new' Barcelona has been welcomed with public acclaim, Beirut's redevelopment has been the focus of some criticism. Charlesworth (2002), for example, reports Beiruti architect, Assem Salaam, describing the Solidere development as 'a paradise for the rich that you needed to enter with a credit card through the Solidere stage design' while the historical geographer, Michael Davie, reports an increasingly unstable and socially divided city where 'the reconstruction process could thus be the spark for another round of violence' (Davie, 1994). Why this difference? In simple terms, it could be said that Beirut got the balance skewed in the public sector–private interest equation. In contrast to the focus on expensive *centre ville* developments of Beirut, politicians and planners in Barcelona focused on the needs of a wider range of citizens through an extensive programme of social housing and new public spaces spread throughout the city. However, the contrast between Beirut and Barcelona is not so much a case of how and by whom urban design and development is funded, but of who makes the decisions and in whose interests. Rob Adams' case study of Melbourne (Chapter 3) is an example of ways in which government planners, urban designers and architects have sought to provide strong guidelines and regulations for an urban design context in which both public and private development can proceed. Yet, while the Melbourne 'Postcode 3000' campaign is seeking to re-inhabit the city core, it is home to less than 1 per cent of the Melbourne population. This situation draws our attention to the second lesson from the case studies.

two

CENTRE VERSUS PERIPHERY

The second lesson to be drawn from the case studies is that urban designers have paid a relatively excessive amount of attention to the central city and far too little to the periphery. The economic and cultural cases for *grande projets* (from Bilboa to Paris) in the city centre are important ones. City centres often drive whole regional, if not national, economies, and investments in heritage conservation projects and the building of new museums, art galleries and convention centres pays important economic and cultural dividends. Such projects, even small pedestrian shopping mall developments, have often been the catalyst for a major reinvigoration of cities. However, their impact is mostly negligible on the daily lives of the vast majority of urbanites who live in the mid- to outer-ring suburbs and beyond in the peripheral sprawl of new towns, *banlieus* and underserviced *ad hoc* residential subdivisions of northern cities, not to mention their lack of relevance to the lives of ghetto and tenement dwellers and the hundreds of millions of people eking out an existence in the myriad informal settlements in the cities of the south.

The potential contributions of urban design to the social well-being of residents beyond the central city core has been too often neglected. The three case studies in this section of the book show that this is not always the case, however. In Chapter 5, John Montgomery reminded us that 'urban peripheries are not a single type of place' and that human choice and political will are needed to ensure an appropriate mix of land-use functions and developments in them. Taking the example of decaying industrial areas, Montgomery showed how the development of cultural precincts that contain work, study, performance, exhibition and retail spaces for artists and associated industries can catalyse the economic and social renewal of one type of peripheral area and one type of peripheral, perhaps marginalized, community.

Life for the residents of outer suburbs is often lived in a car commuting to and from work in the central city. There are apocryphal stories of middle-class and professional Thai families who have shifted their homes to gated communities beyond the periphery of Bangkok, but need to depart for work so early that breakfast for the family is taken in the car on the way to the city and dinner is eaten there on the way home late in the evening, while children do their homework to the sound of the car radio or television. And, for them, life is good. In contrast, the commuting poor spend two hours each way, morning and night, on overcrowded buses without air-conditioning, trying to catch up on missed sleep.

Who made the planning decisions that encouraged this peripheral development, and who failed to anticipate – and plan to obviate – the traffic horrors that are the daily commuting experience of so many millions of people in small, medium and megacities around the world? Perhaps it is not a case of whether someone did or did not make the right decisions. The economic lure of the city, which concentrates employment in nodal locations, may be just too great for business and industry to afford to move to where people live – a clear case of private interest undermining the quality of the public realm and of governments failing to provide adequate planning frameworks and incentives to encourage business and citizens alike to locate work and home in some degree of near proximity. But, then, the powerful capacity of global capital to relocate industry in less regulated countries exerts covert, and sometimes overt, pressure on governments not to make much-needed planning and urban design decisions.

Francine Houben's case study from the Netherlands (Chapter 6) is a response to the perceived well-nigh inevitability of increased commuting ('a rich society is a mobile society', she says). Pressed not so much by the migratory potential of global capital but by the decisions of many Dutch families to migrate away from the spreading office towers of the central city to outer suburbs and formerly rural villages, the view from the motorway has become an important urban design consideration. With the mobility of myriad daily trips to the shop, library, school and other local services to be considered also, Houben argues that architects and urban designers have 'to come up with solutions that break new ground – to produce designs that answer the steadily growing demand for mobility', but thankfully, not just by car but also by, and integrated with, trains, metro, bus and bicycle.

Is the ever-outward expanding spread of cities and such levels of mobility so inevitable? 'New urbanists' might argue that it is not – and that, when it is done properly, a 'new urbanism' development can provide the blend of land uses and sense of community that can bind people to a place. However, new urbanism is grounded in the assumption that the periphery needs to be controlled. Perhaps this is not so, argues Arie Rahaminoff (Chapter 4). Instead, he argues, that even edge cities, such as Jerusalem, beset as it is by dire problems of repression and reprisal, can turn around the metaphors of centre and core, periphery and edge, and pay heed to the potential of the periphery as the forefront of urban redevelopment. Seeking to maximize urban design opportunities for crosscultural mixing and sharing, Rahaminoff notes that the places that mark division and conflict are residential areas and religious institutions while open spaces, markets, shopping centres, cultural institutions and public facilities such as hospitals and universities are 'places of sharing'. Thus, he describes and then evaluates a series of projects that have sought to integrate centre and periphery and maximize crosscultural mixing. These include a religious heritage and tourism planning project for the Holy Basin of the Mount of Olives and the Kidron River area, and the Jerusalem light rail project whose 'route will run through different parts of the city and different communities, Jewish and Arab, religious and secular, ... and we hope will act as a social integrator'.

three
CITIES ON THE EDGE

The third lesson comes from the series of case studies of cities which, like Jerusalem, are divided by direct violence and conflict such as Kabul and Belgrade (Chapters 7 and 8) and/or the structural violence of poverty and deprivation (Chapters 9 and 10). The four case studies in this section of the book are analytical accounts of the strategies and pitfalls in planning the reconstruction of divided and destroyed cities. There is much to be learnt from the wisdom in these chapters. This includes the need for local control and sequenced development as advocated by Ajmal Maiwandi and Anthony Fontenot for Kabul (mirroring the layered approach of Barcelona in Chapter 2 and the incrementalist approach in Melbourne in Chapter 3); the need for strong government commitment, private investment and broad frameworks for consultation, redress and renewal, as advocated by Graeme Reid in his case study of Johannesburg (Chapter 9) and the deeply moving plea by Janice Perlman for rigorous social analysis to underpin any interventions in megacities, and for social justice and poverty alleviation to be the prime motivator in planning and redevelopment projects (Chapter 10). All chapters in this section pointed to the loss of urbanity in 'cities on the edge' but it was Darko Radovic's moving account in Chaper 8 of the impact on Belgrade of the disintegration of the former Yugoslavia followed by the destruction of major parts of the city by NATO bombing and the Serbian and Croatian destruction of Sarajevo, Mostar and Srebrenica, that pointed directly to the terrible consequences of the loss of urbanity.

The term 'city' itself derives from *civitas*, the Latin word from which concepts such as 'citizen', 'civic' and 'civilization' are also derived. Despite drawing people from various ethnic, racial and social groups into one place, cities – as civilized places – are defined not by their differences and complexities but by how well they cope with them. That is, the success of a city as *civitas* resides in how well it develops a civilized means of addressing and sorting out these differences. Radovic indicates with sorrow how, long before the Balkan conflicts of the 1990s, the people of Belgrade had weakened before the 'relentless, uncompromising challenges were made to the values that stood against chauvinistic barbarism' and, as a result,

> As its urban culture weakened, latent nationalism grew into the violent, aggressive and insatiable national-socialism of Milosevic's regime. Every aspect of urbanity crumbled, even faster that the facades of the neglected city.

The case studies in this section may be worst-case scenarios of the decline of urbanity, but the lesson I take from the case studies, especially when I read them against others in this book, such as the studies of the divided cities of Jerusalem and Beirut and, conversely, the attempts to build sustainable communities and cities, such as in Curitiba (Chapter 12) and Melbourne (Chapter 13), is a lesson about the need for urban design politicians, planners and architects to reflect on the potential inadvertent destruction of urbanity – or urban civility – even as a result, perhaps, of their best-laid plans. It may be possible the glue of social capital that integrates the people of a city may come unstuck when the balance of a public versus a private determination of the nature and direction of urban design, or of attention to developments in the core versus the periphery, is skewed. This is the potential paradox of urban design: we can undo a city by building it. Or as one commentator has warned:

> ...the very process of building and developing a city, if not undertaken carefully, can destroy the intangible qualities that are at the heart of urban life. In this respect, the greatest damage that can be unleashed on a city is the erosion of its urban civility. (Architectural League of New York 2004)

There is a strong need, therefore, to emphasize in urban design the importance of building social capital throughout the city, at least as much as the enhancement of economic growth and cultural capital. Without this new emphasis, *grande projets* in the city centre will continue to undermine the funding of neighbourhood transformation projects for eradicating poverty in marginalized areas, New urbanist ideals for the periphery will continue to run the risk of dividing society into homogenous enclaves of divided communities and professionally determined master plans will continue to undermine public participation and local democracy. When integrated with programmes for energy and water conservation, green purchasing and efficient resource–waste streams to ensure the environmental integrity of our cities, this emphasis on social capital, democratic governance and economic vitality is the only pathway to sustainable cities.

four

THE ECO EDGE

Sustainable development is often misconstrued as focusing on the natural environment and, in urban design and architecture, this has meant reducing the environmental impact of buildings by cutting energy and water use and using recycled and renewable building materials. However, as has been recognized in so many international prescriptions for sustainable cities – such as by the International Council for Local Environmental Initiatives, the UN Habitat sustainable cities programme, the UN Global Compact for Cities, the UN Environment Programme's Melbourne Principles for Sustainable Cities (2002), and so on – sustainability is grounded in the four pillars of resource efficiency and conservation, appropriate development, social justice and democratic governance. As the Ahwahnee principles for building prosperous and liveable communities argues,

> *Prosperity in the 21st Century will be based on creating and maintaining a sustainable standard of living and a high quality of life for all. To meet this challenge, a comprehensive new model is emerging which recognizes the economic value of natural and human capital.* (Local Government Commission, 2001)

Thus, one Sustainable Community Roundtable (n.d.) in the USA defines a sustainable community as 'far-seeing enough, flexible enough, and wise enough to maintain its natural, economic, social, and political support systems'. It adds that a sustainable community continues to thrive from generation to generation because it has:

- A healthy and diverse ecological system that continually performs life-sustaining functions and provides other resources for humans and other species;
- A social foundation that provides for the health of all community members, respects cultural diversity, is equitable in its actions, and considers the needs of future generations; and
- A healthy and diverse economy that adapts to change, provides long-term security to residents, and recognizes social and ecological limits.

Underpinning sustainable communities and cities are a set of incontrovertible ecological principles. Life in cities may be socially constructed and post-modern, but it is lived in a material world of energy and matter and nothing we, as humans, can do can deny or brush aside the basic laws of thermodynamics and entropy and their impact on cities through the laws of metabolism. This is the lesson from Mick Pearce's metaphor of 'cities on the energy watershed'. The chapters in the eco edge section of this book show how these laws are being applied at the scale of the individual building (Chapter 11 by Pearce), the city (Curitiba in Chapter 12 by Cassio Taniguchi) and the metropolitan region (Melbourne in Chapter 13 by Stuart Niven and Cathy Wilkinson). Synthesizing the ideas in these chapters, Michael Sorkin's 'Formulatory for a Sustainable Urbanism' (Chapter 14) is a *cri de coeur* for urban designers to recognize that a major cultural shift is needed in the way we think about cities. He argues that 'One of the cultural resistances that must be overcome ... is our own inclination to think in terms of technical solutions'. In distinction to this, he insists on the adoption of a new culture of planning and urban design grounded in respect for localism, resource self-sufficiency, widespread cultural and biological diversity and local democracy.

Principles such as these are central to sustainability and have been incorporated in broader sets of principles for sustainable cities developed by the international agencies mentioned at the start of this section. Perhaps the most widely acknowledged set is the 'Melbourne

Principles for Sustainable Cities' which was developed at an international charette held in April 2002. The charette was organized by UN Environment Programme's International Environmental Technology Centre and the Environment Protection Authority of Victoria, and sponsored and hosted by the City of Melbourne. The Melbourne Principles for Sustainable Cities were submitted to the World Summit on Sustainable Development in Johannesburg in September 2002, and adopted as part of a communiqué delivered to the main plenary on behalf of local authorities worldwide. Designed to 'achieve the creation of vibrant cities where there is respect for one another and nature to the benefit of all', the Melbourne Principles serve as a guide to thinking and practice on the sustainable development of cities.

And as such, there can be no better conclusion to this book.

THE MELBOURNE PRINCIPLES FOR SUSTAINABLE CITIES

Preamble

Cities are fundamental for economic opportunities and social interaction, as well as cultural and spiritual enrichment. Cities are also increasingly damaging the natural environment, unsustainably exploiting natural resources, undermining the social fabric and jeopardizing the long-term prosperity on which these benefits depend. These impacts are of global concern as more than 50 per cent of the world's population live in cities and the trend indicates that this proportion will increase. Improving the sustainability of cities will not only benefit their inhabitants, but also significantly contribute to improving the global situation.

Melbourne Principle 1: Provide a long-term vision for cities based on sustainability, intergenerational, social, economic and political equity, and individuality.

Clarification of Principle 1: A long-term vision is the starting point for catalysing positive change leading to sustainability. The vision needs to reflect the distinctive nature and characteristics of each city. The vision should express the shared aspirations of the people for their cities to become more sustainable. The vision needs to address equity, which means promoting equal access to both natural and human resources, as well as taking shared responsibility in ensuring that natural and human capital is not degraded for future generations. A vision based on sustainability will help to align and motivate communities, governments, businesses and others around a common purpose, and provide the basis for developing a strategy, action programmes and processes to achieve that vision.

Melbourne Principle 2: Achieve long-term economic and social security.

Clarification of Principle 2: Long-term economic and social security are prerequisites for beneficial change and are an integral part of triple bottom line sustainability. Prosperity and social stability are dependent upon environmentally sound sustainable

---

Contd.

development. We need to promote economic strategies to increase the value and vitality of human and natural systems and to conserve and renew human, financial and natural resources. Other issues to consider include: local democratic control of resources (especially land use and watershed management), self-reliance in terms of energy and other inputs, maximizing local multipliers and how to improve health and welfare systems. Economic strategies should also guarantee the right of all to potable water, clean air, food security, uncontaminated soil, shelter, and safe sanitation and to allocate the resources required to do so.

Melbourne Principle 3: Recognize the intrinsic value of biodiversity and natural ecosystems and their protection and restoration.

Clarification of Principle 3: Nature is more than a mere commodity to be used for the benefit of humans. We share the Earth with many other life forms that have their own intrinsic value. They warrant our respect, whether or not they are of immediate benefit to us. Just as humans have the ability to alter their habitat and even to extinguish other species, we can also protect biodiversity. Therefore we have a responsibility to act as custodians for nature.

Melbourne Principle 4: Enable communities to minimize their ecological footprint.

Clarification of Principle 4: Cities draw in significant quantities of resources and have a significant impact on the environment, well beyond what they can handle within their borders. These unsustainable trends need to be substantially curbed and eventually reversed. A convenient way to represent the impact of a city is to measure its ecological footprint. The ecological footprint of a city is a measure of the load imposed by its population on nature. It represents the land area necessary to sustain current levels of resource consumption and waste discharged by that population. Reducing the ecological footprint of a city is a positive contribution towards sustainability. Like any living system, a community consumes material and energy inputs, processes them into usable forms and generates waste. This represents the 'metabolism' of the city, and making this metabolism more efficient is essential to reducing the ecological footprint of a city. Decisions about cities should be based on an understanding of the consequences of a city's metabolism and should aim to reduce the city's ecological footprint wherever practical.

Melbourne Principle 5: Build on the characteristics of ecosystems in the development and nurturing of healthy and sustainable cities.

Clarification of Principle 5: By applying as a model for urban processes the ecological principles of form and function by which natural ecosystems operate, cities can become more sustainable. The characteristics of ecosystems include diversity, adaptiveness, interconnectedness, resilience, regenerative capacity and symbiosis. These

Contd.

characteristics can be modelled by cities to design strategies that will make them more productive and regenerative, resulting in ecological, social and economic benefits.

Melbourne Principle 6: Recognize and build on the distinctive characteristics of cities, including their human and cultural values, history and natural systems.

Clarification of Principle 6: Each city has a distinctive profile of human, cultural, historic and natural characteristics that provide insights to pathways to sustainability that are both acceptable to their people and compatible with their traditions, institutions and ecological realities. Building on existing characteristics helps motivate and mobilize the human and physical resources of cities to achieve sustainable development and regeneration.

Melbourne Principle 7: Empower people and foster participation.

Clarification of Principle 7: The journey towards sustainability needs the support of all. Empowering people mobilizes local knowledge and resources and enlists their support and active participation in long-term planning, leading to the implementation of sustainable solutions. People have a right to be involved in the decisions that affect them. Attention needs to be given to empowering those whose voices are not always heard, such as the poor.

Melbourne Principle 8: Expand and enable co-operative networks to work towards a common sustainable future.

Clarification of Principle 8: Strengthening existing networks and establishing new co-operative networks within cities facilitates the transfer of knowledge and supports continual environmental improvement. The people of cities are the key drivers to transforming them towards sustainability. This can be achieved effectively if the people of cities are well informed, can easily access knowledge and share learning. Furthermore, the energy and talent of people can be enhanced by working with one another through such networks. There is also value in cities sharing their learning with others, pooling resources to develop sustainability tools and supporting and mentoring one another through intercity and regional networks. These networks can serve as vehicle for information exchange and encouraging collective effort.

Melbourne Principle 9: Promote sustainable production and consumption, through the appropriate use of environmentally sound technologies and effective demand management.

Clarification of Principle 9: A range of approaches and tools can be used to promote sustainable practices. Demand management, which includes accurate valuations of natural resources and increasing public awareness, are valuable strategies to support sustainable consumption. This approach can also provide significant savings in infrastructure investment. Sustainable production can be supported by the adoption and use of environmentally sound technologies which have the potential to improve environmental performance significantly. These technologies protect the environment, are less polluting, use resources in a sustainable manner, recycle more waste products, and

Contd.

handle all residual wastes in a more environmentally acceptable way than the technologies for which they are substitutes. The appropriateness of environmentally sound technologies can be informed by using evaluation tools such as lifecycle assessment, which can help formulate decisions, drive reduced impacts over the whole value chain and support businesses embracing product stewardship.

Melbourne Principle 10: Enable continual improvement, based on accountability, transparency and good governance.

Clarification of Principle 10: Good urban governance is based on robust processes directed to achieving the transformation of cities towards sustainability through continual improvement. While in some areas improvements will be incremental, there are also opportunities to make substantial improvements through innovative policies, programmes and technologies. To manage the continual improvement cycle it is necessary to use relevant indicators, set targets based on benchmarks and monitor progress against milestones to achieving these targets. This facilities progress and accountability, and ensures effective implementation. Transparency and openness to scrutiny are part of good governance.

REFERENCES

Architectural League of New York (2004). *A crisis in civility.* Online at URL http://www.worldviewcities.org/civility.html; accessed 31 August 2004.

Charlesworth, E. (2002). Beirut: city as heart, *Open House International* (Special Issue on War and Cities), **27**, 4, 50–6.

Dagher, C. (2000). *Bring Down the Walls: Lebanon's Post-War Challenge.* St. Martin's Press.

Davie, M. F. (1994). Demarcation lines in contemporary Beirut. In *The Middle East and North Africa.* (C. H. Schofield and R. N. Schofield, eds.) Routledge.

Folkes, C. et al. (1997). Ecosystem appropriation by cities., *Ambio,* **26**, 3.

Local Government Commission (2001). Smart growth: economic development for the 21st century. Online at URL http://www.lgc.org/ahwahnee/econ_principles.html; accessed 31 August 2004.

Rees, W. (2003). Ecological footprint as a tool for regional sustainability. Paper delivered to the International Sustainability Conference, Perth, Australia, 19 September.

Sustainable Community Roundtable (n.d.). What is a sustainable community? Online at URL http://www.olywa.net/roundtable/what_is_sc.html; accessed 31 August 2004.

Toepfer, K. (1999). The urban revolution. *New Village Journal,* Issue 1.

United Nations Centre for Human Settlements (Habitat) (2001). The state of world's cities report. Online at URL http://www.unchs.org/istanbul+5/statereport.htm; accessed 31 August 2004.

United Nations Environment Programme International Environmental Technology Centre (2002). Melbourne Principles for Sustainable Cities. Tokyo and Melbourne. Online at URL www.unep.or.jp/ietc/focus/MelbournePrinciples/ English.pdf and http://www.melbourne.vic.gov.au/info.cfm?top=235&pg=1619; accessed 31 August 2004.